D1105368

Conversations with Dvora

CONTRAVERSIONS

CRITICAL STUDIES IN JEWISH LITERATURE, CULTURE,
AND SOCIETY

Daniel Boyarin and Chana Kronfeld, General Editors

Conversations with Dvora

An Experimental Biography of the First Modern Hebrew Woman Writer

AMIA LIEBLICH

Translated by Naomi Seidman
Edited by Chana Kronfeld and Naomi Seidman

University of California Press

BERKELEY   LOS ANGELES   LONDON

PJ
5053
B34
Z7613
1997

University of California Press
Berkeley and Los Angeles, California

University of California Press
London, England

Library of Congress Cataloging-in-Publication Data

Lieblich, Amia, 1939–
[Reḳamot. English]
Conversations with Dvora : an experimental biography of the first modern
Hebrew woman writer / Amia Lieblich ; translated by Naomi Seidman ; edited by
Chana Kronfeld and Naomi Seidman.
p.   cm. — (Contraversions ; 6)
Includes bibliographical references.
ISBN 0-520-08539-6 (cloth : alk. paper). — ISBN 0-520-08541-8 (pbk. : alk. paper)
1. Baron, Devorah, 1887–1956—Criticism and interpretation.   2. Imaginary
conversations.   I. Baron, Devorah, 1887–1956.   II. Seidman, Naomi.   III. Kronfeld,
Chana.   IV. Title.   V. Series.
PJ5053.B34Z7613   1997
892.4'35—dc21   96-37297
                                                                                        CIP

Printed in the United States of America

1 2 3 4 5 6 7 8 9

The paper used in this publication meets the minimum requirements of American
National Standard for Information Sciences–Permanence of Paper for Printed Library
Materials, ANSI Z39.48-1984 ⊗

Contents

Foreword

When I was a young girl and some relatives, Holocaust survivors, would come to visit, my mother would give them my room and make up a bed for me in my father's study. I would put myself to sleep each night by looking at the colorful bindings of his books, neatly arranged on silvery black wooden shelves. It must have been then that I taught myself to read the titles of the Hebrew books standing beside the fat German encyclopedias and dictionaries, and I would chant their strange names like a lullaby. I distinctly remember a slender volume with an antique golden cover, on which was embossed the title *Dvora Baron, From There*. I understood the words *Dvora*, which meant "bee," and *Ba'aron*, which meant "in the closet." But which closet were they talking about? How did the bee get caught in it? Where was the "there" they referred to?

Recently, I tried to find Baron on my father's old shelves, but the book seemed to be gone. Apparently it had been donated to one of the children's institutions my father worked with, along with the dozens of other books in which his daughters and grandchildren had no interest. Who was this Dvora Baron? Even at school, in my Survey of Hebrew Literature course, her name had never been mentioned.

Dvora Baron died in 1956 at the age of sixty-nine. I was seventeen then and had never met her. Yet, I have written this book as a series of meetings between Dvora Baron and myself, twenty-four in number, which presumably took place at her house on Oliphant Street in Tel Aviv from the summer of 1955 until her death one year later. The meetings described here could only have taken place if we were free from the shackles of time and death. And who among us does not crave such freedom?

In my work as a Gestalt therapist (see my book *Tin Soldiers on Jeru-salem Beach* [Pantheon, 1978]), I studied and taught that nothing prevents our engaging in dialogue with someone who is absent, a person who has died or moved away. Our imaginations can break through the walls of time and death to win us this freedom. Having therefore immersed myself in all of Dvora Baron's writings, in everything that had been written about her, and in the stories her remaining acquaintances told of her, I finally raised her voice in my own ear. While I was writing this book, I would often see Dvora Baron in my mind's eye, or see myself sitting in her darkened room and hear the conversations that took place between us. The character described in these pages is thus the great writer as I understand her. Alongside her am I—at the age I am today, with my opinions and outlook on life—interviewing Dvora Baron through a wrinkle in time. She tells me about her life, about her writing and her thoughts, and I contribute my own thoughts and experiences. This, then, is a book about two women who meet in an imaginary time-space. The first, Dvora Baron, is the chief protagonist, while the other is me, playing second fiddle to her lead.

Dvora Baron was born in a small town in the Minsk region on the Eighteenth of Kislev in the Hebrew year 5648 (that is, at the very end of 1887). Her father, the town rabbi, noticed her talents and, in contrast with the way he treated his other daughters, educated Dvora in Torah as if she were a boy, alongside her only brother. When she was fifteen she left home for the district capital of Minsk, in her brother's footsteps, in hopes of acquiring a profession and some secular education. For nine years she made her way from one of the cities of Lithuania and Russia to another with no economic support from her parents, first under her brother's wing and then on her own. During these years, and after an extended period of self-education, she was awarded a high school diploma in the Russian Gymnasium as well as a teachers' certificate, all the while supporting herself as a tutor and establishing a reputation as a fiction writer in both Hebrew and Yiddish. Her stories started appearing in Jewish publications while she was still a young girl in Ouzda, her hometown, and editors frequently solicited new material from her.

When she was in her twenties, her beloved father died, the family nest disintegrated, her hometown was destroyed in the pogroms that followed the first Russian Revolution, and her long engagement to Moshe Ben-Eliezer, a young writer of her generation, was broken off. In the wake of all this Dvora Baron immigrated to Palestine in the winter of 1910 and established a home in Neveh Tsedek, near Tel Aviv. She soon found employment at a publication called the *Young Worker* as the editor of the literary section, and married Yosef Aharonovich—leader, activist, and editor in chief of this newspaper. Dvora Baron did not change her name after her marriage (a fact that elicits no comment in the biographical notes published by her daughter after Baron's death).

Tsipora, the only daughter of Dvora and Yosef, was born in 1914. A year later the family was exiled by the Turkish government to Alexandria along with hundreds of other Jews—foreign subjects residing in Ottoman-ruled Palestine at the time. The family spent four years of poverty and disease in Egypt, after which they returned to Tel Aviv at the end of the First World War and the British capture of Palestine, and Dvora Baron and her husband went back to work at the *Young Worker*. Their daughter, Tsipora, grew up under the wing of her famous parents. She acquired a far-reaching education primarily under her mother's supervision, never attending school or developing her own network of friends.

Dvora Baron learned of her brother Benjamin's death in Russia shortly after her return from exile. In 1923 she and Yosef resigned from the editorship of the newspaper; from that year on, when she was around thirty-five, Baron secluded herself in her apartment, never to leave it again. She continued to write and translate, and she maintained contact with writers and other acquaintances, who sometimes visited her at home. In the second half of her life Baron adopted ascetic habits, keeping a strict diet and spending her days on the couch; for the last twenty years of her life she was virtually confined to her bed.

After leaving the paper, Aharonovich was assigned to manage the Workers Bank. He died suddenly in 1937, and the settlement of Beit Yosef was named after him. Tsipora lived with her mother and followed her rigorous vegetarian diet, and she loyally cared for Dvora Baron until the day her mother died. There is no medical documentation that can account for the life choices or disabilities of mother and daughter.

Baron published between seventy and eighty short stories. Approximately half of them appeared in print in the Yiddish and Hebrew press before her exile to Egypt; the other half, which critics consider her mature work, appeared in collections published from 1927 on. Unlike her efforts at keeping her later work in print, Baron treated the early stories with utter disdain and strongly opposed their republication. She was also known as a translator; her translation of *Madame Bovary* was especially admired.

Dvora Baron died on the Thirteenth of Elul, 5717 (1956), of a cerebral hemorrhage. Her daughter, Tsipora Aharonovich, died childless on the Fourth of Tishrei, 5732 (1971).

As I read more and more of Dvora Baron's writings, I became increasingly convinced of their psychological truth. I assumed that, just as imagined material provides important information to psychologists, Baron's creative works reflected her personal reality, and there was no point in questioning whether the stories she described had ever occurred. This insight arose and crystallized in the confrontation between the two of us—two women writers, the circumstances of whose lives could hardly be more different. Nevertheless, I strongly identified with Baron's personality, and this empathy helped me construct her character until I saw her before my eyes as if she were alive, and heard her voice speaking to me.

This approach to biography would hardly have been countenanced twenty years ago. Members of my generation in the social sciences were taught to separate ourselves from the phenomena we were researching. The place of the researcher (always in the third person and usually male) outside the subject of inquiry guaranteed objectivity, the fundamental basis of good research. Moreover, it was essential to distinguish between fact and interpretation, data and theory, as if the borders between them were etched in stone. This was, of course, the height of the positivist era.

The same stance governed the writing of biographies and case studies. Biographers were supposed to distance themselves as much as they could from any emotional connection or identification with their protagonists. This attitude has only recently begun to change; scholars of biography and psychobiography, literary criticism, historiography, feminism, and sociology have begun to emphasize the reciprocal influences, the mutual illumination, of the writer and the subject of her work. Now, at the end of the twentieth century, interpretation has been shown to be inextricable from the collection and presentation of data; writing, in every discipline, has emerged as a dialectical relationship between writer and subject.

Within this intellectual context, psychologists who study biography have borrowed the notions of transference and countertransference from psychoanalysis, using them to describe and interpret the relationship between biographer and subject. Freud and Erikson had already paved the way for this insight in their studies on, respectively, da Vinci and Gandhi, although neither had made transference or countertransference central to their biographical analyses. The principle of transference maintains, for our purposes, that it is necessary for biographers to relate emotionally with their protagonists, modeling these relationship on others in their past. Instead of seeing the biographer's emotional investment as a misreading, however, it is important to recognize this phenomenon as the source of the inspiration, dedication, and understanding the biographer brings to the subject.

I will freely admit that these issues were not yet clear to me, a psychologist and Hebrew writer, a feminist living in Jerusalem, when the search for a "good" research subject brought me, in 1989, to the life and work of Dvora Baron. It was serendipity, or perhaps the spirit of the times, that led me to writing a biography in which subjectivity and identification were proudly announced, rather than being concealed. Only when the creative process was complete, and in response to the comments and comparisons of my colleagues, did I understand that the postmodern spirit of the close of this century had found expression in the story I had told.

In this book the character of Dvora Baron is woven from the sources listed below.

1. Her own writings, which can be found in the following collections: *Stories* (1927); *Little Things* (1933); *What Was* (1939); *For the Time Being*

(1943); *From There* (1946); *Sunbeams* (1949); *Chapters* (1951); *From Yesterday* (1956); *By the Way: Posthumous Literary Works about Dvora Baron and Her Circle* (1960); *The Exiles* (1970); and *Early Chapters: Stories 1902–1921* (1988).

2. The writings of her husband and daughter: Yosef Aharonovich, *Writings 1–2*, edited by Dvora Baron and Eliezer Shochat (1941); and Tsipora Aharonovich, *Her Letters and Notes from Comrades* (1972).

3. Essays and articles by Israeli literary critics; of these, I will only mention two: Nurith Govrin, *The First Half—Dvora Baron, Her Life and Her Work* (1988); and Ada Pagis, editor, *Dvora Baron—Selected Critical Essays on Her Work* (1975). A complete bibliography of stories, translations, and critical essays on Dvora Baron can be found in these two volumes.

4. Material related to me in conversation with the following people: Friends of the Aharonovich family or their children, such as Meir Bareli, son of Yitzchak Brodny-Bareli; Hadassah Bosel, daughter of Chayuta Bosel; Leah Braudes, widow of Avraham Braudes; Ayala Hacohen-Barash, daughter of the writer Asher Barash; and Shmuel Shimoni, son of the writer David Shimoni.

I also spoke with Nurith Govrin, Hebrew literary critic and expert in the writings of Dvora Baron; Dr. Manya Marari, who lived in Baron's house as her personal attendant and a family friend; Marari's husband, Eliyahu; and Leah Margolit, Baron's neighbor in the building at 4 Oliphant Street, where the writer lived for the last sixteen years of her life; Professor Baruch Padeh, the son of Baron's oldest sister and medical adviser to Baron and her daughter; Rivka Praus, clerk at the Workers Bank, who handled the finances of the family, and a onetime friend of Baron; Chasya Siletzki, who attended and read to Baron in her later years; and Alex Zahavi, literary critic, who visited the Aharonovich house in his childhood. All the conversations were tape-recorded.

5. Additional background material, which I assembled by reading or conversing with people who had some knowledge of the literature of the period:

The Second Aliya (the wave of immigration before the First World War in which Dvora Baron participated); Tel Aviv at the beginning of the century; and the psychology of literary creativity, of women, and of self-imposed isolation. Some of those I spoke with are (in alphabetical order): Nachy Alon, Prof. Catherine Bateson, Chaim Be'er, Dr. Yoram Bilu, Sister Morina Fritz, Roni Givati, Prof. Ruthellen Josselson, Prof. Gershon Shaked, and Muki Tzur. Among the background books I read I would like to mention especially Anthony Store's book on solitude and Caroline Heilbron's book on women writers.

Not repeated here are my acknowledgments of colleagues, students, and editors who helped me in myriad ways in the course of the research and writing in Israel—their names appear in the Hebrew edition of this book published by Schocken in 1991. My family, and especially my young son, Eliav, generously gave me the space I needed, the solitude in which I communed with the figure of Dvora Baron. A sabbatical year in the Department of Psychology of the University of California at Berkeley provided me with the opportunity to meet Professor Chana Kronfeld, through whose eyes I saw *Conversations with Dvora* anew with the perspective of a critic of modern literature, and who guided me in reading the dialogue in the context of literary theory.

The English version has three mothers, and I thank all three of them immensely. Chana Kronfeld generously offered to publish my book in English in the Contraversions series, and found in Naomi Seidman an able translator. Finally, Doris Kretschmer, at the University of California Press, was a dedicated editor, coordinating our international contacts and demonstrating the patience necessary to bring the delicate process that culminated in the book before you to fruition.

In memory of my father and teacher, Dr. M. A. Kurtz, 1909–1994
AMIA LIEBLICH, JERUSALEM, 1995

Translator's Note

I began with the desire to speak with the dead.

—Stephen Greenblatt
Shakespearean Negotiations

The publication in 1991 of Amia Lieblich's *Embroideries* was an expression of two related phenomena: the recent revival of Israeli interest in the first modern Hebrew woman writer, Dvora Baron (1887–1956); and the growing exploration of the field where feminism, postmodernism, and biography meet. We have few enough descriptions of women's lives in Eastern Europe and Palestine during the fascinating times in which Baron lived. This one draws power from both the subtle insight of Baron's modernist fiction and Lieblich's postmodernist biographical technique. In imagining Baron in conversation with the narrator and author, a contemporary woman, *Conversations with Dvora* reconstructs this world and opens it to our own.

The foreword to this work outlines the life of Dvora Baron, the first modern Hebrew woman writer and an important early modernist. I will only note here that Baron cuts one of the most intriguing figures in modern literary history: a rebel and conservator of tradition, a social and literary activist, and a homebound recluse. As Tel Aviv grew up around her, Baron continued to describe the traditional Eastern European life she had left behind, which was disappearing as she wrote. She paid the price of semiobscurity for writing about the past in a literary environment in which young Zionist writers were expected to turn their attentions to the new world rising before their eyes. Baron's self-imposed "house arrest" was also accompanied by her outright rejection of all of her early stories ("my rags," as she referred to them). It may be no accident that these stories contain some of the most explicit—and most powerful—

critiques of patriarchy and religious authoritarianism in modern literary history.

One can trace the recent rediscovery of Baron's work both to growing feminist awareness and to a renewed interest in the Eastern European Jewish culture that earlier generations of Ashkenazic Zionists so decisively rejected. Baron, who, like Lot's wife, continued to look back, is an appropriate emblem for this struggle to construct a usable past; and Lieblich's imagined conversations with Baron are extensions, into the present, of the same project. American Jews have been no less cut off from the world described with such immediacy in *Conversations with Dvora.* Jewish feminists, in particular, should welcome so radical and complex a precursor as Dvora Baron.

In translating and editing *Conversations with Dvora* for an American audience Chana Kronfeld and I made a number of changes in the texts. Since Hebrew prose tends to be condensed (a page in Hebrew usually translates into two in English), we tried to recapture some of that brevity by shortening passages wherever we could. We also changed the Hebrew title *Rikamot*, which means *Embroideries*, to one we hoped would convey more to the English reader. After Chana and I had gone over the translation in Berkeley, we sent the drafts to Israel, where Amia commented on our work. Doris Kretschmer at the University of California Press presided over this entire international enterprise with grace and tact. There were four women, then, working together on this project, or five, if you count the ghostly presence of Dvora Baron; I enjoyed the time I spent in their company.

Conversations with Dvora presents the translator with something other than the usual linguistic knots. The challenge that faced me was to find two distinct and consistent voices to match those of the hybrid text. The first of these was that of the narrator Amia, an Israeli-born writer and psychologist of the 1990s with a healthy ambivalence to the professional vocabulary of her chosen field. The second, more difficult, task was to translate what Dvora Baron might have sounded like in 1955. The Dvora Amia hears speaks a bookish, somewhat old-fashioned Hebrew, albeit a careful, well-chosen literary one. This is not only because Amia "hears" Baron through the pages of her writings but also because

Baron began to write Hebrew before it fully became a vernacular, and secluded herself as this transformation was finally succeeding. Moreover, Baron's voice, in *Conversations with Dvora*, arises from within something like an auditory hallucination, with the uncanny echo that goes with such an encounter. As the translator of this literary séance, I had to transfigure these voices into English, a process that began with Baron transforming the Hebrew of holy books into modern prose and continued with Amia turning Dvora's fiction into spoken words she then set on paper again.

The only way to approach such a project was to hear the voices myself, in English, as Amia had heard Dvora's. In trying to make Dvora audible I thought first of Emily Dickinson or Virginia Woolf, although Dvora's Hebrew cannot be compared with what was, for Dickinson or Woolf, a native tongue. The voice that eventually spoke Dvora's words surprised me—it was my father's. Perhaps that shouldn't have been so surprising: he had the same sharp, unsentimental wit, the same Jewish erudition, the same immersion in a vanished world he still saw before his eyes. And Dvora, after all, had as much in common with her male as her female peers, as her unusual upbringing had ensured. There was something appropriate, I finally decided, in linking Dvora with my father. *Conversations with Dvora* presents a conversation between women, but they are women in deep mourning for the men they have lost (Dvora's brother, Amia's husband), men with whom they were unusually closely identified. Amia's and Dvora's talks, often enough, concern the recovery of these lost voices. I, who joined their conversation in translating it, lost the father I fiercely loved as I was finishing this project. It is to him that I dedicate this translation, and to Chana Kronfeld, who helped raise all these voices in my ear.

NAOMI SEIDMAN, BERKELEY, 1996

Conversations with Dvora

first encounter

It was a scorching day. A Saturday afternoon heaviness weighed the city down, the sidewalk burned through the thin soles of my sandals. A colorful schoolyard gate at the corner of Oliphant Street twinkled in the sun. A few boys were shooting baskets in the yard. It was quiet, as if someone had muffled the clamor of the game and the city itself with a turn of some dial. Only my own footsteps rang in the stillness as I reached number four and climbed to the third floor, left.

When I first met her, Dvora Baron was sixty-eight years old, bedridden, her vision nearly gone. Her daughter, Tsipora, a woman of no particular age with downcast eyes, opened the apartment door. Twilight and the smell of mildew accosted me as the ancient door shut behind us. For a minute I panicked—what was I doing in this place? How was I going to get out? Following Tsipora, who was wearing clumsy boots over white schoolgirl socks, I could just barely make out the foyer and the shrouded silhouettes of some furniture. In the living room a heavy curtain was drawn across the window to the street. A large photograph of the writer in her youth hung on the wall, a dark-eyed beauty in a white blouse with puffed sleeves. Near the window was a high bed, metal frame, covered with red velvet and pillows. Dvora Baron lay stretched out, a black dress falling like a nun's habit to her ankles. Glass-doored bookshelves lined the room, in one corner a forlorn writing table. I seated myself in the chair that stood beside the bed; the hard slats pressed against my back, and my heart surged.

She didn't smile as she put out her bony hand, but our eyes met and locked for a long moment. Your eyes are just like mine, I wanted to say, and then I said it silently, shaken with the palpability of the moment.

1

For some reason, there was no embarrassment in our common silence. I wanted to say too, I came to learn from you, to sit in silence; and I knew she would answer, And I would like to learn from you, to walk among people again—and she would not add, Even if it is too late for that.

I thought I saw a smile flit across her ascetic features. I returned it and said, They told me we looked alike, but I had no idea how much.

She did not confirm it; she held me with her piercing eyes. Beside her head I could see a small nightstand with newspapers and books, the Bible with commentaries, some bottles of medicine, a sewing case.

What do I know about you, Dvora Baron, I heard my inner voices murmuring.

You're one of the last of the Second Aliya pioneers, those fiery idealists who came to this country between the failed revolution of 1905 and the onset of the First World War. A tragic figure. No wonder your husband couldn't survive under the same roof as you.

Why tragic? the internal dialogue continued.

Because you tore yourself from your distant village and never really made it to the land of Israel. Because for forty years you couldn't write about what was all around you here in Tel Aviv. You kept on talking about how it was "there," when it was already long gone. "A tragic stance before the cultural void," they called it at the university. Death liberated some of your peers, some committed suicide, others took to their heels and ran; but you just cut yourself off from life and the present, following your characters to their netherworld, your netherworld. A rabbi's daughter—fiction became your new monastic creed, an end to justify any means—including the exploitation of your only daughter.

If that's so obvious, the voices clamored, then what did you come for anyway?

That quieted them down. The familiar inner stage was silent once more.

Tell me about yourself, Dvora said abruptly, and pulled herself up to lean against the embroidered pillows, one hand over her eyes. I had heard about her weak eyesight, her terrible headaches. I'm a burden to her, I thought, wondering how I could bring the meeting to a graceful close.

I'll get out into the light of day, spend some time among the living, and try once more when I'm myself again.

I am waiting, she said in the silence that stretched out between us, as Tsipora set two glasses of water on the nightstand.

How is it that you can't hear the city in this house? I asked.

We live behind shut windows, Tsipora answered drily. The humidity is harmful for Mother, and in any case, the air is completely polluted with automobile exhaust. My eyes were drawn once again to her boots, to her shapeless brown dress. She left the room silently, the door shutting behind her.

How should I start? I spoke up, answering the question Dvora Baron had asked. She still had not moved. I'm looking for a woman artist whose life I can research. But that's a terrible way to begin!

Why? she asked.

Why am I looking, or why is it a terrible opening? Nothing was going the way I had rehearsed it.

Four years ago my husband suddenly died, I started again, in utter contradiction to all I had planned to say. I've been alone since then, living in Jerusalem with my young son, and writing. I have a full life and the strange feeling that I control my own destiny—even though I've seen how suddenly the ax can fall. Since my world fell apart, I've tried to do only the important things, to choose carefully.

And you, I hesitated, are important to me. A woman who let me see a town or a river, a house, an alley, that were already invisible to everyone else. You brought that alley to me. So I wanted to see you for myself.

Go on, she said when I stopped, without turning her face toward me.

I don't know quite how to put it. I'm looking for a hero, a woman who is sad and intelligent and creative, who will struggle with me, but who will also let me be whatever I am. I don't know if you're the one, but maybe it's enough just to be looking for you. Or maybe—if I can start my story again—I'm just looking for a riddle to ponder.

I prefer riddles to heroes, she answered, turning her head, and our eyes met again. And what else?

She reads thoughts, I said to myself, she sees the words before I know

I am saying them. Now I turned to the lines I had rehearsed during a long drive from Jerusalem one summer evening, when I had worked out a script for our meeting.

I'm a Sabra, I said, a local product. Hebrew is my mother tongue, the Diaspora something utterly alien to me. I have taught myself to feel some connection to the Holocaust, to the extent that it is possible, but what came before that? For years I dismissed the Diaspora, the pale, terrified Jew who once lived there. And here you are, from over there. Yet, you're nothing like that distasteful character; that is, as far as I could tell from your stories. You chose to stay the way you were, you weren't interested in becoming the new bard of the new Israel. Nothing that happens here touches you. I hear your voice inside my head, I said boldly, and I want you to hear mine.

There was no sign of retreat in her face. I smiled.

Have you read *Madame Bovary*? she asked.

I nodded and then said Yes, remembering her poor eyesight. I thought of saying, Your translation was wonderful, but I held back. She must have heard that more than enough times.

Tell me, which one of my stories occurs to you at this moment, is there some section you particularly like?

Like a student who cannot be caught by surprise, I answered, The part of the story "As It Is," where you say that you saw compassion.

She began to speak without pausing, as if reciting from a book: Once, while I was still a young girl in the shtetl, I entered a house whose owners were at market. On the sideboard small balls of dough were hardening in preparation for the approaching Holy Days, and two birds were pecking to their hearts' content from the bounty. Not sensing my presence, they flew out the window and soon returned with another bird. They stood and waited while she too ate her fill, and then they flew off again with her and I saw that she was blind. That was when I knew that I had seen compassion face-to-face.

And here you are before me, an old and nearly blind woman, I thought, my heart going out to her.

It would suit me if you were to visit again, she said after a lengthy pause, and I relaxed in my seat for the first time. Many cherished friends have already long passed on. These days there are few who knock at my door. If you wish, I will tell you the story of my life, as it appears to me now. I have lost my sight, but in my mind's eye the scenes appear clearer than ever before. When you get home, look up the dedication to my book *Chapters*, it was taken from the story "Fradl."

In that place, in those days, they did not believe in shielding the eyes of a child by throwing an elegant prayer shawl over life's nakedness. And so, along with the song of sun-dazzled birds and the scent of dew-drunk plants, she also absorbed impressions of daily life, bits of local color, of heartache and joy, which in the course of time—when they had been refined and illuminated by the light of her intellect and experience had bound them into life stories—became for her, in the solitary nights of her wanderings, a source of pleasure and comfort.

second encounter

Today I will tell you about my family as I remember them from my childhood in the shtetl, she began our second meeting, lying on the bed as if she hadn't moved a muscle since last week. It stunned me to watch words break through such immobility, but I was grateful she was speaking.

My rabbi father was an interpreter of dreams, like Joseph in the Bible, she said, gazing at the ceiling. "Sweetening the dream," they called it in our village.

I think there's a prayer like that in the prayer book, to make sure that nightmares don't come true.

Dvora's expression hardened for a moment. Was it rude of me to interrupt? I flushed with embarrassment, but she went on as if I hadn't said a word.

If someone had a bad dream one night, he would show up the next morning at our home—the rabbi's house, which was called "the community house"—to unburden his troubled heart. As a tiny girl, still unfettered by studies, I would listen from a corner of the room, invisible. And what strange night visions they were, she said pensively, such as the man who dreamed he was floating all night in a black void. No matter how dark the dream, my father interpreted everything as a good omen; people left with their minds at ease. There were those who would go on to read a chapter of Psalms or light candles in the synagogue, as my father had instructed. After a lengthy silence she added, But the catastrophes they envisioned, all of them indeed came true, and even worse.

Of course I did not know that then, she continued, recovering and turning her eyes to mine. My father in the community house, interpret-

6

ing and sweetening dreams, is my first childhood memory, or maybe only the first page I have turned for you. I could have told you as well about my father on the eve of a holiday passing judgment on whether a woman's chicken was kosher, or drawing up divorce papers for a barren woman whose husband had spurned her. For I was always there, a girl with eyes and ears that missed nothing, invisible in a corner of the room. Neither he nor my mother ever tried to stop me from seeing the things that took place in our home—things unsuitable for a little child, you would undoubtedly say today.

I'm in the dream business too, I told her, and explained how images in a dream—people, objects, or even words—were expressions of the various parts of the dreamer's psyche. By interpreting what each part means for you, you could decode a message about yourself.

She lay on her back, staring at the ceiling. There was no way of knowing whether she had heard anything I said, so I stopped. But then she turned her face to me again as if waiting for me to continue.

I read your stories the same way, I said boldly. That is, I thought of everything you wrote as an expression of where you came from, your inner world, your deepest beliefs. I could feel you behind the words, serious, longing, sometimes angry and protesting, once in a while humorous. You spoke to me woman-to-woman. I studied your life, your texts. And even though my literary friends always remind me that there's no direct connection between a writer's life and their work, I couldn't help thinking that way. Would I have thought the same if you were a male writer? I don't know.

And what did you do when the images contradicted each other?

But aren't these the contradictions we all live? I answered. So in one place you talk about a warm, close family, and in another story the family is exploitative, inconsiderate, even hateful—they don't cancel each other out like an equation in algebra. They're different facets of the same experience, or the same experience remembered in different moments of a life.

So, she declared, I have had many childhoods, as many as my memories.

You could put it that way. Truth is always relative to the speaker, the listener, the time, and the place. Our memories change when we do. There was a wonderful sentence in an Italo Calvino book I recently read that went something like this: "A traveler's past changes according to the path he follows."

And what are the contradictions within you? she suddenly asked.

It's hard for me to answer when you won't look at me; it's hard for me to feel that I exist, I heard myself say, and wanted to take back the words immediately.

And I have difficulty looking at the here and now, not only because I do not see very well. I am no longer really here, you know. For many years now I have retreated from direct contact with the present; I remain cloistered in my inner world, mainly in the past. I once thought that since my world no longer exists, I must preserve its images, as if they would vanish in sunlight and fresh air. Today I know well enough that nothing can ever be erased—nevertheless. . . . She was silent for a minute and then added, I am a hard woman.

I am too, very often.

And what contradictions do you hold within you? she asked again.

I get terribly lonely. When I'm alone, I want so badly for someone to be with me; but when I find that someone, I want freedom, privacy, my own space, I want my loneliness back again. I smiled at her eyes.

Can you sweeten a dream? she gazed back at me, searching my face.

When people have faith, miracles happen, I said for her sake, for mine, as if I believed such things.

In the course of my lifetime it has become very difficult to believe, Dvora continued. In my house they had faith—but I lost it. Did you know that the primary meaning of "security" in Hebrew is "faith"? she asked in a teacherly voice, looking sternly in my direction. Then she immediately continued: I remember my mother, the young rabbi's wife, during the ten days of atonement before Yom Kippur. For all of that period my mother would pray each day in the synagogue together with the congregation. Mists of purity swaddled her childlike eyes, their whites large and prominent; the black scarf covering her wig redoubling her modesty. The devotion with which she murmured the prayers! The other women in the synagogue gazed at her with genuine love, the dying sun setting the golden curls of her wig aglow. And when she descended from the women's section at the conclusion of the prayers, the hem of her simple linen dress would trail, step after step, in her wake.

Later, at home, in a cotton apron tied below the waist, she would stand over the blazing stove, talking with the neighbor-woman and preparing the meal. Her small hands spun and flashed, peeling large American potatoes at breakneck speed. How I loved to watch her shampoo her hair in the washbasin on Friday afternoons, the "good" soap beside her in its colorful paper wrapper, its embossed surfaces still unworn. She drew the shade over the window and unloosed and shook out her abundant hair in the dim light, standing a moment at the dusky mirror. Sometimes I would see her at daybreak shaking her head to spread out her silken hair, which filled the room for a moment, and angrily run a comb through it, complaining about how thick and unruly it was; then she would capture it in a kerchief, tie a firm knot, and turn to the day's work.

The main thing was, however, that she believed in the God of her fathers and knew the correct path to follow. I remember her fulfilling the commandments in the most natural manner, never talking much about what she was doing. That was how it was with Bashinke-Basya, who helped my mother with the housework. Basya didn't work much, just two or three hours each day. The wages she received—half a ruble per week—went for rye flour, with which she baked her family enough bread to last the week. The "ruin," they called the house in which Basya the widow lived with her six children. It stood at the end of the community alley, and people said it was sinking into the ground. And indeed, each year it would be a little lower. But when Basya arrived in town with her six children and a few possessions in a rented cart after her husband had been murdered in a pogrom, my mother advised her to rent the shack. "A roof over their heads," she said in her usual shorthand, and then I was sent over with some of the buckwheat cakes my mother had baked that day. When these had been accepted, I brought over some hot potatoes freshly plucked from the glowing embers. Then my mother opened our closet and took out some of our underwear and my brother's wool suits, folded them into what looked like a postal parcel and deftly dropped it through the door of the "ruin." "For the orphans," she said, when she saw me watching. She had a light touch when it came to giving.

In another memory I see how my mother would support a woman who was about to be divorced against her will. While the men were busy in the community house with the divorce papers, she would bring the unfortunate woman over to the window seat to gaze at the meadow, so the serenity of nature could soothe her tortured heart. My mother firmly believed that the sight of the solitary willow growing in our courtyard, standing strong against the gales that often lashed its isolation, would provide solace for the poor woman in her travail.

In the pause that followed I awoke to myself for a dim moment. But soon enough she continued.

And then there was my father's faith. It was different, of course. I can still sometimes hear him in quiet moments, which is why I have always loved silence. It is his melodies that come back to me, the ones he would sing to himself. Sometimes an ordinary tune, an arbitrary, unimportant tune, like one you would use to quiet someone or put them to sleep; sometimes, at night, from the other side of the partition, the chant of the Torah portion as he prepared a sermon. And sometimes, a lament, a piercing, tremulous meditation on human destiny—a melody that poured the wine of sorrow into me.

Do you like music? she surprised me by asking.

Very much, I answered. Listening to music is one of the most soothing things I know. To me, composers are the greatest of artists.

The talent for composing a melody must certainly be God's most wondrous gift, said Dvora. My father's melodies implanted in me a love for the musical phrase, which I only developed much later in life. But sometimes when I listen to Tchaikovsky, or Mendelssohn, especially to the extraordinary violin concertos, it is my father's religious melodies I hear.

In the corner of the room stood an enormous old-fashioned Victrola, its oversized ear cocked toward the center of the room as if to confirm her words.

Something in my father's singing could lift the curtain that veiled my future, she went on, so I could glimpse it: all gray and mournful, with no passage or exit, like those stone walls between which I ran back and forth years later, pursued by oppressors, fleeing the jaws of their dogs. I can still hear, from sometime later, his harsh, metallic cough, hacking and rasping through the day from his seat in the synagogue. And after that, at night, when his cough worsened, I could hear my father through the falling rain, gasping for breath as he tried to hold on to the verses of the bedtime prayer, dejected. The melody and the cough, and she stopped, as if silently reading through a score inscribed within her.

Do you want me to leave? I asked as the twilight deepened in the room. Tsipora was nowhere in sight. I thought, I shouldn't leave Dvora alone, but maybe she has had enough for one day.

Paying no mind, she went on in her deep voice. I remember him in the synagogue, a young man with an aristocratic beard, long and dark, without a trace of silver in it yet. On Sabbath he would stand beside the Holy Ark and deliver his sermon on the weekly Torah portion. As if flesh and blood, his words stood before his listeners. His voice sent an imperceptible shudder through their hearts. He could weave the Torah verses into the everyday fabric of their lives, and lightly ornament them with the golden shimmer of the legends. His words were wrung from a weakened heart, but they set all faces aglow, warming the chilliest soul among his congregants.

But I also see him on weekdays, alone in the synagogue. A solitary shepherd whose sheep had scattered across the furthest slopes of the mountain. Tired of poring over the book, he would stretch out along the naked bench, his caftan hanging limply over the side and his yarmulke slipped down onto his forehead. Too powerless even to fend off the flies that hovered and landed all over him.

He was my first teacher; after him, I learned from my brother. My father taught the boys, among them my brother, Benjamin, in the old study hall. I would sit alone, imprisoned in the women's section, reciting the "Well of Jacob" or "The Great Midrash" out loud. From time to time I would call through the lattice: Papa, Benjamin, what does this mean?

Many of the young boys envied my scholarly diligence, and my father encouraged and guided me through the Mishna and Talmud as if I were one of the boys.

After he fell ill, he would pace the dusty, echoing study hall like a man who has lost his proper place. When none of his congregants needed him and my brother was immersed in studying for his rabbinical ordination, there would be no one with whom to share his newest Torah insights but me. I sat on a bench in the rabbinical court, a girl of no more than ten in a thin dress, legs dangling in the air, and he would stride rapidly back and forth before me explaining all the while, and my eyes would tire of watching his rabbinical caftan flicking round and round. He taught me to read the special script of Rashi's commentary by lecturing on his reading Genesis. The small script underneath the solid, self-satisfied letters of the main body of the text struck me as so flimsy and powerless, just like those pickets that separated poor people's plots in the gulch. One day he lectured to me about the dilapidated bridge of time, which connected the depths of the abyss—the world. I didn't understand completely, of course, and I envisioned the community house itself perched on the edge of a chasm, about to tumble in. When the sun had set and my father had left for the synagogue for the evening prayers, I raced with my girlfriends over those fences to the open meadow on the other side of the gulch.

From an early age, my father made me feel that I could understand things and that he appreciated the quality of my mind. More than once I acted in his place, and quite naturally at that, as if there was no need to take notice that it was a little girl who was delivering the rabbinical judgment. Once when I was about twelve, for instance, my father had to leave town. That Sabbath eve, an agitated woman rushed to the community house because a catastrophe had befallen her: She was alone in the house, and had lain down to rest and fallen asleep. When she awoke, the Sabbath had already begun—but she had not lit the Sabbath candles. What should she do now? How many candles do you ordinarily light? I asked her. "Two," she answered. From now on, I ruled, she must light an additional candle each week, as atonement for her omission. The woman left with great relief, and I went back to the book I was reading. I did not say a word to my mother; but when my father returned, I told him what had happened and he said, "You ruled correctly, my daughter. I would have arrived at the same decision."

And didn't he think that was strange? Didn't you? Or anyone else?

That was how I lived, so how could it seem strange to me? Perhaps that was how rabbi's daughters lived in other towns as well.

But how about your sisters, I argued, they weren't like that.

True, she considered, I was different; but I did not often notice it. Only when I compare myself now with the other boys and girls I knew, and not only to my brother and sisters, do I realize that perhaps I really was rather special.

She stopped, lost in thought, and finally said, We will speak about this at greater length, I am sure, but today I wished to draw a portrait of my parents.

I'm sorry, I said, should I not ask you any questions and just let you tell the story your own way?

Dvora gazed at her slender hands on the blanket.

A good conversation finds its own proper course, like a stream flowing down a slope, she finally spoke. If it comes up against a boulder, it bypasses it naturally and finds bedrock once again. We will proceed then.

I want to sketch for you my everyday Mama and Papa. I remember my mother waking each morning at daybreak. While my father is still praying with the "old-timer" quorum in the synagogue, she lights the kitchen stove, moving back and forth by the flickering light of the flames, her long hair spread out and not yet covered. A little later I see her busy selling yeast at our marketplace stall. On the way home, she picks up wood shavings from the neighbor's new building site and gathers them in her enchanting maternal apron as she walks, piles them in a cone under the cooking tripod in the oven, and sets the pot down on it to simmer. As the fire catches, the smell of the meal spreads through the house—American potatoes with an onion-pepper sauce—an aroma that mingles with the damp river breeze wafting through the open window. That is my weekday mother, the smell of home. From the window there is a glimpse of meadow and green grass. The motionless river flashes in the sunlight and the solitary willow in our courtyard radiates repose.

There were, however, things I had a hard time understanding. While my father was alive my mother had no close friends, and it seemed to me that she really missed that. In my childhood there was a young woman on our street, Chana-Gitl was her name, who worked in the provincial capital to help support her orphaned brothers. When she arrived before each holiday to visit her elderly mother, she would hover near our house. Sometimes I would see our mother go out then too, as if she had something to do in the yard, with a candle end to light her way. Once outside, she would carefully extinguish the candle, and feeling their way in the darkness, the two of them would meet. From my bed I could hear her whisper, "Chana-Gitl?" On moonlit evenings, I would see my mother stealthily take her shawl and go out to meet her friend. They would slip through the gap in the fence to the meadow, and sit on the bench by the priest's courtyard, facing the gulch. This fascinated me, but I did not dare question my mother or older sister about it. Was it a sin to want to stroll a bit in the evening breeze with the neighbor's daughter? Was it because there was still household work to be done, unwashed glasses still standing on the table beside the lukewarm samovar? Was it because she was the rabbi's wife, and her friend was the daughter of the dead shoemaker?

What those two spoke about I will never know. Once I hid beside the window to await my mother's return, and the stars had already grown pale by the time the two soulmates arrived. Another time I saw them returning at dawn, in a close embrace, laughing and crying at once. When I played with my friends Mina and Gitl, the thought would sometimes cross my mind: When I grow up and get married, will I not be allowed to tell stories and laugh with my girlfriends? she finished and sank into thought.

Silence descended on the room, and I tried to remember if I had ever heard any of my female friends raise this question so poignantly. Then Dvora continued.

I see my everyday Papa in my heart, in isolated images from our summer life in the resort. Once I tagged along with him and his friend the old merchant on their afternoon walk through the countess's wooded grounds. The old man asked and argued, and my father, quick on his feet, answered and explained clearly, briefly, and with a sharp wit, until all difficulties had been worked through and the text had become translucent and clear. The light of Torah shone then along the shaded trail through the forest. When the old man turned down the path back to town, I could walk shoulder to shoulder with my father. And he, in a good mood after his conversation with his friend, with eyes sharpened by the minute strokes of Rashi-script, would discover berries for me hidden among the bushes and he would help me pick them. Then, he seemed like any other father, the divine cloud that always went before him in the community house somehow dissipated. Once, when the kitchen shelf under the milk can broke, he came and fixed it: he set a nail into the wood and stood back and hammered it in, just like one of the folk.

In the resort town Mama and Papa sometimes acted like one of the regular couples. Once my mother told him that the water in the barrel had run dry; and he told her that he had seen a fresh spring between two hills at the edge of the forest and he could show her where it was. So she took a container and went off with him, radiant and shy. Her headkerchief blew off in the breeze, exposing her wonderful hair streaming out behind her. I was amazed to. see them like that together, for the first time it seemed to me, man and woman.

A man and a woman, she went on, just as when they arrived to take on the rabbinical duties in the town, as they told me many years later; after my father brought my mother from the big city, a newlywed, the entire congregation with their women and children fanned out along the roads to the train station to welcome them. A motley crew wearing colorful rags, many of them barefoot, and at its head two of the more prominent members of the congregation, the rabbinical contract in hand. New woolen sleeves poked out of their shabby Sabbath coats with an odd innocence. My mother, the young rabbi's wife, watching all this as she gracefully leaned on her big-city parasol, could hardly believe her eyes. And so the procession moved from the train station back to the town to the beat of drums and the blare of a trumpet and the trill of a shepherd's pipe, a jubilant rabble raising great clouds of dust; and in the carriage sat the rabbi's wife in her suede gloves and an ostrich feather in her hat. Thus she arrived at the small community house, which was propped up by wooden supports like the other houses on the street, where a white and wide-eyed goat was standing on the heap of garbage in the courtyard waiting to be milked. And they told me, Dvora smiled, that the rabbi's wife refused to enter the community house; finally, she threw herself down on the bench outside and wept bitter tears.

It was my father, apparently, who comforted her, calling her a young and inexperienced goat. Thus began the long, bewildering summer in the remote little Lithuanian town, and my mother's heart was soon enough drawn to the charms of the town and to its ways. The affection that the congregation and my father had for her softened her disappointment and her face lost its gloom. In the long winter nights, when my father chanted the weekly portion and his voice was tremulous and gloomy and soft, my mother could stand it no longer and would rise and stretch out her hands to him. And he did not call her "little foolish one" now but rather soothed her with intimations of the child she would soon hold like our Mother Rachel in her day, and he waited affectionately until she had calmed down.

You have a holy woman and an everyday woman inside you too, I said. When you turn to your inner world, when you look inside yourself instead of at me, I see before me a saintly recluse. Your voice gets deep and you speak the language of some faraway world.

And the everyday Dvora? she asked, laughing.

Like everyone else, a human being, speaking an everyday language.

Looking at how the neighbors live through her window, preoccupied with her body, her illness, the food she eats—you know very little yet. But leave that for now. So I saw my father in holiness and in daily life, in health and in sickness, but there was never the slightest conflict in his character. Their lives were hard, but nevertheless the people I remember from my town were not torn in two the way we are these days. That faith we spoke about earlier knitted the jagged edges together. One noontime I was waiting for my brother in a corner of the synagogue when I saw an old neighbor woman come in. I knew that her son was ill, and that Pavlovski, the Polish doctor, had pronounced him not long for this world. The old woman marched straight to the Holy Ark, where two lions gazed down at her with kind eyes and the flame of a single memorial candle spluttered sadly in the white daylight. She did not open a prayer book, which would have been usual, nor did she recite a prayer by heart, but instead she turned directly to God in her everyday language, as if she were standing right before him. She asked him if it was proper that he should take a father away from his sons while they were still young, when there was no one else to support them. "You could cure him, after all," she said, leaning over to stroke the silk curtain. I watched as she turned to leave, an expression of confidence on her face. Later I heard at home that the father—that is, the old woman's son—had taken a turn for the better, and soon he rose from his bed and went back to work.

When I would feel helpless, I would search for such a faith, for a strong conviction that could prod me forward, as it used to when I was a young girl. She made a listless gesture, smiling ironically. Then she lay back against the pillow. Evening shadows filled the room, and for a moment Dvora looked like a child, mother and father hovering beside her bed.

In the doorway stood Tsipora, her hunched silhouette rooted to its spot. I had no idea how long she had been standing there.

Shall I turn the light on for you, Mama?

No, not yet. The dusk is beautiful. Open the curtain. And you, Amia, she said without looking in my direction, run along now. You have spent enough time with a hardened old woman.

You know very well that I don't think of you that way, I said, but I got up anyway and said my goodbyes.

When you come again, Dvora called as I reached the threshold, be so kind as to ring the bell twice, two short rings. That way I shall know it is you and answer the door.

On Oliphant the streetlights had been lit. The days were getting shorter, next week was the Jewish New Year, and the heat had still not let up. Tomorrow will be the fourth anniversary of my husband's death,

I remembered, as I walked to where I had parked. Cars galloped by, their horns blasting me forward, pinning me with their headlights. People coming home, going out. And the past is still always with us.

In the car on the highway to Jerusalem I played back the cassette I had just recorded, making sure I had captured that deep, monotonous voice. Excellent, I thought, she's safe with me now. I ejected the cassette and inserted Mendelssohn's *Songs Without Words*, and I drove on home to the notes of the piano.

third encounter

A few days after the Jewish New Year I received a short note from Tsipora, asking me when I was coming to visit her mother again. She wondered if I could find the time on Tuesday afternoon, when she herself had a doctor's appointment.

At the agreed-upon time, Tsipora stood ready at the door, and I took my place beside the bed. Two tall glasses of water and lemon had been prepared on the small bedside table and the curtain was drawn shut, sinking the room into twilight. Dvora looked pale and tired in her black dress with the high white collar—a dress of the sort I had never seen outside an antique shop. I offered her a glass of water, but she waved it aside.

Can I prepare you something to eat, I suggested, or a cup of something hot?

You are a perceptive woman, she said. I do feel a bit unwell today and thought of canceling your visit; but Tsipora wanted to go out, and refused to leave me alone in the house. She said she would sit for a while in a café after her appointment and write, which would do her a world of good. She has almost no life of her own, you know.

Why do you think that is? I ventured.

You are the psychologist, she said, with a bitter grimace of a smile; the daughter of two eminent people, you would say. They sacrificed her, you would say, except that it always looked to me as if this was her freely chosen path. Many and wondrous are the roads a human being chooses.

I kept silent, sipping the cool, lemony water.

And you will certainly ask, as everyone does, why we did not send her to school.

You wish to tell me, I said in a voice that was half-statement, half-question.

Not necessarily. We are, after all, dealing with my childhood, not my daughter's. You are a highly methodical woman, they tell me.

Who could she be talking with about me? I wondered, but I let it go. Let her talk about me as much as she pleases.

I am not one for womanly intimacies, you know. Where a person takes stock of his soul is a sanctified place, my mother would say, and no one else may approach. I was often silent in my life, and when I did converse, it was usually with men. Most of my friends were men—writers, editors, translators, people I met through my work. We spoke about the important things, literature, philosophy, the events of the day. But who among them remains a friend today? Which of them still visits? Her voice was lost in thought. The ones who are still living, she added.

Only very belatedly did I develop friendships with women, she continued, and with them I could speak my heart about everyday concerns, the house, our troubles, Tsipora, our health. When I was young, women were . . . she stopped. This was the first time I had seen Dvora Baron at a loss for words. Different, she concluded dismissively. And I, ever since childhood I played with my brother and his friends and learned with my father and his students—I was a tomboy. I had an older sister, Chaya-Rifka, and after her my brother, Benjamin, was born, and we had two younger sisters, Tsipora and Chana. I was considered a bit of a mischief maker. Girls' games held no interest for me whatsoever. I never once played with dolls. I hated to be reminded that I was a girl, because that meant that there were things I could not do, or was not supposed to be able to do. So I would pump myself up like a lion and try with all my might to lift a heavy boulder or run like a deer, just to show the boys that I could keep up with any of them.

But Benjamin was always at my side. He was four years older than me, and wherever he went, I followed. He would protect me from the other boys and take revenge on anyone who hurt me. My brother, Benjamin, she said dreamily, how I loved him! He was exactly like me: his nature, his character, his appearance, the way he moved. We both had a dark complexion, black wavy hair, but my eyes were blacker and more beautiful than his.

Even now your eyes are amazingly beautiful, I thought, careful not to disturb the delicate embroidery of our common dream.

How I loved him! she repeated, and he loved me too. With our band of little boys we played wildly in every moment we could snatch. We would swing on the hoist of the well and play "Mount Sinai" at the top of the hill, while the girls played with their dolls. One would take a kerchief, one would take an apron, and they would make large dolls and small dolls. One doll was the mother, another the aunt, and suddenly it would be Sabbath and the first doll would take her little dolls and go off to visit her friend. I had no patience for such pursuits. Rather, my brother and I loved helping my father. Once my brother even snuck me into the old synagogue storeroom; but I always knew that it was only by special dispensation that I was allowed to do such things—not by right, as it would have been for a boy. One complaint from me and my brother would say: "Go play with the girls! Your dolls are crying for their mother!"

Once, on the eve of the Ninth of Av, when the whole town was preparing to mourn the destruction of the Temple, the boys acted as if they were actually happy I was joining them. Unfortunately, it was my curly head of hair that made me so welcome a playmate. As was the custom on the Ninth of Av, each of them took a handful of thistles and stuck them in my hair, my brother, Benjamin, first and foremost. Dozens of hands, big and small, rained stinging thorns onto my scalp, accompanied by a flood of laughter. And although I ran for my life, even I laughed along as I fended them off.

And then, when we had returned home from battle and found mother and grandmother seated on low stools, reading Lamentations by candlelight and crying, my brother whispered to me, his eyes glinting mischievously, "Now we can see what's hidden in grandmother's treasure box." So we found the box in the darkness and had just managed to get it open when we were caught red-handed. And what was in that treasure chest? The secret was revealed only after grandmother's death: two small sacks of earth from the Land of Israel, one for my grandmother and one for her daughter—that is, our mother, for their burial after one hundred and twenty years. This dirt, you understand, protects a Jew in the grave from maggots and worms. There you see faith, she sighed, as we were saying last week.

Many years later, she went on in a different voice—by which I knew that she was with me and not "there"—when I disembarked from the boat at the Jaffa shore, I was amazed to see a whole country full of white sand, all of it soil from the Land of Israel. And everyone just ignored it! All I could think about was how this dirt they were walking on so obliviously was such a precious commodity for the Jews back home, a guarantee against the ravages of death itself. And here it is, all around me now.

From the sacred to the profane, I commented.

The profane Land of Israel, of pioneers and Arabs, of the writer Yosef Chayim Brenner and the *Young Worker* and everything I found when I arrived—and the sacred one, of prayer and Torah, of my mother and grandmother—could not have been more distant from each other. As long as there was still a way to get from one to the other, however, there were bridges connecting them; while today there is only one left, she stopped, her voice absorbed in its own mourning.

I also remember a small sack among my grandmother's treasures, I spoke up, surprising myself with a memory that seemed to come from nowhere. When my grandmother and grandfather arrived after surviving the war in Siberia, my old grandmother, who was blind in one eye, was wearing a ragged shoelace around her neck. Hanging on the shoelace was a little old cotton pouch that had soaked up all the smells of her body in all the places she had hidden after she was driven out of her home in Poland. She wore the pouch between her breasts day and night, and I only saw it poking up from her dress once in a while. When I asked my mother, she told me that Grandmother had put her gold rings and diamonds and a few coins in the pouch—"sovereigns," my mother called them—a horde that had kept her and her old husband alive among the gentiles. By now there is certainly nothing left, my mother whispered, aside from a few pictures of a house that no longer exists, and of her parents and her young son, Nachum, an officer in the Russian army who died in battle. My oldest son is named after him, I added.

Perhaps we should have brought the dust of the shtetl here to Israel, Dvora said.

You were telling me about your brother, I said when the silence lengthened.

He was a child prodigy. He was supposed to inherit the rabbinate from my father, and we expected greatness from him. And even though my father loved me fiercely and taught me everything he taught Benjamin, for as long as I can remember I knew that sons were more important than daughters. I always longed to be a boy, a son, like my brother. I thought that that was the way to make my parents and grandparents happy with me, and that it was too difficult for a daughter to give them the same joy. I saw the boys saying Kaddish after the death of their parents and I knew that although I could pray as fluently as they, I would never be allowed to do as they did. I fantasized that I could unite in myself a woman's gifts with all the things that only men were allowed to do then—study, freedom, wandering. I felt this desire from the earliest age, even if I could not, of course, articulate it even to myself. Instead, I clung to my brother and tried to do everything he did along with him.

But he also followed my lead. I would ask my mother to let me take my supper outside, and then I would share my food with beggars or with animals that happened by. Benjamin was my partner in crime. Once I found a stray dog wandering around the neighborhood in the most desperate condition. The other dogs in town despised him and never let him get a crumb of the leftovers that people threw in the gutters for them. He was scarred from fighting, blind in one eye, just a bag of bones. I asked Papa to let me take him into the house, but he answered, "My little savior of the downtrodden, now you want to bring dogs into my house? What would people say? They're raising a dog in the rabbi's house, just like some Polish esquire!" One night, my brother came with me to bring the dog some of my supper and we found him lying lifeless. Dead of starvation.

And you, she turned to me, do you have a brother? And added, Or sisters?

I was startled and hurt for a minute. If sisters were of so little interest to her, then why was she speaking with me? There were three girls in my family, I answered coolly. I'm the oldest. When my mother gave birth to my twin sisters, a woman in the hospital said to my father when he arrived to see them, "Mister, don't be angry with her, the next one will be a son!" There were only girls in my family, but I never once felt that my mother or father regretted not having sons.

How come?

I don't know. It's all in the family, I laughed, forgiving her. I knew the entire grace after meals by heart by the time I was five, and Papa would boast about my talents to the guests, "Such a head—and on a girl!" I went to the synagogue with my father every Friday night, and sat next to him until I turned twelve. After that, my father could no longer fight the congregation's disapproval and I was exiled to the women's section; that was the end of my going to synagogue.

All this in our own little shtetl of Israel, she said. But at least they let you go to school, like the boys.

A girls' school, but still a school. I had good friends there, I said, remembering, and immediately asked, Did you really have no girlfriends at all when you were little?

Of course I had some. When Benjamin grew a little older, he studied in the yeshiva all day; later, he went off to Pinsk to prepare for medical studies. During those years, until I joined him when I turned fifteen, I was already shy about playing with boys; and although I still studied with my father as if I were a son, in my free time I was a girl in a girl's world. My best friend was Mina, the baker's granddaughter, who had come to our town to help her grandmother. In the street they gave her a nasty nickname, "Spotty," because she was covered with freckles. She was not much of a beauty, more like a simple earthenware vessel, but one which holds a rare wine.

Since she worked all day in her grandmother's bakery in our street, sometimes I would go over there to lend a hand. The first time was in the days between Passover and Pentecost, when the bakery was busy with all the weddings to be celebrated in the town. Mina would work at the ovens with clumsy zeal, and everything she baked came out looking perfect; but she had a hard time dealing with customers, so I would keep track of their accounts, making a list of the cakes purchased on credit with charcoal on the wall.

While we worked she would tell me about her siblings who had remained in the city. I heard about her relationship with her mother, no love lost between them as far as I could tell, and I could feel Mina's pain about this. She told me that as hard as she tried to please her mother, she could never satisfy her, and sometimes her mother would turn on her with a truly mad fury.

From the way she leafed through my books I saw that Mina could not read, so I decided to teach her. In our free time, which was generally in the afternoon, I began to show her the alphabet: first, with an "Alef-Bet" chart, and later, when she could connect the letters to their sounds, with a prayer book. Before long we were at the Bible, which we used in those days as a Hebrew primer. We couldn't find a place to study in either of our houses, so we used the upstairs corridor of the synagogue. There, in the dark confines of the hallway, the story of creation slowly unfolded before her eyes. I added as many legends as I could remember, just as my father had done when he taught me years before, and my commentary made the story lucid for her. A spark would brighten her eyes whenever she suddenly grasped something I said. This is the spark I would notice in the eyes of my students in later years.

When I saw how she longed for something from her own world, I found her some Yiddish books we had lying around the house, and soon she was transported. A world with undreamed-of horizons opened before her. She shared in the characters' pain and sorrow, especially if they were poor or oppressed; and I was the same way.

And so our lessons progressed, until finally she could drink up a chapter of the Bible like wine and top it off with a few pages of *The Love of Zion*. I especially remember the story of the three weeks, when Mina and I, sitting in the corridor of the synagogue, read the historical account of the destruction of the Holy Temple together. Here, look, she said thoughtfully, all those prophecies, which seemed like empty threats, came true in their smallest detail.

We were the closest of friends, beginning with the bakery, then in the world of books and in our hikes through the meadows that surrounded town. Through our friendship Mina "straightened out," her rough edges became smoother. She learned how to carry the water buckets from the well as lightly and with her back as straight as the local girls, and I knew that it was her soul that had grown tall within her.

My second friend was Gitl, the daughter of the Jewish lumber dealer, who later immigrated to Palestine and set up her home in a village. While our mothers spoke in their kitchen, my fiery friend Gitl with her unkempt braid and I would go out to play in the lumberyard by the house. First we would set up a see-saw between the rows of lumber, and shriek with delight as we flew up and down on the plank. Another game we played together was "House and Garden": one crate became a house, with a row of "trees" before it, and sometimes, by Gitl's insistence, it was a faraway homestead in the Judean hills with lemon and orange trees on all sides. I remember a large doll slumped against the "house," watching us with empty glass eyes.

Once Gitl's nursemaid was ill; she was let off her lessons, and she suggested that we lay out a real garden. We set off a medium-sized square of ground outside the gate to the yard and planted vegetable seeds in it. Some sprouted and quickly blossomed: radishes, beets, and turnips, exactly like a real farm. When we were a little older we would together to the Daughters of Zion organization, which Gitl's older sister Shifra and her friends had started, but that was much later, after I had already begun writing Hebrew short stories—sketches, we called them. I will tell you about that some other time, she promised.

Is there anything else you want to tell me about your childhood home in the shtetl? I brought us back to her previous story.

Its beginning and its bitter end, about these things we have still not spoken. I have often thought about the day of my birth, the birth of a daughter, and have written about it as well, and as you say: truth has many faces, according to when it is told; and in this instance you and I are not, of course, dealing with the facts at all, but rather with a fictional world as I imagined it. In my youth I saw my birth as a dark day. Just like a rebellious adolescent, you will probably say. Here I was born, yet another girl in a family that still had only a single son, how bitter was my father's disappointment! As I grew older, however, the day of my birth changed too, growing more compassionate and filled with light.

Tell me, I begged.

Her voice deepened again into her storyteller mode, and she spoke as if she were reading aloud from an invisible page.

The day I was born was a short and meaningless winter day, with low and utterly ungladdening clouds in the skies over my town. It was 1887, around Chanuka time. My father had been called to preside over the circumcision ceremony at the home of one of the wealthy men in town, and my young mother was left alone with only her mother-in-law, an ill-tempered old rabbi's wife, in attendance. If I had been graced with understanding from the moment I was born on that hard wintry night, when the stove had been stoked by so stingy a hand and the flame of the lamp had no faith in its own powers, I would have felt a silence in the house, stranger than I have ever felt or would ever feel. With the first morning light, I could see from my cradle the meager kitchen furniture, desolate and bare. The naked stovepipe peered hopelessly into empty space and a single screw stuck uselessly out from the expanse of the ceiling, which later became my symbol for everything superfluous and forlorn in life. From the other side of the wooden partition I heard the squeak of felt slippers, storming back and forth more and more thunderously as the day brightened. In short, my rebbetzin grandmother, wife of the rabbi of Tokhanovka, was unhappy at my arrival into the light of this world: another daughter in the family.

So passed my first day in the house between the two rabbis' wives— my weakened mother and my angry grandmother. The day was already darkening and my father had still not returned. When I saw that it was dark and silence surrounded me, I did the thing that any person would do if she were lonely and abandoned and salvation were distant: I raised my voice and I wept. Then a miracle happened, all of a sudden—as all miracles, the nature of which is to come suddenly and from a distance—

the ringing of a bell was heard from out of the darkness. Immediately the door rejoiced in being opened and into the house walked the man, who without having met him, I knew was destined to be dearer to me than all life's pleasures. Already from the sway of his sheepskin coat a pleasant smell wafted that could only belong to Papa. He approached the wooden partition, parted the curtains, and called out, "Mazel tov!" And I, I lost my breath in my excitement and within a moment had hushed. Then the lamps were lit on both sides of the partition, and warmth and a goodly atmosphere reigned in the house. While the smell of the meal that had been hidden in the oven all day spread through the air, my father told my mother about what had happened to Reb Shimon bar Ami: On the day his daughter was born the great Reb Chiya said to him that now the Holy One Blessed-Be-He had finally begun to favor him. Even my grandmother's face lit up, like a chunk of ice on which the sun's rays had suddenly fallen.

Dvora's drawn face lit up as she remembered. I sat silently, until she turned in my direction.

In this story, if you don't mind my commenting, you express your sense that it was your father who provided warmth and ease at home, while your mother was helpless to act on her own: weak, beaten into submission by her mother-in-law, confined to her bed.

Maybe so. That was how I sometimes felt, and that was how it seemed to be in my own family here in Israel. The father, he was the one who could provide his daughter with confidence, more than the mother. You know well enough, however, that the truth has many faces. Sometimes I write the first day of life very differently. On the blank page I see my mother, so beautiful after the birth, approaching the cradle and gazing at me, a smile slowly illuminating her face. After a long silence she continued: The same smile I will see again perhaps—how dearly I would love to believe this story—when my mother welcomes me into her arms once more on the day of my death.

My presence has been practically forgotten, I felt with a quiet satisfaction, sitting in the dark room in the lengthening silence.

I have another memory from my first days, she continued after a while, as if hypnotized. When I was still a baby I would suddenly fling myself onto the floor and sob wildly and bitterly for no apparent reason. At first they tried to calm me down, but when that had no effect, they would just leave the room and let me cry my eyes out.

Later on this story aroused various feelings in me: first of all—self-pity, that when I was still at the breast, still at the threshold of life, I was left alone like that, abandoned by everybody. And more than that, I resented my mother for behaving that way, even if she had her reasons. I was amazed that she could treat a tender and helpless creature so coldly. Most importantly, much later I was persuaded that this had not been some sort of childish tantrum but a foresight, a premonition about the future, a kind of forecry, which however desperate it was, still could not begin to grieve for all that was to come. If my mother had guessed this, instead of punishing me she would have showered me with enough love to safeguard me from the pain in my future.

Indeed there was no shortage of pain: death and separation from my father and brother, after which my entire world disappeared without a trace.

You said earlier that you would talk about the end of the family when we were done talking about its beginning, I remarked, but maybe you would rather leave that for now?

Turn on the light, she said briskly. My stories are so dreary. I have no idea what pleasure you could possibly take in them, a young and healthy woman with the whole world ahead of you.

There seemed no point in protesting. Instead, I turned back to something that had been occupying my mind.

You wrote a great deal about your father's death in the stories about Chana's childhood in the shtetl. But I immediately realized that you weren't speaking directly from your own experience, since Chana's father died when she was still a young girl.

True. The young rabbi, Chana's father, died of consumption, as did my own father, but my father died ten years later than Chana's. I was about twenty years old then and already living in the big city. What do these experiences have in common? The fears of a little girl, who hears her father coughing through the night, the man who had always shouldered his burden with a smile; and my mother's muffled cries, filled with utter hopelessness. Thus, the terror of what might befall us—we lived under constant threat—found its expression in the figure of the father, adored, ill, on the verge of death. Why did I turn my literary mirror image into an orphan prematurely? Why did I widow my good mother while she was still young? Who knows? And perhaps, she said, her words reaching me as if from a great distance, it was in recognition of the essence of the thing, which is that a woman is alone and can never depend on a man for very long. On the poetic level, if one can speak that way, Chana's fiction is the truth of my life. My father could not give me any real support after my early childhood, and the world never treated me as tenderly after that.

Tears welled in my eyes. It's been a while, I suddenly thought, since I had a good cry.

So when my father fell ill with consumption in my childhood, our family found out that only pure forest air could help him recover. With the help of a well-to-do friend, we traveled to a summer resort run by a man named Yotka. Our family occupied an entire coach, surrounded by our kosher dishes, and so we traveled like the rich people of the region on holiday. Our journey led us down the road that passed the villages, on one side the Usha River and across it the windmills on the countess's estate waving us along our way, until the carriage entered the darkness beneath a sort of roof, a thicket all aquiver with whistles and piping and the flapping of wings. Those were the pine woods; there, my father and the coachman got down to pray in their prayer shawls, and then we continued on to the forest resort. First my mother took all the crucifixes down from the walls and nailed a mezuzah by the door, where honeysuckles peeked innocently through the leaves: open during the day and shut like sleepy eyes when evening fell.

How wonderful it was to awaken in that rosy warmth pouring from some silent, invisible sun, Dvora said dreamily. From above, from the corners of our thatched roof, rare and wondrous birds plunged down again and again while the forest sang around them. A sort of earthly paradise, my father said, full of holy stirrings in the face of its glory. Across from us shimmered a grain field and beyond it a stream meandered along the foot of the hill. The shepherd boys would bring their sheep down to the stream in the evenings, and the farm girls would come to scrub their laundry.

A Torah scroll was brought from a neighboring town for my father, and a few of the vacationers used our house as a synagogue. My mother took the lacy curtains out of storage, where they had been since she had first brought them from the big city—they were too fancy for the community house—and made a kind of tent beside the summer house, in which my father could sit in the healthful air and study his Talmud, a pine needle dropping from time to time onto the page. Vacationers from the big city would walk by, staring at him from beneath their colorful parasols: "Look," they would say, "Der Rabbiner is praying!"

Our hope knew no bounds in our early days at the resort. The forest sang and smiled at us, promising an instantaneous cure; but the nights, when the forest filled with stifling mists, were restless, and our hearts groaned even as we slept. My father was short of breath and at night his cough grew hoarser. Once there was a party in the old mansion and my mother said sorrowfully: "Run over and see." And what she meant was: "There has not been much joy allotted to you in this life; go then, and find some pleasure in other people's happiness."

And so the autumn arrived; the forest darkened and made no more promises, and my mother's hopes for my father's recovery began to fade. From here our ways part, my little Chana, she continued dreamily. The father of my literary sister died soon after, and as was prophesied for her, she knew no more joy after that. And I? But you know. My father lived for another ten years and died before he could witness the troubles that came to our family after he was gone. While he was alive he continued to encourage my brother, Benjamin, and me in all our plans to study. In his own way he always kept us company, even taking a look into the "modern" Hebrew and Russian books Benjamin would get from Minsk and read on the sly. He was even able to give us his blessing when we left to study in the big city among the gentiles, she finished sadly; but all that is from different days.

fourth encounter

I had been busy all morning doing errands around Tel Aviv and finally, in the early evening, about an hour before my meeting with Dvora Baron, I sat down to rest by the Jaffa waterfront, sipping an iced coffee and gazing at the peaceful autumn sea with the fishing boats floating on it like a dream. Just a few more minutes here, I thought, before I immerse myself again in that other dream, my heroine's story.

A car festooned with colorful ribbons came to a screeching halt in front of the café. A bride stepped out, followed by two little girls in pink carrying the long train; the groom, in a bow tie and dark suit, in their wake. A frenetic photographer ran behind them, immortalizing every step, orchestrating their every glance and smile. A choreographer of happiness, from the festivity factory, I thought derisively. But Dvora once got married in Jaffa too and probably smiled just as proudly. The bride noticed my stare, and ashamed for having intruded on her happy moment with my skepticism, I smiled and called out a guilty Mazal tov! She returned the smile and for a moment looked almost beautiful under her heavy makeup, and then the young man dragged her off to look at the sea and I got up and went on my way.

What was the manner of life in the town of your birth? I asked Dvora, after we had exchanged a few words about her health and the promise of relief from the heat in the autumn air. Dvora Baron smiled gratefully at my having phrased the question in her style, and immediately began reciting: fields and forests and gentiles, many gentiles, and in the midst of it all, a narrow strip of land, blanketed in snow all winter and drenched in sunlight all summer, and saturated always with the scent of Torah.

The town of my birth was Ouzda in the district of Minsk, she continued, which is Zhuzhikovka in my stories, and Ouzda resembled Zhuzhikovka as it resembled every other remote village in Lithuania. Our house, the community house, that is, was poor and humble. The large room was the community headquarters, with tables and benches, the eastern wall lined with overflowing bookshelves that contained the Babylonian and Jerusalem Talmud, the Torah with the various commentaries, the midrashic collections, Maimonides and the later rabbis. The family slept on the other side of the wooden partition. There was a china closet in the kitchen, with glass dishes that caught the early morning sun and reflected the mountains across the way, and an entire shelf of charity boxes, around whose curved sides were printed the acronyms of all the yeshivas, all the Talmudic academies, around the world. Outside, there was a shelf with slices of cheese drying on it, swallows circling above with thievery in mind. A solitary tree with a bench at its foot rose in the yard outside. Across from us was the well, with its hoist and its deliciously pure water, where the women gathered each morning, chatting as they filled their buckets.

The community alley led from our house to the synagogue. It was a domed building, heated with a stingy hand, with rows upon rows of benches with wooden lecterns separating each row. A small lamp hung at the western corner, over the table where the daily page of Talmud was studied. A single memorial candle burned at the eastern wall above the plaque that read "I have set the Lord always before me." On the eve of Sabbath and holidays, the beadle would drape the community prayer shawl over the pulpit and light the chandelier that hung before the Holy Ark, a gift of the wealthy owner of a nearby estate. The large windows would instantly darken, and the engraved letters—"I have set"—would shine forth, looking bright and freshly scrubbed. A permanent semidarkness reigned in the women's section, and only a ray of light or two ever penetrated the letters of the stained glass "EAST."

I can see the village houses of our alley in my mind's eye, crowded, lopsided, propped on either side by supports. Among them were dilapidated hovels on the verge of collapse. Other houses were large with many windows and their own sheds behind. These houses had yards with vegetable beds, where radishes and onions grew alongside beanstalks and pumpkins; the pumpkin seeds were our Saturday night treat. Still farther away was the house of the rich man in town, sun-drenched and sturdy, its balcony rising above the roofs on the street and a wisp of smoke curling from its chimney. The house had a porch enclosed in glass and was set in a garden, its paths strewn each morning with fresh sand. In the garden were flower and vegetable beds, and a hen house, from which the angry screech of a turkey would periodically erupt. Curtains fluttered in the open windows, and a servant girl beat the carpet against the fence. A piano spilled soft music onto the street, and a large dog guarded the house, pacing before it or stretching out in the garden at his master's feet.

I set foot in the rich man's house only on rare occasions, when I accompanied my mother on a social visit; but I spent many hours in the houses in our alley. I first saw the world around me on those days that I wandered around town, free from the fetters of Torah school, she said dreamily, and nothing I ever saw afterward added a jot to these impressions. The doors of the houses whose owners were at market were closed but not locked, and I could enter any of them I chose. They were alike: a mezuzah on the doorpost, an "EAST" drawn on the wall, and a great tower of pillows on the bed. In one corner a broom stood over a small pile of dust as if it were trying to hide it, and the clock had a human face and a mournful tick. If it was around the High Holidays, small balls of dough would be spread out to dry on the sideboard, and anyone who entered the house felt compelled to give them a stir.

Rich people's houses had parlors, corridors, dim stairways. Hat stands and leafy plants cluttered the entry hall, and once I caught a glimpse of myself in a mirror—from head to toe—and nearly slipped on the polished floor. The parlor chairs were upholstered in plush fabrics and golden taffeta covered the walls; there were airy curtains and flowered carpets. The black piano reflected a silver candelabrum, tea was served in delicate china cups, and a green-marbled lamp stood on the sideboard, on a doily. While mother was busy with the hosts, I stared, hypnotized by all I saw.

But I lacked for nothing at home. On Fridays my mother and Basya, the one who helped my mother with the housework, washed the windows, scoured the copper pots, polished the candlesticks, and scrubbed the floor until the house glowed. The casseroles in the oven spread a delicate odor through the rooms, and my mother's handiwork was everywhere. She crocheted tablecloths and runners, quilted appliqués onto the pillowcases, and embroidered a landscape and a proverb to hang on the wall. Potted plants lined the windowsills and colorful fabric hung between the beds. The neighbor women never sat idle, their hands were always busy crocheting or embroidering. The women would sing together as they sewed; the ballad about the orphan girl and the man who left for faraway regions would always just break my heart. I was supposed to learn how to crochet, too. My mother knitted while I dutifully watched the soft yarn draw submissively behind. Sometimes my aunt would recruit me to help her unravel her wool. She would wind the wool over my hands, my fingers spread wide as if I were performing the priestly blessing, and setting herself down in the meager shade of the roof, she would pull the yarn slowly and listlessly, like someone dragging out a monotonous, laborious life. I hated these contemptible jobs, this women's work! They were always singing the praises of this work, she continued, the patience and morality it teaches those who do it, those old women forever darning woolen socks.

Silence reigned in the room.

So you didn't like either women's work or girls' games, I commented.

No, I never did, although I did my share of embroidery when I was young and sometimes even enjoyed it, when it wasn't forced on me.

On the bedside table, beside her Bible and midrashic commentaries, I noticed her sewing case again. Even now, with her eyesight so bad.

I'm the same way, I told her. At my girls' school they taught us crafts, especially knitting and sewing. I'll never forget the yellow socks I was supposed to finish by the end of the school year to get my report card. The other girls were just spitting out amazingly symmetrical socks with those slippery needles—I was the only one who was always getting tangled up, and my wool was ratty and black from being taken apart so often. When I finally finished one, lopsided and twice the size it was supposed to be, I timidly brought it to the teacher; but she asked, "Where's the other one?" At home, I lied, it's exactly like this one. I laughed, remembering.

So, did you finally learn to sew and knit?

Not at school. When my children were born, I wanted to make their clothing, so I taught myself to sew and knit. I particularly enjoyed sewing my daughter little cotton dresses—until my children grew up and found the clothes they saw in stores more to their taste, and since then I haven't sewn a thing.

Dvora lay on her back, covered with a light summer blanket, her eyes gazing vacantly beyond me, and I knew that she was "there," lost to me across some inpenetrable frontier. I sat and waited for her return, and after a few moments her voice reached me again: And there were, of course, poor people starving for a piece of bread. I see their houses, gloomy and cold. Patches of mold crept along walls that seeped moisture in the winter, a sooty stove belching smoke into the house; and in the middle of the room, a large washtub, overflowing with dirty laundry. Babies' wails and the squeals of the hungry goat. . . . It always pained me to see the cozy house of the rich man in the very midst of this misery. But there was nothing I could do about it.

The poor people lived in the gulch in our town, while the wealthier houses were built on the streets along the rise, and on the mountain itself were the gentile neighborhoods. The road up the mountain branched out into the paths that led to the surrounding villages, where the peddlers hawked their wares during the week. At the edge of the town stood the slaughterhouse. Rows of acacias and vegetable gardens separated the Jewish neighborhoods from those on the mountain. A grove of pine, one of the countess's forests, darkened the mountainside, drowsing in the heat of day; and farther along the slope, a group of buildings nestled around a windmill, fanning themselves with its blades. On the other side, where the alley ended, a flock of slovenly, heavy-uddered goats grazed the blue meadow. The garden plots flowed down the mountain and at its foot ran the river, with fishing boats and barges bearing lumber from the countess's forests.

Of all the landscapes of my childhood, I loved the grassy meadow beyond the alley best. It was a broad field, a cushion of grass, with flowers growing without anyone tending to them. Once I had played among those flowers, I never wanted any vases of flowers in my house, she added emphatically. I can still feel the touch of my bare feet on the warm grass, with thousands of puddles sparkling in it. On the banks of the river I caught my first glimpse of water lilies, which I thought were living creatures. At sunset, the harvesters' sickles flashed in the faraway wheat fields. One mountain turned purplish-pink and the seven hills opposite darkened; the windmills lifted their blades in turn as if waving goodnight to each other.

But I also loved the landscape of the village of Khmilovka, two miles from our town, where my aunt lived. The village had just a single street that lay abandoned in the midday summer heat. The dull thud of a hammer surged from the forge, and the smell of hay, unripe apples, and fresh rye bread sweetened the air. Here, too, the village was built on the slopes of a mountain, surrounded by vegetable gardens, and the river at its base smelled of damp reeds. Young women shrieked with laughter as they did their wash in the river each morning, and at noon they pulled carts full of clean laundry down the street. Wagons loaded with cucumbers, bundles of dill clinging to their edges, bumped down the road, leaving great dust clouds in their wake.

One summer there, in the village across the river, I got my first glimpse of an estate. It was set in a famous garden, protected by an iron gate, and to me it was paradise itself. Only the baker is allowed inside, my aunt told me. He brings them egg bagels every morning. Once when we were sitting across from the estate the gate opened and something blinding could be seen through it, something that looked like a rainbow, which my aunt explained to me was called a fountain. It was a shimmering column of lights, a vision that stayed with me all that winter and eventually led to the first adventure of my life.

And what was your adventure? I asked, as the silence lengthened.

A journey, she answered, a journey I took across the river on ice floes, she snickered. It was the end of winter, and I had come for another visit to my aunt for her milk, fresh from the cow, which was supposed to keep me from getting sick. Finally the river "opened": the sun shone, the ice began to melt, and all the streams flowing into it began to swell. Following the cracking sounds, I made my way down to the valley, where I saw the river, broken free of its constraints, alive from one bank to the other with ice floes in overlapping scaled rows, moving downstream. And I saw that across the river, on the now-green hill, the gate to the estate had been left open and unguarded. So I stepped onto an ice floe that seemed fairly solid and off I sailed.

She stopped, a slight smile on her lips, and I asked, as expected, And where did you sail off to?

Not to the other side of the river, my dear. As with many of my other journeys, this one did not take me where I wished to go. At the end of it all some farmers rescued me and brought me back to my aunt's house. The children laughed at me, the adults were furious, and only my aunt looked at me with open sympathy and understanding; for she knew that mine was a truly courageous act, an attempt to pass from an ugly world to a different, more beautiful one.

At the forest resort too, a few years later, I saw an estate that seemed like a palace to me, with the wicked dog Nero at its gate, allowing no one to get close enough to take a good look. But the dairyman's daughter told me there were lamps inside the mansion that were lit by the press of a button and musical instruments that played on their own; and that the two daughters of the squire, clad in splendid silk gowns, held dances in the countless ballrooms of their palace.

Those were the landscapes of my homeland, and they changed, of course, with the seasons, and even now, while I lie still, she added, they continue to change. The transformations of the river at the edge of town were especially dramatic. This was the Ouzda River—"Harness" river in Lithuanian, because of its shape—whose water we drank, and in which we bathed and washed our clothes. Sometimes I wonder which was the soul of the town: the synagogue at its center or the river at its edge? The river was not very wide, but it had been flowing through our valley for centuries without end. In the summer the whole town would gather at its wide sloping banks, now transformed into a lush green carpet. As children we would splash around in the shallows and make ourselves flutes from the reeds along the shore. In the winter, when the entire town was blanketed with snow, the river was elegant white marble. No one disturbed the river then except for the gentiles up the mountain, who would split the ice with their axs on baptismal days. It enraged me to see the river desecrated, and I prayed for the frost to return and whiten its wounds. In the spring, when warmer winds blew, the snow in town would begin to melt and we would ask each other, Is it still quiet? And when the sun finally broke through, the frost on the river could be heard crackling into sections, the water raging up through the cracks to overflow the banks, swelling until it flooded the houses on the street. We hurried to help the adults clear out the pillows and featherbeds as the river continued to rise, licking at the walls of the houses and rinsing them clean. The next morning, at dawn, the river would begin to ebb, retreating into itself again. Then we would return to our houses to find them scrubbed and sparkling in the sunlight, all koshered for Passover.

Yes, spring was the most wonderful time in my childhood. As you scrubbed the windows for Passover you could peek over the sill to watch the river, now erupted into rivulets in the meadow, and the people standing at its edges dunking their new dishes, and the gentiles from the mountain netting agile pike, with their sharp fins and merry golden flecks on their scales. Broken fences were mended, and each day flocks of sheep descended the steep path from the mountaintop. Once again the shepherd played carefree springtime tunes on his tremulous flute. Briskly and confidently swiveled the wheel of the mill at the foot of the hill beside the river. The furrows crouched in their sun-drenched rows, the smile of creation in their folds.

A week before the holiday the storm windows were taken down and the house filled with a powerful whiteness and seemed to expand, she continued. After Passover, although the evenings were still a bit chilly and in the synagogue they were counting the days of the Omer, the air already carried the delicate scent of summer clothes and the smell of pastries being prepared for the town weddings. The doors to the boys' school stood open, and the merry shouts of the children let out for recess could be heard. Only the ringing of vespers in the Christian church sounded melancholy, as the sad moon rose from behind the dense Lithuanian forest.

Half the Sabbath was given over to God; but in the summer, on Sabbath afternoon, the family assembled in the grassy yard in the shade of the pear or nut tree. Across, one could see the open fields and the groves of white birch, and a little farther on flowed the river, and in the summer its soft murmur was audible. Sometimes there would be a sudden cloudburst and afterward a rainbow appeared on high, clasping the entire town from one end to the other in a powerful hoop. The thatched houses seemed to grow smaller and a strange luster illuminated the windowpanes. Women, with the light of grace on their faces, recited at the doors to their houses: "Blessed is the One who remembers His covenant with Noah."

It's been years, I broke into her trance, since I heard someone say that blessing.

And was there a time when you knew such things? she asked in wonder.

Yes, of course, I answered, we learned that one in my girls' school, and I knew blessings for thunder and lightning and many other blessings, and I have forgotten just about all of them. But you remember everything, after all these years! Here I am again, interrupting your story; do continue, I apologized, noticing again that I seemed to be picking up her strange style, which sounded so natural in this monastic room, as I sat there, looking at her world through my eyes.

I loved laundry days in my mother's house in the summer. The servant girl helped my mother take the washtubs out to the yard and fill them with water and I would tread on the soaking laundry. Stamping my feet, I would shatter the clouds in the soapy water, and then stand still to see them form anew.

In the dead of summer, however, during the three weeks of mourning for the destruction of the Temple, the town lay desolate. The dark square we had left unpainted on the wall in memory of the Temple seemed to expand until it filled the house. On the first day of the month of Av everyone would begin the mourning rituals: clothing was not laundered, dishes remained unpolished, no one went down to the bathhouse on Friday afternoon. On Sabbath mornings, the Torah portion was followed by

Isaiah's harsh prophecies, and for the rest of the day the alleys lay abandoned. Only the hay gatherers on the mountains continued their work, sickles glinting in vertiginous flashes.

Sometimes a dark summer night would be suddenly transformed into broad daylight: fire had broken out in the gulch. There were no firemen in town. From the mountain the church bell tolled, and the Christians, when they saw the sky reddening over the town, scrambled to save their own possessions. The blaze hurled firebrands in all directions, long red tongues that licked the roofs and threatened to swallow everything. Then there was the crash of falling beams, girders heaving and falling, a roof struck and crushed scattering sparks everywhere. In the inferno frightened cows moved blindly about, huddling against each other and lowing, dogs barked, and roosters screeched. Barefoot, half-naked women raised their hands to the crimson sky, children clutching at their hems and wailing. By morning the fire would have died down. From the ruins, a column of smoke twisted up, mixing with the stink of scorched hides and melted tallow. Piles of singed belongings and broken furniture accumulated in the meadow, and babies lay sunk in slumber atop dirty pillows and featherbeds.

One bright summer day in my childhood, the sky suddenly darkened. From afar something like a black column could be seen surging forward from behind the forest and approaching the pumpkin patches, and at high noon it suddenly turned night. Where the sun had been, jagged lightning bolts flashed across the sky, and to the unceasing roar of thunder hail struck the windowpanes, breaking through and bouncing inside in icy pebbles. The doors in the hall blew open in a single mighty gust, and for a moment I saw the world tilted askew. When it was over, there was nothing left but the flash of the hail crystals and the shattered glass, glinting in the maimed sun. People went down to where the cows had been grazing, and women whose husbands were off peddling in the villages stood at their thresholds and sobbed. I will never forget that storm. I connected it in my mind to the barber, who had given me an awful boy's haircut on my mother's orders. When the heavens thundered, I knew it was a divine punishment for those who had done me wrong.

When the month of Elul arrived, it was time to begin preparing for the High Holy Days. The summer canopies were taken down in the gardens and the men went solemnly off to the house of God each day in their wrinkled caftans. On the New Year, the women wore white, as on their wedding days and on the day of their death. Then the winter approached and lifeless leaves fell from the trees as lightly as feathers.

Her voice was rich with remembering, intoxicated at having entered so completely into her story. From somewhere in the distance clouds broke through and crept into position like troops at the edges of the horizon, and the town lay under siege. The last vegetable was carried in from the garden, and the chickens and goats were brought inside. The supports for the bridge by the watermill were mended, and a kerosene lamp burned there each night. And then one day the air went dark, and from within the pregnant silence arose a rustling sound, as if someone were scattering lead pellets on a tin roof. The streets grew increasingly waterlogged as the rain continued, deteriorating under our feet until they were impassable. When the women did go out, they wore boots and carried the children on their shoulders. The chilly rain, thin and ugly, penetrated the woodsheds and the potato cellars. The trees stood dreary and naked, and the bucket on the well dripped and creaked, full of misery and complaint.

But at the end of autumn the puddles froze, the cawing of crows split the predawn sky, and the first snowflakes began to fall. All deliveries of wood from the forest stopped. At the risk of life and limb a few last potatoes were brought over from across the river, and the opening of the well was blocked. The snowstorm went on forever. The churchbells tolled dejectedly over the barren marketplace, and at night the dogs howled from the other side of the river.

Sometimes, however, winter would come on with no warning. One morning I got out of bed and saw that the whole mess of mud and mire was gone, and the mounds of garbage were nowhere to be seen. It was white clear across the horizon. The sky was washed clean, the birds chirped sweetly in the transparent chill. Together we sat around the blazing fireplace, bundling planks for firewood. At seven o'clock each evening the schoolchildren would begin to pass in the alley on their way home. The reflections of their lanterns flickered like a flock of golden sheep on the dark wall behind them. A horse pulled a low wagon, which left deep furrows in the snow, tracks for the sleighs to slide along on their way to the villages or on to the big city. And so it went until spring arrived, all the days of my childhood.

fifth encounter

A week went by and again I presented myself at Dvora Baron's house in Tel Aviv. A faint early-autumn chill was already palpable in the musty old stairwell. The postman was distributing the day's mail, and a cheery-eyed old woman stood beside him, waiting to see what he might bring. She watched curiously as I slowly climbed the stairs, tape-recorder on my shoulder, ringing the doorbell, second floor, left. "Dvora and Tsipora are home," she remarked, as if another possibility existed.

Through the door the sound of a typewriter suddenly stopped and Tsipora stood in the doorway before me, stolid in her strange clothes.

How's your mother? I asked.

Fine, except that her blood pressure has been rising recently.

And are you taking care of it? I asked.

She gestured noncommittally and I was already facing Dvora, who was lying on the bed exactly as I had left her, another shadow lost in the shadowy autumn afternoon.

Hello, Amia, she said heavily, are you still at it?

Certainly, I laughed, trying to lighten things up a bit. It's your beautiful stories that keep me coming back.

And I still haven't left the world of my childhood. I suppose this chapter is the longest of them all, the way it is with old people who linger in the past.

Except, I thought, that you started living that way very long ago indeed.

I will try to describe for you the characters of my town, the ones who were not relatives. In town, of course, there were Jews and gentiles, poor people and rich; that was how the world appeared to me at its root. A

44

Jewish woman covered her hair with a kerchief or wig. On weekdays she wore a voluminous striped apron, in which she walked to market and went about her business. On Sabbath she wore a stiff satin dress and a narrow coif, smooth and black, with two tassels that leapt and shook with every movement, and in the morning she went to pray in the women's section of the synagogue. On Sabbath afternoons the women would sit under the tree in the yard or on their front steps and their colorful dresses would glitter in the sun. I would stroll up and down the alley and stare, bewitched by the sparkling, blinding watchchains and earrings. When evening came on a sweltering summer day, the women would go out on their front steps again, barefoot and half-naked, cooling off in the meadow breeze. The unmarried women went out on ordinary weekdays in housecoats with simple colored headkerchiefs; but for weddings and other celebrations, they would take out their finest muslin dresses with velvet sashes, tearing up the floor in a dizzying dance.

And what are your memories of the men in the town? I asked, when she fell silent.

Usually they were in patched woolen suits, all alike, she said meditatively, but on Sabbath they would put on satin caftans and be transformed into lords and barons. The rich men of the town were better dressed, of course. When I was young, a contractor and his family moved to our town from the city, and they had the strangest city ways. They had an enormous, good-natured dog, John was his name, who was one of the family, and the neighbors said that there was a room and bed in the house just for him, as if he were a human being. The father had an aristocratic prayer shawl, actually more like a narrow scarf, and the prayer book he brought to synagogue had a foreign translation. But their young daughter was the most marvelous of all, arriving in town wearing her high school hat. She was supple and tall, skin untouched by the sun, and beside her, the local girls looked rather insipid and dull. Her unadorned summer dress was gathered below her waist with a ribbon in a loose knot that was the very image of nobility, and when she walked among the fragrant orchards beneath her parasol, blond braid spilling down her back, your heart just raced.

Then there were the gentile girls, she added, her eyes on the invisible procession of figures; they wore the national costume, panels of embroidery dappling their cotton shirts in a blinding array of colors, with their hair gathered in two heavy braids, tied in an enormous loop at the neck.

Dvora stopped and asked me to bring her a glass of water. Tsipora had apparently left the house, as she usually did when I arrived. This is the first time, I thought, she has asked me for anything. Something in me shrank from entering the antiquated kitchen. It looked clean, but there was a sourish, moldy odor that reminded me of my grandmother's room in the old-age home and the stale candies in their sticky wrappers she would serve me yet again each week on visiting day. Old age, I thought, smells exactly like this. I filled the glass from a pitcher on the table, as she had instructed, and went back into the living room, shrouded in its heavy gloom. As usual, I offered to draw the curtains or turn on a lamp, but Dvora asked me not to.

The community revolved around its families, and unattached individuals had a hard row to plough, she said when I was seated again. There were families that had carried on the same traditions from time immemorial. Members of the family were named after their dead forefathers—Hayim, Meir, and Leyzer, and then the whole thing all over again—and they all worked at the family trade. In the baker family the old man would draw water from the well for kneading the dough, a graying man moving painfully slowly, his bent back perfectly suited to the depression in the yoke. His son, who was stronger than he, would do the baking. He was a man who inspired confidence, with a thick beard descending importantly down his chest. When he went for a walk he always carried an oak walking stick, and one day, during a pogrom, he beat the drunkenness out of some hoodlums from up the hill. From that day hence the gentiles left a wide berth if they happened to cross his path. When I returned to town from the city he had already grown old, and he was the one carrying the water and his young son was baking in his place. Things had always been that way; that was why it was so tough when there was no one to continue a family line.

I remember our barren neighbor Dinah, the one for whom my father wrote divorce papers after she and her husband had been married for ten years. She would cry literally without respite. Passersby on the street would hurry by her without slowing down. And really, who likes to see a fellow human being weep over things that should bring only joy: a child's smile in the sunlight, a young girl singing over her embroidery, the smile of a mother bouncing a baby on her knee?

But fate was also unkind to the woman who failed to bear sons for her husband. In our alley that was the shoemaker's wife. She gave birth each year like clockwork, during the three weeks of mourning for the destruction of the Temple, and only daughters emerged from her womb. Her shoemaker husband would beat her and the little girls, and hurl his tools at her. Once I peeked as she showed my mother her arm; she rolled up her sleeve and quickly turned her face away in shame. My mother snatched a hurried glance at the reddish bruises, the marks of a sledge-hammer, and turned away as well. In my hiding place in a shadowy corner of the kitchen, I crouched over in pain. One summer in my childhood, after the shoemaker's wife had given birth to a new baby girl, her husband dragged her up the street, her barefoot daughters clinging to her and wailing. Inside our house, the man pounded on the rabbi's table in a rage: "Divorce," he roared, "get me a divorce." But my father managed to placate him, and when the sun began to set and my father left the house for evening prayers, the shoemaker was right behind him.

Wretched also were the orphans in town, especially the girls who were left without a mother. That happened in little Muscha's family up the street; her mother died when she was three, and after her father lost his wealth when Muscha was just thirteen, her stepmother turned her into a servant-girl. She would wash the dishes on the bench outside, milk the cow, haul water from the well, scrub the wooden floor with sand and soap, polish the brass. Once I saw her during Passover spring-cleaning, blowing on her frozen fingers to warm them up, her face taut with pent-up fury.

I knew many girls who by the age of ten or eleven were already running their widowed fathers' households. I remember Leah, who was brought from her uncle's house in the village when she was eleven to run the house for her widowed father. She made herself an apron from some old dress of her mother's, tied a kerchief around her head like a full-grown woman, and before long the neglected shack began to look fit for human habitation again: the pillows were gathered and heaped in a great pile at the head of each bed and the shelves lined with shiny cooking pots and dishes. At sundown a bright fire lit up the stove, where the young girl was cooking a soup of buckwheat groats or oatmeal, according to her mother's recipe.

She, at least, had her father's house, where she was loved and protected; there was a homeless girl in our alley who was also brought from a village after her parents died, and she had nothing of her own apart from a bundle of bedding and what little warmth remained from her mother's loving hands. A villager had brought her to some women in the gulch, and for a few days she was passed from hand to hand like a useless implement. Those who put her up in their house just barely cleared a spot for her in a corner, and before they agreed to do so they insisted on making sure she had no skin disease and that the belongings in her bundle were clean. She walked around in her farmgirl's housecoat, her hair unkempt, without a trace of charm on her face. This abandoned girl scraped together a living from the age of eight by helping the gulch women with their chores. By the time she was twelve she could heat a kettle, light a stove, and bring water from the well, and the laundry, when she had finished wringing it over and over in the washtub with her great big "paws," was blindingly white. Because no one had a kind word for her, she grew accustomed to being alone in a world of mute objects, and in the silence that surrounded her, her speech became heavy and muffled. When she passed with her basket, the children playing on the street would call after her: "Here comes Chaya-Reyzl, Crooked-Crazy-Chaya-Reyzl," and she would limp on as if she had not heard. That was when I first noticed that when they encounter something that disturbs them, grownups tend to put a sort of quarantine around it, as if they were withholding the intricate filaments of intercourse that normally connect one human with another. Thus the space around such an unfortunate creature empties out, and she is left alone within it.

Amazing, I blurted out.

What is so amazing about that? she asked.

Your last sentence really struck me, I stammered. I once had a very similar experience.

What experience was that? she asked with great interest.

When I arose from the week of mourning my husband, I told her, my heart pounding, it was just before Rosh Hashana. My sister had taken all the preparations for the holiday upon herself, and the house, which had been full of visitors all week, was suddenly empty. I put on a khakhi dress that seemed appropriate to my new status and went downtown to buy holiday gifts for my children. I strolled through the familiar streets of Jerusalem, but that day they seemed alien. His feet will never walk these streets again, I repeated to myself, we'll never walk together again. People hurried on their way, holiday eve with all its bothersome details, and I walked among them at a different pace, like an invisible spectator, someone from a distant planet. Suddenly I saw a famous psychiatrist I knew quite well heading in my direction. He fixed his eyes on me—and continued walking, as if I were transparent. To this day I shudder when I think of that moment. Had I died too, along with my husband?

Now you've confirmed what happened to me that day, I continued, as if only you could see me when I was invisible to everyone else. I met the psychiatrist again a few months later, and he spoke to me perfectly naturally. So why wasn't he able to see me that morning when I so much needed to feel that I was alive too?

Dvora didn't answer, but I had no need, for a moment, of her voice.

What were we talking about? I asked after a few moments, as if I were shaking myself awake.

I was telling you about Chaya-Reyzl the orphan girl, Dvora smoothly continued. Have you ever known young girls who had to grow up so quickly?

Not that I remember. Of course, I've read about children in distress, how they can sometimes keep things together and comfort their little brothers and sisters, acting as parents to them. There were stories like that in the Holocaust, I offered.

In this country all children go to school. But even that is a burden, she said. How many times have I watched the little children being taken to kindergarten each morning? Mist from another world still covers their infant eyes, but the burden of existence is already lodged across their shoulders along with their school bags.

That's exactly how I felt the first day my oldest son went to school, I said, remembering. I dressed him in a striped shirt, buttoned up the front like a man going to the office, and like that, his messy hair falling in his eyes, I watched him walk into the doorway of a big building, a factory for education. I boldly opened a sensitive subject: But you never even sent Tsipora to school!

True. Tongues wagged over the unusual way Yosef and I behaved in this matter. Those were different times. She was a fragile and sickly child, and I was a professional home-teacher; for these reasons the decision seemed logical enough to us at the time. We would create a beautiful, enlightened world for her at home, we thought, and in it she would blossom like a flower. I taught her on weekdays and Yosef brought her some of the culture of the new settlements and, for her sake, we once again started celebrating the Sabbath and holiday rituals we had abandoned when we first came to Palestine. Over the years we became accustomed to this life. Tsipora never completely recuperated, nor did she ever express any desire to go to school, and I did not insist—perhaps because I enjoyed her presence and saw how well her studies were progressing. Only for her lessons in mathematics did we have a tutor come to the house. She acquired a comprehensive education, she knows many languages, and it is only recently, seeing her in her loneliness, that I have wondered whether we wronged her by educating her in this manner. As would be true of any one who dared go over his accounts at the end of the day, she finished in a whisper, mistakes, alas, were made.

In the stillness I understood that she would speak no more of this today. So I sat there in silent sympathy, as she had done for me a short while before. Let her lead her story wherever she wants it to go, I said to myself.

The world is cruel to the weak, she said suddenly. Even these days I sometimes see through my window the delivery boy walking from house to house, carrying a box of fruits and vegetables larger than he is, and I wonder, Where are his parents? Is he an orphan?

But there were many good people in my childhood, she continued in her storytelling voice. I was always watching for a few souls who could light up the darkness with their goodness, the way a Jew awaits Elijah the Prophet. One such generous man lived in the village outside our town. He was amassing a fortune with his mill, and since he had no children, he spread his wealth among strangers like a swelling river, which, having no tributaries, overruns its banks. In the early mornings, when no one had yet ventured outdoors, his wagon, reined to a powerful and large horse, could often be found in our alley, his faithful servant Cyril unloading sacks of flour and beans to deliver to those in need. Like his master, the servant would make his deliveries so skillfully that those who received them were inclined to believe that the food had been brought on credit, just until they could pay. Here Dvora smiled with an innocent pleasure I had not yet observed on her face. Moved, I stretched out my hand and stroked hers gently through the layers of blanket, as one would stroke an infant.

And there was, of course, Grandma Henya, she returned to her visions. Everything she earned through her nighttime labors, in her feather-plucking business, she gave to the town's poor. All day long she would walk among the houses of the poor people down in the gulch in her wide apron, the skirt tucked into her waistband to hold the food she would distribute to the destitute of the neighborhood. She gave handfuls of nuts and candy to the little children and brought medicine to the old. Once when I was still a child I saw her carrying two sick infants who had just been orphaned. Benjamin and I followed and watched as she lay the infants down on her bed and fed them until they rallied. An Elijah of the female sex, she smiled.

There were many festivals in our town: Jewish holidays, wedding celebrations, circumcisions, and Bar Mitzvahs, and as the rabbi's daughter, I often took part in them. How joyous was a holiday in my childhood, when it came with the pleasures of a brand-new dress. In honor of the holiday my mother would buy a new silk scarf for her head or a cotton kerchief with silk trim. For us girls she would get a roll of fabric from which the seamstress would sew some dresses to size—but large enough to fit us next year as well. What happiness I had in my childhood from azure fabric the color of the heavens and the stream that flowed through the meadow. I would take the cloth from its place, refolding it and drawing into myself its scent and pleasant rustle. I could scarcely wait until

Passover. I knew that my mother would choose a pattern and all sorts of crinoline and lace trimming so that, come the night of the Seder, my new dress would adorn me as if I were a princess.

Weddings were about the most important celebrations in the town. An arranged match always preceded the marriage, of course, and a young couple would never dare forge a connection without their parents' consent. There were many couples in my day who married by the arrangement of their parents without ever seeing each other until they met under the canopy. I remember our neighbor Shloyme, the old man whose son died at an early age and who wanted to marry off his grandson. The older granddaughter bundled up her satin dress in a kerchief and went to the nearby town where a match had been proposed for her brother. Since Shloyme was very much smitten by the father of the prospective bride, a poor preschool teacher, the arrangement was concluded to the satisfaction of both sides. So the bride, a girl of tender years, was brought to her in-law's house to marry our young neighbor. The wedding ceremony took place in the synagogue courtyard under a shiny satin canopy stretched above like the blue skies, while I stared at the bride standing between the groom's strapping sisters, who were supporting the canopy poles. I would meet the young girl at the well every morning; she was not yet used to the intricacies of hair-covering and raised her hands every few moments to adjust her kerchief with a touching shyness. I could see that her heart ached with love for her husband, although he had been chosen for her by the old people. Indeed, it was much the same in my parents' case.

But another time I witnessed a bride, my young aunt, taking leave of her friends before being married off to a stranger. The day before the ceremony the girl went down to the field with her friends, and like Jephthah's daughter in the Bible, she mourned her youth there. "I'll never see the world," she said, and her friends cried with her. Only then did she let her beautiful hair be shorn and submit to the guidance of her mother-in-law, who had come to instruct the new couple. A short time later, while I was visiting their house, I found that hair in one of the trunks in the corner of the bedroom, still gathered in a braid with a colorful silk ribbon at one end. It lay on a white cushion in the trunk like the body of a decapitated creature, a much beloved corpse.

A terrible picture just occurred to me, I shuddered. Your stories arouse the strangest images in me!

What now? she asked.

Last year I visited Poland and saw the death camps, I whispered. In one of them I saw, behind an enormous glass window, hundreds, thousands of those braids, cut off the heads of Jewish girls before they were gassed—or maybe after. Who knows?

She was silent for a long time, covering her eyes with her hands. I could not have borne such a vision, she finally said. One braid is enough for me, my aunt's braid lying headless in the trunk. She was also killed, as they all were, she added in a harsh voice; and immediately continued, but marriage ceremonies were joyous and festive in the town. The bride would be led to the canopy decked in white, weak from the prenuptial fast, and after the ceremony the street children would escort her, cheering, to her new home. Those same children also escorted the town's dead, reciting Psalms after the bier on the dead man's final journey. Joy and sorrow are not so alien to each other.

We had our local holidays, too, she said, after a silence. I especially remember the burial of damaged holy books in our town, which my father organized. Two rows of musicians—drums, trumpets, and a high-pitched violin—escorted the wagons, which carried thirty earthen vessels containing the holy fragments to be given a proper Jewish burial. And the horses, as if aware of the importance of their task, cantered with a stately gait through the market. It was then that I saw our community, which usually seemed to me such a scanty bunch, the finest of whose sons had been streaming overseas for decades, magically swell to an honorable four-hundred-year-old assembly, a row of fifteen distinguished rabbis at its head, with its priestly families, its leaders in every generation and its fallen heroes who had been martyred for the sanctification of God's name.

In the middle of Dvora's story about the book burial Tsipora had entered the room, lighting a lamp that threw dim shadows across the floor.

Listening, her eyes wide, she gazed at her mother and then at me, maybe wondering when I would leave her mother in peace—or when I would stop stealing her mother from her; but Dvora just turned to Tsipora for a moment and went back to her story.

Weekdays and holidays in our town, like the seasons of the year, are accompanied in my memory by their distinctive foods and smells, which exist no more. The staples of the poor were a potato cooked in its jacket, fish stew, homemade rye bread with greens, and brewed chicory. The bread was served with a stalk of onion and cheese when these were to be had, and for variety, the order was reversed: the onion was served first and then the cheese. Carrots and radishes were stored in the basement and a wreath of onions hung in the attic. The third Sabbath meal was prepared from red or white radishes, sliced and sunk into buttermilk, and sprinkled with a little salt; this was far from being considered the shabbiest of Lithuanian dishes. So it was with the scallions, which were eaten uncooked, whole or grated and soaked in vinegar, and also new cucumbers, which were often crumbled into beet borscht for their aroma and flavored with sour cream and egg yolks. We so loved the compote in honey and the kugels seasoned with cinnamon that were prepared for holidays. For the Sabbath supper, the woman would make semolina flour challah, noodles, and dessert. There would be a kugel and a cholent of pearl barley and beans warming in the back of the oven for the next day's hot stew. What was there to complain about?

In the summertime the fisherman would bring deep-sea fish, still alive. As they gasped their last on the table, my mother would light the stove and dice onions into a pot. Sometimes she would stuff the fish for Sabbath. Late summer, during the three weeks of mourning for Jerusalem, was the season for wild blackberries, which were a snap to prepare. Two or three spoonfuls of fine sugar and a little flour for flavor and we all ate our fill, and if the children's faces were streaked with blue and purple and red, the stains just set off their bright eyes all the more. On Sabbath afternoons in the summer we would eat new fruit—pears from the countess's gardens and bunches of ripe cherries—and in honor of my grandmother, when she came for a visit, my mother would bake a rich sugar cake. We would crack pumpkin seeds and drink cherry nectar with the guests, while the adults sipped the tea that had been brewing at the back of the oven. On Rosh Hashana there would be little round dumplings simmered in broth, and the challahs and the sliced vegetables were round as well, so that the new year would roll nicely along. Toward the winter my mother would get cherries by the bushel from the gardens of Usha, which she cooked and canned. With the stores of radishes, pickled cabbage, and cucumbers, our house lacked for nothing in winter.

Rich people ate different dishes, she continued, pouring her descriptions into our amazed ears. They used parsley and other seasonings, and sometimes prepared a custard that looked like snow, and once I saw a brown pudding in the shape of a bear in a rich man's house at the end of the alley.

I burst into laughter, but Dvora continued to declaim, But finest of all was the sublime orange. When people brought an orange wrapped in silk paper back from the city, there was no better gift. At the summer resort my father would sometimes peel an orange and divide it among us. We would sprinkle a little confectioner's sugar on the slices and slowly suck the delicious juice, and all the sorrow within us would melt away.

Mama! Tsipora cried out excitedly. If you only ate a fraction of all those treats you described. We have as many oranges as anyone could want nowadays. I added my own admiring cries, You remember so much!

And a lot more than this, she answered with a gaiety that was new to me.

You could dictate a Lithuanian cookbook to us, I joked.

Why not, there might be some profit in it, she said, laughing.

When I left the house, the smiles still prevailed. I wondered how this meeting, which had touched on such somber topics, had ended in such light spirits. I would have to listen to the tapes again to understand.

sixth encounter

I arrived at Dvora's house the next time tired, preoccupied, and late. Piles of unfinished worked cluttered my office desk and the telephone had not stopped ringing for days. Moments before I left the house my son complained that his throat was sore and had been all day, and the girl who regularly babysat for him suddenly looked out of her depth. While I was calming him and giving detailed instructions and looking for those candies that helped soothe his throat the last time, I remembered that the car had been making suspicious noises that morning. I wondered how I could possibly leave. They're waiting for me there, I explained, pushing aside all worries about the car. I promise I won't be back late tonight, and so I left.

What an oppressed expression on your face today! Dvora Baron said to me as I entered the room. Startled, I stopped in my tracks. She's a witch, I thought. In fact, she looked pretty frightening today. As I had heard others say, her black eyes in their sunken caverns were both virtually blind and able to see right through people. This must have been how she had watched the women who came to consult her father or who sat whispering in her mother's kitchen, seeing what was in their hearts.

Suddenly a lively sympathy spread from one ear to the other. For a moment she laughed her rolling laugh and her eyes shone through the gloom. Have I frightened you? Dvora asked with a smile. I always seem to do that.

They say you people's read thoughts.

Nonsense, she answered dismissively. All I do is listen to what they tell me. There are many ways to send messages, you know.

I told Dvora about some of the mundane troubles that were bothering me, most of all my worries about my son.

A woman's life is always diffused among so many diverse goals—unlike a man's life, which is dedicated to his great pursuit, she said. I was not able to bear that, and I suppose that was why I fell ill.

And your illness freed you from all the womanly distractions, I asked, so you could devote yourself to your work? By now I had so concentrated my attention on understanding her that my earlier worries had disappeared.

It was not that simple, she laughed again, but I promise that we shall discuss it at the proper moment. In the meanwhile we are still in the midst of my childhood in the shtetl, she said. Pour yourself some hot tea and ask your questions.

I set up the tape recorder between us and turned to my notes.

I thought that today we might speak about the things that disturbed you as a young girl in the shtetl.

Her calm, organized voice emerged from the shadows after a long moment.

As would have been true of any place, there were brushes with death that disturbed and frightened me. But greater than these was the hatred of the gentiles and our fear of them.

Tell me about that, I asked.

Life was so short! Death lurked in every corner. Knowledge of this suffused my own house as well. Even before I was born, my mother had two sons who died in infancy. And then my father's illness appeared and worsened over time. We lived in the shadow of mortal fears and illness, and it was only later, in my adolescence, that I learned that sometimes death is not so very frightening at all.

Life was carried out in the open in my town and everything was known to me, a curious little girl. I secured myself quite an education in the neighborhood yards. Old people were not sent off to die in hospitals. One elderly man in our alley, whose face was eerily pale against the beard that framed it, would sit in an armchair or, when he grew weaker, lay on the ledge, sipping medicine mixed with sugar water. People around him would speak in slow, careful voices, waving the flies off him. Once I passed and saw him playing with his infant grandson, and a sort of breath of compassion freshened the air around him, diluting the medicinal odor of the Polish Doctor Pavlovski's drugs.

A breath of compassion with the odor of medicine, I whispered. How you express yourself!

It is not the figure of speech I meant to get across, she explained impatiently, but rather that illness and even death were handled in a more human way in the shtetl. I have heard Tsipora's stories about the hospital, so I have some basis for comparison.

On the other hand, I argued, even you would have to admit that there are still certain advantages to modern medicine.

I certainly do not, she said heatedly. They prescribe drugs without considering the condition of the patient that do no good at all. If I had not discovered for myself which foods to eat and which to avoid like poison, I should be long dead.

I kept silent.

When the old man's condition worsened, she continued, a sheet was spread out for him under the tree, and his aching limbs were covered with fallen leaves, warm and healing leaves, someone explained to me. His wife slowly fanned him with her handkerchief. He died that spring, one Saturday night, just when the pear tree had begun to bloom by the gate outside and the river downhill was sounding its deep, full murmur. I watched the members of his family recite "The Righteousness of the Judgment" in the corner of the yard, and then they cried for a long time, the warm sobs of a family.

Another time, our neighbor Abner got lost in a swampy part of the forest and caught an ordinary cold. The Polish medic from the hill brought him some spirits and medicines to make him sweat, and he drank and perspired—but even so it was clear that somehow he was still wandering in circles through the bog, dank water sloshing around his knees. He was a widower, and his two married daughters were summoned from their husbands' houses to care for their father. They brought him chicken soup, but it did no more good than the medic's tinctures and the man died in the very prime of his life.

Then, as now, the doctor could relieve people's ailments only very rarely. When paralysis struck, or sterility, all the ointments or bath salts or the various drugs in Dr. Pavlovski's satchel were of no use whatsoever, of course. Many people fell ill with malnutrition. I would often play with my brother and his friends in the garden of Dr. Pavlovski, whose beautiful maid, Pauline, loved children. Once I saw the porter from our alley, who also cleaned the synagogue when his services were needed, half-carrying his sickly son, who was lagging and stumbling beside him. The doctor impatiently drew the boy toward himself, thumped him here and there on his chest, angrily pushed him back to his father and said in Yiddish: "Haven't I already told you that the boy is simply starved; instead of dragging him up here, it would be better if you found him something to eat. Give him milk, porridge, cocoa—and he'll get better." But where could a poor Jew like our porter find the money for cocoa?

When my friend Mina's father became very ill, she added, she would bring him each spring morning to sit in the shade of the linden—the tree that stood in our courtyard in all its vernal splendor, spreading its mighty limbs over us. There, on the bench at its base, the sick man rested. He would drink a bottle of goats' milk in the shade and watch the birds set the branches to rustling. Soon enough, he felt so much better that he no longer needed anyone to accompany him, and he walked only with a stick, carrying it more than leaning on it.

I watched her describe these people, the dying and the recovering, thinking about her own state, a bedridden old woman, a bundle of bones, legs atrophied from years of lying still, obsessively interested in what touched her lips.

Prayers for the well-being of the sick person were recited, of course, with great devotion in the synagogue; but when Pavlovski and the medic threw up their hands, some people would also make pilgrimages to holy men or beseech the dead. Once I heard the women at the well murmuring about barren Dinah, how she had traveled to the district seat to receive a blessing from the saint who lived somewhere on its outskirts. He was a pious Jew, around whom lingered the smell of holiness and old books. As he instructed, the women said, Dinah added a third candle to her two Sabbath candles—symbol of the threefold braid—and pulled her headkerchief down further on her forehead. But as time went by the women began to doubt whether the man's blessing was worth very much at all; and Big Basya, who came every morning to the well, even expressed her doubts about how holy he really was, seeing as she had never heard his name mentioned in the home of her departed father.

In other cases of mortal illness I heard that the grandmother had been sent to the "field" to intercede with the dead, or that relatives had gone down to the poor people in the gulch, pockets full of ready coins. Miraculous recoveries were said to have followed such expeditions.

Nothing disturbed me so immensely as my father's illness. I had been hearing him cough for as long as I could remember, and the worry in my mother's eyes did not escape me. One morning my father suddenly began vomiting blood. Dr. Pavlovski came and announced, "It's from that synagogue of yours. Get him some fresh air!" That was when we first went to the resort in the forest. And when the doctor would come for a house call and see him bending over his books, he would become furious: "Talmud, Talmud! Better have some honey cake and a glass of port to put some flesh on those bones."

At each death I witnessed in my childhood, each funeral, I would picture my mother, my brother, my sisters, and myself accompanying my good father on his final journey. Once, a woman who was considered saintly in our town was laid to rest. The horizon was already heavy with rain clouds, for autumn was approaching. I stood in the yard and watched the procession pass. The pupils from the local elementary school, the cheder, went first, reciting Psalms from hearts filled with sincere sorrow, since the woman used to provide them with beaverskin jackets and woolen coats each winter. His eyes glued to the coffin, her husband walked among the mourners as if he were being drawn along solely by the pull of his gaze, legs stumbling behind. This is how it will be when my father dies, I thought with dread; and when that day arrived, she said in a pained voice, I did not even make it to his funeral.

When I grew up a bit, she continued, I was allowed for the first time to attend the funeral of our old neighbor. He was brought to the graves of his ancestors, to the row of Levites in the cemetery, on whose gravestones the family names rose and fell in recurring cycles, as in life. At the edge of the cemetery, I saw the markers on the graves of the children, among them my two brothers who had died before their time. From afar, I could hear the older women clapping their hands and wailing; to me it sounded just like the rustling of wings in the treetops.

Then everyone went back to the mourners' house. In the shtetl people were scrupulous about the commandment to comfort mourners. They did not speak much, but their portion in the sorrow—which was no more than its reflected light, tempered with compassion—radiated from every countenance. Sometimes they would sit and read from the Book of Job, and in the face of that poor man's story, every other grievance paled.

You are talking about compassion again, I said.

There is no greater virtue than compassion, I would think, not even justice, she said.

That is a feminine stance par excellence, I said and immediately regretted it.

Says who? she asked irritably.

There's research comparing the ethical decisions of men and women. They use a different terminology, but basically it seems that men prefer to act with justice and women, compassion.

Dvora burst into laughter. Do not be offended, she said when her laughter had subsided, but I cannot bear such nonsense. Surely you do not believe it yourself! she continued, as if she were trying to mollify me.

Don't worry about it, I said, the main thing is that I got you to laugh. Now I know that you don't like either psychology or medicine.

Even a mediocre writer knows more about the human soul than a whole staff of trained psychologists, she added mischievously.

Well, you're no mediocre writer, and I'm only a single psychologist, so I bow to your judgment, I nodded in mock concession. But you first started talking about the gentiles, I reminded her.

About our fear of the gentiles, she corrected me, and immediately her face was transformed. When I think about the gentiles in the shtetl, I immediately feel that same ancient, primeval fear; and even if that fear was sometimes lulled into forgetfulness, the church bells would always awaken it anew. The ringing of any bell tower has always sounded thunderous and alarming to my ears, and when I hear it, I feel what I have long recognized as the eternal Jewish terror. It is the same fear of the great darkness that fell upon our ancestor when first he struck a covenant with his God, and was told that he would be a sojourner in a land not his own, she intoned, and there he would be afflicted and oppressed.

Even after I went up the slope one fine day to gather wildflowers, she continued, glancing suddenly toward me, and first saw the "idol" I had been told was their god and realized that he was nothing more than a lumpy mass of misshapen clay that would no doubt have long crumbled to pieces if not for the massive cross holding it together—even then the terror continued.

I once saw it in my father's face when I was still in the cradle, when he woke up one night and looked out the window that faced the fields and said, "The miller Abba-Itche is burning." My mother said with a shudder, "Oy, a solitary Jew in a sea of murderers!"

And one Friday afternoon at my grandfather's house, I was helping my grandmother bake a cake and one of the neighbor women knocked on the window and said they were coming this way. The house had an attic with a secret entrance and we scrambled up into it. My grandmother was already pulling the ladder up when my old grandfather announced that he needed to go to the synagogue to rescue the Torah scrolls. He climbed down, put on his good coat, set his hat upon his head as he did at the start of every Sabbath, and left the house, with all of us watching him through the small attic window. The mob was already flooding the street as my grandfather walked calmly and steadily along, as if he were navigating a raging river. He and the sexton appeared a few moments later, the Torah scrolls wrapped in prayer shawls in their arms. No one dared touch them as they made their way through the crowd of rioters.

Later on I knew two widows who had arrived, one after the other, in our alley. The first, Chaye-Chave, had six small children. They were living in a village when it happened. Her husband was an innkeeper, and the villagers got along well enough with him; but one unfortunate day, they rose up against the father of the family and murdered him after stealing his watch and purse. Since she could not hope to beat them off, the woman tried only to protect her children and the Torah scroll. The drunken men desecrated the scroll, but she managed to save her children from harm and she came with them to live in the community alley.

After that came the turn of Hershl from the square up the hill, a peddler who sold his wares in the surrounding villages. He provided the farm women with haberdashery—buttons, ribbons, and emery boards—and in exchange for these luxuries they gave him eggs, beans, and bundles of flax. He was killed solely for the thrill of murder, they never even touched the bundle of notes in his pocket. His widow and four orphans were brought from the gentile section of town to our alley as well. And who helped the wretched woman get back on her feet, if not Chaye-Chave the widow. What heroic strength coursed through those two women. Together they baked cakes and sold them at market, sitting on a bench with no back, supported only by their own faith. I would see them exchanging pleasantries with those who had darkened their lives, for they had to make a living, my mother explained to me from the counter of her yeast stand. I would stand in our yard nervously awaiting their return, for what would become of their children if something befell them? When I heard the drunken carousing outside, I knew that market day was over, and soon I saw the two widows hurrying back to their children with baskets filled with bread, groats, and sugar. Only Basya, who helped my mother with the housework after her husband was killed one night by gentiles outside town—I have already mentioned her—lost her confidence. She told me she would never look for work uphill or along the riverfront because "they" were there, and one must stay far, far away from "them." During the quiet times there were, nevertheless, business dealings, neighborly relations, the exchange of advice between Jews and gentiles; but even in those normal times their dogs would bark at me through their gates, and the young toughs would throw sticks and stones at me until I arrived safely at the entrance to town. Once I was walking with my girlfriend to the meadows on a harvest day and two hoodlums, Stasz and Antosh, attacked, and as their fathers watched, went after us with their sickles. We were trapped on a narrow path with ditches on either side. My agile friend leapt across the ditch and hid from our attackers, but I, who was a little behind her, could already hear the metal whistling behind my ear before I managed to escape.

These childhood memories are now mixed in my imagination with some other childhood wars I fought, she continued thoughtfully. The son of the rich Jewish landlord of the estate that bordered the pine forest would often torment me, in very nearly the same way the gentile hoodlums would. He was exactly my own age, and we were even related somehow, my mother told me; but this boy was a thorn in my side more than once. The first time we met, on a summery Sabbath afternoon when I was still a frail child, he set the courtyard dogs on me as I wandered through the forest. Then, too, I was caught between dank and impenetrable walls with no escape, and climbing the gate to escape the dogs was beyond my powers. I shrieked with all my might, and finally, hearing the bloodcurdling cries, the servant boys came out and rescued me. From afar I could see that master's son, standing in his short silken socks, his shaven head bare and a flash of malice on his well-fed face. How I hated him then, she finished with a certain forgiving note.

In those days I saw them, bare-headed and rich Jews, as a hybrid species beyond my comprehension. On holidays I would stare at them in all their finery when they came to pray in the synagogue. As it turned out, my brother and I also left the ways of our father's house behind us, as you know, and became "free," as Jews of our sort are called; but we never crossed into the camp of the landowners and rich men, she said emphatically, although during the years that I taught in rich Jewish houses in the city I learned much about their ways.

So then, I tried to clarify, did the rich Jews and the gentiles represent the same sort of threat?

Certainly not, she answered abruptly, turning her head away from me. The line that separated Jew and gentile was absolute, an unbridgeable chasm.

For a moment I sensed that she was tired of trying to explain her life to a boorish Israeli—a girl growing up among pious Jews, assimilated Jews, gentiles, men and women, threatening dogs, damp walls with no exit. I could feel her shut down, slip back across the moving ice floes that separated our worlds, the gap that Dvora Baron had spent her life trying to bridge, telling us here in Israel, in Hebrew, about her life over there. And maybe she didn't bridge it at all, I thought for a moment, since she never really lived here—at least not in the last thirty-five years. But is there ever, I continued to myself, true communication between people, however similar their worlds?

While I was still searching for the words that could mend the delicate fabric that had momentarily ripped between us, I saw her face return to its dreamlike expression, and her beautiful voice sang out into the room again.

Until one day a different wind suddenly blew and the horizons darkened, as on my visit to my grandfather. This had already happened in my parents' house once during my childhood, when I was in bed with a fever. In the morning stillness I heard the crash of breaking windows and that same shout, which it seemed to me was responsible for shattering the glass. In the same moment I was lifted and carried up a ladder to a hiding place, and through a tiny window I saw the hoodlums waving butcher knives at a crowd of our neighbors, who sat silently before them without moving a muscle. And I remember being amazed that these big people were doing nothing to defend themselves; but from within my fever I explained to myself that they couldn't stop what they were doing, since they were obviously in the middle of the morning prayers. But who am I to judge them, she added sadly, I, who no longer move at all.

When I emerged from my delirium, I was back in bed again, listening to the sounds of prayer and lamentation coming from the synagogue. Through the window I saw the stars hanging apathetically in their places, the skies themselves seemed sullen and shut down, and I joined my voice to the mournful wail.

Another time I woke on a summer's night to a bloody redness from which emerged panicked screams and the faint creaking of the well hoist across the way, where people where rushing to fill buckets of water to put out the blaze. The fire, I was told, had been set by the young Cossack from the slaughterhouse at the edge of the valley, and the flames were spreading down the community street and threatening to engulf the synagogue roof. But apparently the prayers of the community were heard, because the heavens thundered and sheets of rains began pouring down, swift as diligent messengers.

That is what a Jew knew to do in times of distress: to pray to his God, she said, without a trace of mockery. On rare occasions I saw a brave Jew rise up against the hoodlums and strike them with his wagon whip, until they fell to their knees. But even as I enjoyed the delicious taste of revenge, the familiar dread did not loosen its hold, for the surrounding gentiles would surely hear of this and take up arms against us, and we were few against their numbers.

I remember, she said dreamily, that in my childhood I believed that we could get back up on our feet after any blow. For that was how it was in my childhood: The dead were laid to rest and on the ruins of the destroyed houses new ones arose. As soon as the ashes cooled, people would begin building, replanting gardens and mending fences and plowing furrows. And when the head of the family had been murdered, his wife would come to town and set up her house here, as if she believed that peace and quiet would reign among us from now to eternity. Here Dvora Baron stopped, and I thought I saw tears in her extinguished eyes.

Only a few people understood the situation, she said with suppressed rage, and they packed their bags and went off to build a homestead in the land of Israel. One of those from our town was Sholem-Noach, the son of the man who had been slaughtered by the uncircumcised, and he was the first to kindle our desire to go rebuild the ruins of our inheritance—rather than dusting our town off yet again. Not many listened, and even I, in my childhood, saw things differently, because I intended to study in the big city with my brother, Benjamin, she said mournfully. If only we had emigrated then, with Sholem-Noach and his friends, my brother would be here among the living, and I know he would have found a cure for my illness.

It's the same in every family, I said. Those who left Europe torture themselves for not persuading the others to come along. My mother came to Palestine after her older brother had been living here for a few years; but their widowed mother did not want to leave her husband's grave or turn her store over to strangers, and so the rest of the brothers and sisters and all their children remained behind.

Although there were no evil people in it, torrents of fire and brimstone rained down on the shtetl as if it were Sodom, and no one looks back but I, she said, and suddenly I saw her drawn to her fullest height rising in the air like a spirit, like a Chagall painting, in her white dress.

My heart pounded furiously with the force of my emotions, sorrow, terror, admiration. At the same time I wondered: Am I hallucinating, am I losing my sanity here?

I stood up and went over to the window as if an invisible hand were propelling me. Without asking permission, I drew back the curtain and gazed for a long time through the unwashed pane at the street. Two little girls were swinging a rope on the sidewalk, while their friends skipped to a rhythmic chant. This innocent sight steadied me and I felt the dizziness that had alarmed me pass. Tears rose to my eyes again. What can we promise you? I said in my heart to the girls. Here, too, there is no peace, no security, the bridge is narrow and there is no railing, and beneath it the waters rage. Nevertheless, the sight of the lit street had somewhat eased the heaviness in the room.

Dvora was silent behind me. I thought of bringing her bed to the window, but I knew that she could no longer see the cheerful, ordinary sight outside. If only I could open the window, at least, and let the sounds enter the room! No, she could not hear them either, I suddenly understood. She was somewhere where the girls at play, the eucalyptus trees spreading peace over the street, could no longer reach her.

But the speed with which Dvora's mood lifted surprised me.

It was about the time of that fire, she said again in her hypnotic storyteller voice, that my brother and I learned that somewhere the spirit had taken hold and people were leaving to rebuild those other ruins, in the Land of Israel. We were not the least bit surprised; sitting in the garden one evening we read about it together, in the pamphlets my friend's older sister received from the city. And whether it was because the hour had brightened after a rainfall or because it was so perfectly still around us, the image burned in my memory is of that same red that appears at the edges of the sky after a storm, and which prophesies sunny days ahead.

In the end it will be you who shows from whence cometh our comfort, I said, and knew that she understood, and that the rip I had felt between us earlier had been seamlessly and magically repaired.

seventh encounter

The first rain of the season was falling the next time I visited Dvora Baron. It was cool and smelled fresh on the street outside, but the air indoors was literally the same as it had been. The apartment was shut off even from the seasons: the same familiar sourish smell, which was no longer as unpleasant as it had been on my first visit, and the same eternal gloom. Once again I was struck by the modesty, or maybe it was impoverishment, that pervaded the apartment and the possessions of the two women who lived in it. Dvora lay on the living room bed in an old white dress I had seen her wearing in the summer, with a crocheted sweater over it and a few layers of quilts covering her.

She looked distinctly happy as I greeted her and asked after her health. We must hurry, she said, her eyes burning.

Where to? I asked, not understanding.

Not to anywhere, she smiled. I only mean that the day is short and the task is great. Now that we have begun, I want to see my life through with you; we have been speaking for many hours, but I cannot help feeling that we are treading over the same territory without making progress.

One night recently I felt ill, she continued, and I thought that my journey had ended. Tsipora ran to the neighbor to call for help, but after all the fuss, I felt better even before the doctor arrived. What will happen next time, though? I am fading fast, it won't be long before I reach the end of this path. That same night, I thought, she said as if she were talking to herself, that I must prepare for what lies ahead. So why do I feel so unprepared? I have been preparing for the moment of my death for over thirty years now, after all.

Still, you're careful with what you eat and worry enough about your health, I commented drily.

My shaky, damaged health.

What I mean is, I hurried to say, you always had the will to live, didn't you?

Perhaps, she answered evasively, or perhaps only the will to suffer less while I still lived. In any case, someone like myself is always prepared for death.

So you've been feeling that time is short and the work the two of us have begun is still far from complete? I asked.

Yes, the story I am telling you seems to be the preparation I had hoped to accomplish on my own. You arrived at the perfect moment, Amia, and that must be why I welcomed you so warmly. I am not often quite so courteous. More than one of my old friends has written to me to suggest a visit and I refused. Some came and waited outside in the foyer and I turned them away without receiving them.

As I was imagining I could detect the pride of a much-courted woman in her voice, she added, I did not feel well, and did not wish to be seen in so low a condition. Shoffman, whom I admired, was never allowed to visit.

So you don't actually know him? I tried to understand.

And why not? I have read his work, and he mine. Many letters have passed between us, and he is a dear friend of mine. But I have never met him face-to-face, she said mischievously, which makes it easier for him to love me. The point is, it is better for people to remember me as I was in my youth or in those beautiful photographs that appeared in my books.

I hope you are not about to ask me to leave, I said lightly, trying to hide a certain apprehension.

On the contrary, she said impatiently, we must hurry and finish what we have begun.

I suddenly remembered the little prince preparing to return to his star, which was calling him home. Was she too hearing this call? Had the autumn winds somehow managed to penetrate her apartment? And maybe, like Scheherazade, we could both go on living as long as our story lasted? A shiver ran up my spine. I wanted to shake off these thoughts, but I felt as if I were transparent before Dvora's blazing eyes, the eyes of her soul, since as usual her gaze was glued to the ceiling. There was no place to hide in this room, I knew.

You're making me anxious, Dvora, I said softly.

These are the facts of life, my child, she answered gently, and there is nothing to do but face them, perhaps not bravely, a bitter smile twisted her lips, but at least squarely.

After a moment she added, Let us continue, then. Today I will tell you about my youth, which began in my hometown and ended in the city where I studied and in the wealthy houses in which I worked as a governess and tutor. That is, until I immigrated to Palestine in 1911, by which time I was a grown woman of twenty-four years.

I remembered what I had been told about this period, the nine years from her leaving her parents' house until her emigration, during which she lived in various cities and wrote many short stories. I was eagerly anticipating the next chapter in the life story of Dvora Baron.

Years went by, and I went from being a little girl to a young woman, she began in her storyteller voice. When I was twelve years old many crucial changes began to take place within me. My brother, Benjamin, was already acquiring secular books in Hebrew and other languages from Minsk. I read everything I could lay my hands on; I was like a sleep-walker. I also tried my hand at writing for the first time and found that I was quite good at it. Before my newly opened eyes, the town was undergoing a metamorphosis. It may be that the unrelenting hardships were taking their toll, and it was the town itself, which had seemed so beautiful when I was a child, that was changing. But I rather think that the changes were taking place within me, and that the young woman could see things invisible to the little girl.

I remember that suddenly I was observing the people of the town as if I were outside it, or hovering above it, or straddling the fence that separated it from the new world that I was finding both so alluring and terrifying. The pictures I remember from those days are accompanied with a great deal of criticism and sorrow.

Now, for instance, the picture of old Pesya arises in my mind, standing in the women's section one weekday. It was one of those short winter

days, and from the kitchen I had heard my father talking with an itinerant preacher, who was asking permission to address the congregation
following the afternoon prayers. After the matter had been settled, I stole
into the women's section, where it was always dark, to hear what the
preacher had to say. By the light of a few solitary rays that made their
way through the eastern window, I noticed an old woman standing in the
first row of the balcony and listening to the sermon, knitting all the
while without once glancing at her work. It was clear from her dumb-
founded expression that she could not understand much of his talk, for
the biblical verses and rabbinical aphorisms were lost on her, but no matter; she had her sock and ball of yarn with her, and in the meantime,
she was getting her knitting done. But now the preacher was arriving at
the heart of the matter, the parable, and the woolen sock slipped unno-
ticed from her hand. It was a parable about the people of Israel, who were
like an abandoned woman whose husband, which would be God, naturally, left her to pine away. I remember how he embellished the story,
not noticing that the time for evening prayers had arrived and the congregation was eager to get home to their suppers. At the beadle's signals,
the preacher brought his sermon to a hurried close without tying up
the loose ends, closing with some verses that promised salvation to the
people. It was over, and the old woman, still shaken, stood there in the
dark with her mouth agape. Seeing me walking toward the stairs, she
tugged my sleeve and asked, "How did it turn out with her, that abandoned wife? Did her husband return to her, did he?" And as I—in my
own estimation an educated, broad-minded young girl—explained the
concept of allegory to the bewildered old woman, I no longer felt any
admiration for that simple faith that had charmed me in my childhood;
I felt nothing but disdain at her ignorance. Nature, she smiled at me,
abhors a vacuum, as we know, and when wisdom takes flight folly sets
up house.

I laughed. You're so witty sometimes! I said, but it isn't fair that you
let yourself make generalizations, yet when I do, you won't stand for it.

Of course I don't when you make your solemn pronouncements in
the name of psychology, as if that gave them extra weight; but as a joke,

in jest, anything is permitted. I have always said that laughter is the dew of life.

But why do you reject psychology so utterly and absolutely? I asked.

Psychological insight is a personal matter to me, like compassion. To teach psychology to a person who is not a psychologist in their soul, in their nature, is like prescribing spectacles for a blind person. Whether the room is dark or brightly lit, they will not see their way around.

I hope you don't think I'm blind, or perhaps I should say deaf.

She glanced at me affectionately: Would I be letting you see the sparks of my soul if I believed that? But let us proceed.

On many occasions during those years I observed the town in all its pettiness, noticing the deficiencies of our community. I remember the death of the widow Rochlin's son. She lived alone on the gentile street, cut off from the Jewish community. She spoke Lithuanian rather than Yiddish and had a great big dog living in her house. So when a postcard came from a stranger with the news that her son, a student, had died somewhere far away, the women sighed with relief when they realized where the disaster had struck, and no one took it upon themselves to pass along the news. People waited for the right moment, and until it came, the town seemed a place devoid of pity. That was when I saw that, even in my beloved town, the sufferings of others were like a fire at the neighbor's house. Those who came to watch were frightened and even sad, but they were also warmed by the blaze.

Finally, one of her gentile neighbors went in and brought the old mother the terrible news. Only then did the townspeople who had been waiting in the shadows outside her window burst into the house, professional bestowers of comfort and succor. The women scrambled through the drawers, searching for smelling salts and tranquilizers and poultices. The men tore the woman's dress over her heart as prescribed by law and convened a prayer quorum. And even if the women's hearts grew tender in the course of the prayers and they managed to squeeze out a tear, I knew that in the final analysis their mourning was nothing but an occasion for self-pity: for their children who were home alone, who cried for bread and were treated to blows and curses instead; for their hard-bitten, angry husbands, working themselves to the bone to earn a meager living; and for their own grinding lives. And so, when the sorrow had run its course, the women returned to their homes, their minds a little easier in the perfect faith that they, the saintly ones, would not be abandoned by God.

I had never heard such bitterness in her voice, and I remembered how important compassion was in her work.

Don't you think you're being a little harsh on these people? I asked timidly.

Well then, so be it. I am a judgmental woman, and was even more so in my youth, when my eyes first opened.

Judgmental and compassionate at once, I thought in wonder, and for a moment I saw two scenes of her town, embroidered by her artful hand like the enormous tapestry I had seen in the museums of Europe—one picture beside the other—Battle and Victory or Winter and Summer. Here it was, the colorful, warm shtetl of the little girl on one side, and the fraying, gray shtetl of the maturing adolescent on the other.

Other sorts of things also became apparent to me then, she continued after a prolonged pause. At the well or on the streets I could see how all my innocent girlfriends were turning into young women. I remember them blossoming into their summery dresses and light blouses. The boys, too, were growing taller and maturing. Sometimes I could actually see love taking form and ripening within them, as in the Hebrew romances by Mapu, which I could recite from memory. A boy and girl could meet only very infrequently, in the marketplace or on the avenue of lindens, and he would incline his head toward her politely; but at the same time, you could see an excited flush rising in his cheeks. Sometimes the girl would be indifferent to his overtures, her face would shut down and she would hurry off. The boy's friends, who could see through to his heart, would take him on summery Sabbath afternoons to the Countess's wheatfields, where the girl was likely to be strolling. Her perfume would mingle with the scent of the wheat and the boy would nearly faint with giddiness. I would pray for this couple as if I had made the match myself, but it did not always work out. The parents were still in charge of such matters then, even if the heart did not always obey the wishes of the elders.

On our street it was Basya, my friend Mina's older sister, who chose Sholem-Noach as her true love. Like Benjamin, he was a yeshiva boy who had given up studying the Talmud. He took his first steps toward a secular education under the tutelage of Basya, who had studied in a state school before they moved to town. She taught him as best she could the basics of language and some arithmetic, until he could stand on his own two feet. From that time on their souls were bound one to the other. After he had gone to study in the city he would return armed with all sorts of knowledge and this time it was he who helped her with school-work and brought her textbooks and novels.

Like my brother, Benjamin, Sholem-Noach would come home twice a year to visit his mother for the holidays. Between these visits he would send her affectionate letters and she, who was less skilled a writer, would pour her heart into the cheesecakes she sent him at every opportunity. I would see her impatiently awaiting the mailman, just as I awaited Benjamin's letters, and I would automatically calculate the days that re-mained before the upcoming holiday.

When he came for a visit and evening finally descended on the town, Sholem-Noach would stroll around the square, while Basya would off-handedly come out to shake the tablecloth or take down some laundry, and the two of them would chance to meet. For us, who were younger than them by a few years, it was as if two characters had sprung to life from the pages of a novel to grace us with their presence. Before long it was I who would just happen to meet a boy who was a little older than me, and we would stand together in the moonlit square, separated by our enormous embarrassment, only our lengthening shadows touching.

A smile lit her face and I asked, So did you too find the man of your dreams in the town?

No, no, she anwered quickly. After all, I was fifteen when I left, and only Benjamin was truly dear to me. In any case I was a scholar and had no intention of marrying young, as other girls did.

And as if determined not to continue in this vein, she changed the subject: People were quite afraid of the draft in those days. The boys in town worried about being called up to the Russian army, and those who had left town to study in the big city were even more apprehensive. There you were under the nose of the authorities, and they could call you in to take the conscription exam. The boys were clever at dodging the draft, but concern about the issue was nonetheless immense.

As she was quiet for a few moments, I asked if she wanted me to leave; when she shook her head no, I asked what else she recalled from this period.

The thing that excited people my age was the first spark of Zionism in town. During that period we began to hear echoes of the movement that was called, in faraway regions, the Revival. The pamphlets and newspapers eventually reached us as well, and we, who were versed in the visions of the prophets and the laments of the poets, awoke like kernels of wheat in springtime. When Sholem-Noach came back from the city after completing his exams, he became the leader of our group, and all the young people in town gravitated toward him. Sholem-Noach told us about the oath he had sworn to himself: If he could avoid being drafted, he would dedicate his life not to vain pursuits but to the service of his people; and that is what he did. We would congregate in the front room of his mother's house several times a week. I was the youngest of the group, and sometimes I would watch Sholem-Noach standing before an open window and gazing with unseeing eyes toward the horizon. I knew he was seeing a distant land. Our club was called the Seekers of Zion.

When our membership increased and the widow's house could no longer hold us, Basya asked a relative if we could use his farmhouse outside town. In the capacious front room we set up benches and hung pictures on the walls. Basya covered the table with green paper and placed a lamp with a round globe on it. A bluish light would emanate from the windows in the evenings, a signal to the members that a meeting was to be held that night. When Sholem-Noach spoke, he did not use lofty language but always explained what he had gathered us to hear in the simplest words. And I, who was conversant with the synagogue and its customs, could recognize the quotations about redemption from my father's sermons; but there was a small difference here—while father saw the verses as merely a hint of future glories, Sholem-Noach believed they had been written with our very generation in mind. He explained how all the phenomena that tradition told us would immediately precede the redemption had already come to pass: the despair of the people, their impoverishment, the decrees against them that proliferated daily. The power of that young man was incredible. If he spoke about those who had been martyred for the sanctification of God's name, all who listened felt the knife at our throat; and if he spoke about the fervor of the pioneers, each of us burned with the desire to go to the land of Israel as well.

Once one of my friends asked him, "What would happen if someone were to burn all his bridges behind him and invest everything he owned to live there, and others did not follow in his footsteps?" Sholem-Noach confidently answered that they *would* follow, they *must* follow: the matter could be compared, for example, to a ship sinking in the ocean as the people on board spy land in the distance. Would not all of them leap into the ocean and swim for shore?

Before long, in fact, three of our group, enthusiastic and brave young people, were among the first to make the ascent to the Land of Israel, and others began preparing for the journey.

Among the members of the group was my good friend Gitl, who clung to this idea with all her might. In our clubhouse she would always sit beside Reuven-Asher, the carpenter's son, of whom she was very fond, and it was there that their love blossomed. I would see them walking in the field at dusk, silhouetted by the setting sun, lit up themselves by emotion and their dedication to a single ideal: to take sail for the longed-for land. At night, as we walked back from the farmhouse, I could hear them weaving their dreams together, and I knew that they would be the first of my friends to leave us and go off to the promised land. I also knew that they would do it without their parents' consent, and my heart swelled with terror and anticipation.

Reuven-Asher took a job for a year tutoring the children of the landlord of one of the estates in the district so they would not have to leave for Palestine with empty hands. That entire year he did not touch a cent of his earnings, because it was all set aside for the Purpose. On his short visits to town he and Gitl continued to spin their common dream. In their great love for the land even their feelings for each other were submerged.

During this entire time, Gitl continued to manage the club business, selling shekels to rebuild the Land of Israel and distributing announcements and pamphlets. One summer night, when a fire broke out in town, she was the one who remembered the clubhouse, running to save the pamphlets and stamps and account books from the blaze. I remember that on that night, as we waited in the meadow for the flames to die down, Sholem-Noach spoke about the dead rolling underground to be resurrected in the Land of Israel and about the suffering of the Final Days—the birth pangs of Messianic times—and with suppressed excitement called out, "You see, thus will our light rise from the ashes anew!"

In the darkening room it seemed to me that tears were streaming down Dvora's beautiful face, but there wasn't the faintest tremor in her voice.

After the holidays, Reuven-Asher returned from the estate and Gitl began transferring her possessions to the old shed little by little, in order not to arouse her parents' suspicions. At the appointed hour the two of them left in a carriage through the backroads and arrived at the county seat, where the members of the club had arranged a wedding for them at the Jewish innkeeper's house. There were witnesses, and a canopy was set up in accordance with Jewish law. After the necessary documents had been signed, the two proceeded to that other homeland. Sholem-Noach, who had accompanied them to the city, told us the story when he returned to town.

And you, did you not consider going up to the Land of Israel?

Certainly I did, but I knew that I would not be following them soon.

Why not? I asked.

In those days Benjamin was already living in the city, preparing for matriculation and then for medical school. My brother, Benjamin—I have already told you about him—was someone who charmed everyone around him. For me, he was the world and all its glory, and I wanted nothing but to follow where he went. So we clasped hands to seal the bargain, and he persuaded our parents to allow me to study in Minsk.

He promised he would take care of me and that we would share the same room always; and they, aware as they were that the days of our town were numbered and that the best and brightest had already left for America or Palestine, could resist our united front no longer. Benjamin comforted me for not going to Palestine like my friend Gitl by assuring me that we were working toward that goal, and that we too would immigrate. They need doctors and teachers in Palestine, Benjamin would say, and our education will come in handy there, even if it takes us a little longer to leave.

But perhaps there was also a trace of fear in my decision not to accompany Gitl or the other young pioneers, she continued; I was afraid of leaving my parents, especially my sick father, for who knew how long and for a distant land. After all, they always respected our wishes, even when we went off to graze in foreign pastures. Even when my brother, the Talmudic prodigy who was to inherit my father's rabbinical post, chose to follow the path of Enlightenment, they never opposed him. So how could I abandon them in their old age?

But what a daring move it was to let a fifteen-year-old single girl, a rabbi's daughter, leave home to work and study in the big city! I exclaimed.

True, I was the only one among my girlfriends in the town to do that, but I was also the only one whose father studied Talmud with her. Leaving home was another expression of my difference; I was stubborn, she said with a mischievous grin, and with my brother's help the matter was settled.

I still have a hard time understanding your parents' point of view.

Would my own parents have let me leave home at fifteen to make my own way in the world, far from their supervision? I asked myself, and immediately rejected the possibility as absurd. And there, in Dvora's youth, it would have been all that much more dangerous: a girl among men, a Jew among gentiles, when distances were greater and communication so much more uncertain. What could explain the motivation of parents as devoted as hers if not for a sense of utter despair, an awareness that there was no future at all in the old way of life? They must have felt like those parents who threw their children from the windows of the cattle cars a generation later, I thought, and a shudder shook my limbs.

That was the quiet before the storm, Dvora answered, echoing my thoughts, and my parents understood that well enough. We were three girlfriends and our paths diverged from that point: Mina stayed in town, got married, and prepared to follow in the path of her ancestors; Gitl eloped with her lover and went to Palestine to till the soil; and I followed Benjamin to the city to acquire an education. Those were the directions the wind was blowing. Many, of course, went to find their fortune in America, she reminded herself, but that was a path I never considered.

In my vocabulary we would say that you stood at the crossroads at that age, I said, and you have three directions to choose from: to stay in the shtetl, to immigrate to Palestine, or to study in the big city— three impulses that wrestled it out amongst themselves. In the end these options aligned themselves as a set of priorities, and this hierarchy determined your lifestyle; or, as a psychologist would say, your identity. You were an adolescent, the age when people construct their identities through the struggle between competing paths and values.

Very nice, she said with a touch of disdain, but even in my old age I am still left with these parts competing within me.

True, which is why you wrote about the shtetl, although you chose to leave it; it's also why you came to Palestine after you had your fill of the city.

Perhaps, she said reservedly, but there are many facets to things, many more than three. I have an ongoing disagreement with your friends, the scientists of the human soul, who cannot count beyond three and so try to put every man and woman in the same triangular framework.

I'm not interested in a framework, only in you, Dvora Baron, I said, happy that our relationship had progressed to the point that I no longer needed to defend myself.

A powerful wind was gusting through the treetops at the entrance to Jerusalem as I drove home. The noble height of the cypresses brought Dvora's image to my eyes again. The courage, I thought, to leave one's home at fifteen for a cold and foreign world. But how does that fit with the image of Dvora the mother, who wouldn't let her daughter go off even as far as the nearest elementary school? If I were Dvora, I said aloud in my car, I might hold a grudge against my parents for letting me leave so easily. I'll be a better mother than that, I would say, I'll guard my daughter like the apple of my eye.

Home! I shook myself out of my reverie and turned up the volume of the radio, as if I were skirting the edge of a whirlpool.

eighth encounter

When the time actually came to leave for the city, it was not easy parting from my friends and family, Dvora began with little ceremony the next time we met a few days later. I felt sure she had been preparing for our conversation, rehearsing her memories for me just as I practiced listening for her.

Gitl had already arrived in Palestine, as the colorful postcards she sent to the clubhouse informed us, and now it was my turn to leave home. It broke my heart to say goodbye to my friend Mina. Although we promised to stay in close touch, something warned me that Mina would be unable to keep her end of the bargain—either because she would have no free time or because she had never learned to express herself on paper. In fact, I made many inquiries before I learned that Mina was continuing to support her family, had married off her sister Basya, had fulfilled her old mother's greatest wish by sending her off to see the big city before she died, and finally, that she had wholeheartedly entered into marriage with a man who owned a piece of forest near town and had gone to live in his house in the country.

The last days at home before I left to study in the city were just wonderful, she continued, as if she were drawing the last flickers of warmth from her departed childhood. It was winter, but the house was cozy and the steam that rose from the oven where the groats simmered in fat was enough to make me a little drunk. On my last day at home my mother took in the yeast to keep it from freezing, shut the door of her stall, hung the great big lock on it as if it were a Friday evening, and came back to the house. A bundle had already been prepared for my trip; two pillows cinched together with a belt, some books, a jar of preserves. Toward evening my mother set to work on provisions for the road, baking me some cakes with the morsel of cheese she had acquired from the dairyman and cooking up a soup from the old hen who had been reared in our courtyard. I have already told you that she had an undemonstrative nature, and anyway, everything had already been said between us; but as she stood there before the stove I saw her suddenly turn away, her face quivering and twisted in a weird grimace.

Even the ants that marched across the tablecloth after supper and the blossoms of frost on the windows melting in the heat of the stove were precious to me that last night. When the lamp was extinguished and the room plunged into darkness, a still, black, and very, very long night descended on the house: All night long I could hear the lonely footsteps of the old night watchman in his heavy sheepskin coat, walking back and forth outside, rapping his stick with a muffled thud. When I heard the creak of the well hoist, I knew it must be approaching three o'clock, and our baker neighbor was drawing water to knead his dough. From the corner where my parents slept I heard my mother sighing as she tossed and turned, and then my father's murmur. Apparently they, too, were having trouble sleeping that night. My father's voice floated faintly over to me as he comforted my mother, reassuring her that I would be all right. My dear, kind father! He always found the right thing to say, the perfect words to keep the light of comfort flickering through such an endless night.

In the morning the carriage stood waiting at the gate. My father blessed me, and I saw the same strange grimace of grief on my mother's face again. "Be careful not to break the jar!" she warned, snatching another kiss, her distracted gaze already focused off in the distance, like the gaze of our neighbor who saw visions of the end of days. I extricated myself from their embraces, taking one last look at the domed roof of the synagogue, the yards with their dilapidated fences, the snow-covered meadows and the expanses beyond, freezing and clear on this blindingly white morning. I am going off to the city, to my brother, Benjamin, I said to myself as I climbed into the carriage, like someone afraid of losing their bearings. After all, how long had I been dreaming of being the prodigy of my gymnasium class, of conversing in two or three or four languages and playing the piano, of becoming that impeccably dressed teacher who earned her keep with an honest day's work.

The carriage moved with a tinkle of bells, she went on in her musical and resonant voice. The houses of the town passed by, the old synagogue, the slaughterhouse, and the bathhouse, and then the distances opened around me. From the carriage I climbed onto the train—on my own for the first time—for my journey into the great wide world. The familiar landscape of home stretched out before my eyes, rolling the fabric of a new world before it like a scroll that prophesied a wondrous future. My head spun as the train lurched, and the earth beneath us quivered at the warning blast and moved backward. The windmill behind the grove waved and dipped its wooden arms, children with open mouths ran wild alongside the tracks, and a rider on horseback galloped beside the train until it surged and lost him. Did I feel then that I was just as free as that galloping horse, a young girl in charge of her own affairs? Did I know then how lonely I would be from that moment on?

I waited for the answer, but it did not come.

It seems to me, I hesitated, that in times of transition, we often don't comprehend the significance of events while they're actually happening, or realize how much they're going to transform our world. Maybe it's only now, with the knowledge of what came afterward, that your life can fall into place.

Dvora nodded, faintly.

The most striking thing about this part of your story is that your parents didn't try to stop you from going off into a world so different from their own.

We have already spoken about that, she said. In the end they understood that I would go no matter what they said, just as my friend Gitl had eloped and run off to Palestine. As the intelligent parents they were, they accepted what must be—and did not oppose me, Amia. If only we were wise enough to treat our own children that way.

I try, I said, but I was thinking of something else. Maybe the reason you could stay true to the happy memories of your childhood is because your parents let you leave home. You didn't need to replace the shtetl with another setting for your stories the way other writers do. You clung to your good memories even when you described the shtetl ambivalently.

We Tel Aviv writers who immigrated before the First World War often discussed that sort of thing. Although most of us wrote in Hebrew, the group was divided between those who wrote about the old country and those who described the homeland rising around us in the Land of Israel. I belonged to the first camp, and was much criticized for it; but criticism never had the slightest impact on me, she said. Let them try writing before they criticize the work of others. Years later, after it all vanished, she added with some satisfaction, those same writers scurried back to the old world, trying to make up for all the time they lost.

But you never lost any, I commented.

Even when I paid attention to people here in the Land of Israel, she said, it was only insofar as they reminded me of characters from my town, and that was what I chose to describe. Even oranges tasted delicious here only because they reawakened the taste of that first orange my father brought back from the city, she smiled. Very few of my stories were set in the Land of Israel, although I was often asked to write about our revitalized land and people. Can all this be traced to the fact that my parents gave me their blessing when I left home? Who knows?

Of course, I had no idea how difficult the years of wandering would turn out to be, she continued, a homeless young woman moving from one city to the next. The more I think back on that time, almost nine years, the more I see it as two parallel paths that never once met. Outwardly I was a pretty and popular girl, with a brother who loved me and many friends, moving steadily down the path I had chosen, scraping out a rather poor living—but by no means in desperate straits—completing my studies, writing, and establishing a reputation as a Hebrew and Yiddish author. "A success story," you would undoubtedly call it, she laughed bitterly. But at the same time, in my inner world, in the things I saw around me, there was nothing but gloom and sorrow and despair. Perhaps the wound of my premature separation from home was still raw, a wound that never really healed, one that became inflamed again with my father's death and the cruel knowledge that now there was no home to go back to anymore. But perhaps it was also the heartache of a young woman who had not found love or begun her own family, either because she was not suited for such things or because she had failed to find her mate.

Tell me about your life in the city, I requested as the silence lengthened.

How diminished I felt as I stood in the arched municipal railroad station with my bundles and with my brother, Benjamin, who had come to meet me. Will I, too, cut my hair short and look like those women? was my first thought.

And did you ever cut it? I chimed in.

She shook her head no, with a certain satisfaction, it seemed to me, and I saw her standing tall and erect, in one of her dresses with the high collars, long black hair gathered at the nape, her gaze clear and penetrating as a clairvoyant's. Dvora the prophetess, as she had signed one of the first stories she wrote in the big city. This was not a woman to be swayed by passing fashions, I could see perfectly well.

The wintry city, on that first evening, seemed an extension of my hometown, warm and welcoming, even a little thrilling, she said, groping for words. But then morning came, and the world that met my eyes was gray and new. The snow piled by the side of the street was unfamiliar, dull, devoid of its usual glitter. The intoxication I had felt the previous night was now a hangover. Everything seemed ordinary and insipid. Cobblestones and asphalt, instead of pine trees; factory mills that exhaled steam, instead of windmills; sullen barracklike buildings circling the city, instead of the dense Lithuanian forest; and instead of the chime of church bells, the chattering of a municipal clock that never slept, diligently counting the hours draining away. The sorry sight of worn-out streetwalkers, whom I had never seen before, under the ruddy glow of the streetlamps. When evening fell my eyes searched for the skies of my childhood, but all I saw was a distant and faded sky, with two or three alienated stars.

In Minsk my brother was boarding with a Jewish family, and I joined him in his room. He was already attending the state gymnasium, and I took advantage of his textbooks and knowledge to begin preparing on my own—I was what was called an "external student." The work was considerable. A Russian gymnasium in those days was truly an institution of higher education, more comprehensive and advanced by far than any Israeli high school, and a gymnasium education lasted, for most students, at least until the age of twenty. The degree had some worth, essentially qualifying the graduate to work as a teacher. For years I prepared to enter by studying languages—Russian, French, and Latin, of course—and the best literature in these languages. I filled in the gaps in my knowledge of mathematics, geography, history, and other such subjects. Since I had decided, as Benjamin had before me, that once I left home I would take no financial support from my parents, even if they had been able to send us money, I could not dedicate myself solely to my studies. With no help coming from our parents, we supported ourselves by giving private Hebrew and Russian lessons, and later by tutoring subjects in which we had gained some competence. We saved every penny we earned toward tuition. We just barely survived, she said, without elaborating; and I, who had seen how modestly she lived, could imagine the poverty concealed by her words. Only at very great intervals, for the holidays or summer breaks, did we manage to get home to visit our parents or our older sister, who had meanwhile married a rabbi and lived in Radoshkovitz, not far from Minsk.

So you were pretty cut off from home.

We truly were. My father sent us a steady stream of affectionate letters and made sure to keep in close touch, and my mother sent packages of homemade goodies, called *Pshilke* in Russian. She must have known that we were sometimes on the verge of starving, and perhaps she also wanted us to eat her kosher food.

Many catastrophes struck my family in the years I was living in the city. My father died a while after my departure following a protracted illness; and since Benjamin had no desire to assume the rabbinic mantle, my mother married my sister Tsipora off to a rabbi who was a family friend, and so was able to remain in the community house, alongside which another two room house was built for the new rabbi and his wife. But only two years after the marriage, she continued in a whisper, my sister Tsipora unexpectedly died, returning from bathing in the river with her girlfriends. Girls and young women seemed to die much more easily then, it seems to me. It was always the most beautiful girls, the ones with shining hair and wide eyes, who died young.

Her sorrow touched me and I wished I could comfort her, but the room seemed too full of her own wondrous presence, her world and its shadows, to leave me any more than an awkward witness, at a loss for words. It was Dvora who finally shook herself free of her sadness.

Perhaps it was better that way, she said abruptly, to die without warning after spending a summer day with friends. At least she was saved from knowing the evil that descended on the others, not so very much later.

But while bonds with my family slackened, she continued, my connection to Benjamin grew stronger and deeper. He was my spiritual guide, my friend and teacher both. He introduced me to the world of young Jews searching for enlightenment in the cities of Lithuania. He encouraged me to write my first stories and supported me in my dealings with the editors of the various Hebrew and Yiddish newspapers in which I was published. I know that if he had been blessed with as long a life as I have been and had told his story, it might have been his voice you hear now, describing our closeness in those days of poverty and wandering as a light piercing the darkness.

The two of us earned a living by tutoring. I came to know many people that way and learned their way of life, which had been so foreign to me before. Benjamin and I lived just as the other displaced Jewish students, the "external" ones, she said as if weighing her words especially carefully, but for the most part I do not think we saw ourselves as quite so miserable and degraded as the other shtetl youths who had flocked to the cities in search of a new, adopted world. Perhaps it was because we could always depend on each other or because we were relatively successful at finding work. The hopes of immigrating to Palestine I continued to sustain during this period kept up my spirits and saved me from despair and ennui. I was usually the only girl among groups of men, an independent young woman living the same life as the others, a writer with a brother who protected her good name. This image earned me a privileged position in the big-city world of young Jews from the provinces.

My life progressed from Minsk, Kovno, and Mariampol, and back again, punctuated by visits to my mother, who had moved to live with my other sister in Radoshkovitz. There she was helping my sister, who had been widowed, raise her six children. We lived in Minsk, Benjamin and I, for about a year, and from there we moved to Kovno. At times I also lived in people's houses, working as a tutor or governess, apart from my brother. It was only in 1907, I think, that I moved to Mariampol and entered the gymnasium. After I had completed my studies and obtained a teaching certificate, I went back to the Kovno area, working in one house after another in order to save money for the journey to Palestine. By then Benjamin's path and my own had diverged. He was studying medicine in Königsberg, Germany, while I chose to try my luck in the Land of Israel.

Today, as I try to arrange the pictures of this period of my life before you, Amia, she turned toward me, I have some difficulty remembering what came first and what came later. The houses and towns of my youth have blurred together in my memory and become a single image, less focused than those of my childhood.

Whom do I see in this picture? At the center were we, the young Jews who had left their homes in the small towns and come to the city to study, some with still fresh hopes and some old-timers, moving sluggishly along in their studies for years on end, undernourished and worn out. Then there were the Jewish bourgeois, in whose homes we managed to eke out a living. I abhorred their exploitative ways, but their children were my students and some of them became really attached to me. Later, these same children worked beside me in the Zionist youth movement. All around, of course, were the gentiles. I especially remember the young gymnasium students we so envied: walking happily to school each day, agile boys standing tall in their school uniforms and bright-faced girls in their lace-up shoes.

Exposed, beyond the protection of my good parents, I also met gentiles who wished to harass me, as they had done to Jews from time immemorial. I saw them everywhere, the Staszes and the Antoshes, grown-up versions of the Lithuanian boys who tormented me in my childhood. That same familiar spark gleamed in their mocking eyes, she said. I understood then that they were everywhere, and on lonely nights in the city, in nightmares, they would fall upon me with ferocious weapons in hand, while my friend Gitl called to me to join her in the refuge she had found. But in the dream this refuge was so far away, and in the meantime the axes and knives had multiplied around me; and I knew, with that terrible certainty that comes only in dreams, that escape was no longer possible and that here, in a strange land, evil would finally overtake me.

There was yet another scene—whether it is a memory or a nightmare I do not know—that often arose before my eyes in those days, she said pensively. One summer day in my childhood, when we were at the resort, my mother sent me to buy some bread from a bakery in the neighboring town. This town was surrounded by quicksand, which I had never seen before. Following my mother's instructions, I crossed the bridge and approached the entrance to town; but before I could reach the bakery I sank into the sand. I walked toward the bakery I could see before me without making the slightest progress, lifting each leg only to sink deeper and deeper into sand.

What a stark image! I exclaimed. But actually, I continued, we all have such dreams, where we walk and walk and get nowhere, losing our way or arriving late.

And you, like your friend Freud, she said mockingly, undoubtedly interpret these dreams as unsatisfactory sexual encounters.

Not true, I protested heatedly. You know I'm no Freudian! I explained to you during our first meeting how I work on dreams.

She smiled, and I saw that she had only been teasing.

Do you want to go on? I asked, strangely gratified. Tsipora must be home by now.

Dvora, ignoring my question, had already turned her gaze back toward the ceiling.

The frame around all this, the Jews and non-Jews, the rich and the poor, is a sprawling city with its houses, its factories, and its mills. The streets of the city are lined with impressive red-roofed buildings, with shop windows facing each other at street level and trams rushing noiselessly back and forth between. Far outside town trains roar by, blasting their tiresome shrieks at the city. At nightfall electric streetlamps illuminate every corner, and during the day governesses strolled down the boulevards, shading their little charges with colorful parasols. At the center of the city, among the other buildings, rises the proud gymnasium, with its bright sloping roof and its three rows of tall windows, precisely ninety-six in all.

The first group of people I came to know were the external students, those preparing for the gymnasium entrance examinations. The boys who had failed in their attempt to pass the old gatekeeper guarding the entrance to the school left the deepest mark on my impressionable soul. Young Jewish refugees from the small towns, growing older with each successive failure, with the hard choice before them: to gird one's loins and keep at the books, or give up the fight and go back home without the coveted certificate, or perhaps marry the grocer's ugly daughter here in the city. Their hair was already thinning, the studies had drained them of whatever vitality had once been theirs. Some had taken the exam five or more times, and were too exhausted either to leave or to find a way out.

They would lock themselves in their dark basements, as I did, where a weak lamp flickered through the day, casting thin, twisted shadows against the low ceiling. We would review our foreign languages, parsing and memorizing, study history, Russian literature, world literature, mathematics, and geography, laboring to better our Russian so our accents would not immediately give us away. The weak ones would trail behind the brighter ones, and some cleaned rooms or cooked breakfast in exchange for a private lesson from a friend who was a bit ahead. They worked out complicated mathematical equations in neat notebooks, hitting the same dead end over and over again. As the examinations approached, I would see them hunched in their tiny rooms, dark circles around their eyes and faces as white as the page before them, undernourished boys immersed to their eyeballs in schoolwork. The stench of sweat and unwashed bodies filled the stifling air. At night the little Primus stove on which the tea was made gurgled from its stool in the corner, sending tongues of flame in all directions and emitting the acrid smell of kerosene. I can still hear their hoarse voices, drenched in the music of pain and hopelessness. Their sole pleasure was a cigarette stuck between the lips, dissipating the black thoughts for a moment or two.

Meanwhile it was spring outside, and the glory of new life shone everywhere. The bright sun spent its radiance lavishly, the trees budded, and determined blades of grass pushed their way up the cracks in the gymnasium courtyard. But in the rooms of those studying for the exams, panic reigned: Someone had spread a rumor about a decision that no external students would be accepted this time; tomorrow was the written examination and we would all fail. And one of the young men would fling himself down on the stool in despair and groan, "Help!" or smash a plate on the floor, sobbing like a baby about how he was up the creek without a paddle and nothing could save him now. And how could we, his friends, comfort him? Our own throats were thick with tears.

That was how it was, she said in her storytelling voice. And then someone would go over to the table, pound his fist and proclaim, "That's it, if I fail again I am going to get married, married to a grocer lady"; and we knew he meant the landlady's daughter, an old maid with stained, rotten teeth that smelled foul.

You were friends with people like that? I asked in surprise.

I was not so different myself, she said. After a pause she continued, as if correcting herself; I tried to study with that group—although I was more advanced than most of them and I never lost that spark of hope. When I looked at them I would think: even if they pass their exams, what is the best they can hope for? An appointment in a village tutoring some rich man's brats. No wonder they often thought of suicide.

These things sound so foreign! I blurted.

Apparently you have not read any of the memoirs of my generation. But who remembers all that today? The world of my youth was destroyed forever in the great wars.

Sometimes I really envy young people growing up in Switzerland, I said, or in Scandinavia. Life wouldn't always be like starting from scratch, suddenly, in the twentieth century, in a brand-new language, over and over again. In general, people who can just go visit the house where their grandfather or great-grandfather lived a few streets or the next town over, instead of having to listen for voices in the ruins. What a difference that would make.

A new language, she said without explaining. How right you are!

I am very tired, she said after a few moments, her voice growing fainter. Be so kind and call Tsipora now. I want to sleep.

ninth encounter

What was it we were speaking about last time? Dvora asked as I walked in. The room seemed darker than usual—the days were growing shorter.

Until now she had always remembered. Was her mind going? Was I going to lose her? I wondered, thinking about the dark hints she had been dropping. Then I remembered that she had nearly fallen asleep at the end of our last conversation, and maybe that was why we had lost the thread of our story. In the meantime autumn had come to the streets of Tel Aviv, sending shivers through the eucalyptuses.

We were talking about the young Jews in the big cities and how they tried to get into Russian schools.

So we did. We stood before those institutions like beggars at the back door. The gatekeeper sweeping the courtyard, the teacher going in that gate each morning, the students walking up those wide steps, they seemed as distant from us as east from west. If one of us spotted a teacher in his black suit walking down the street—or, more amazingly, the principal himself—we nearly fainted with excitement. Could they really be the same as other human beings, with wives and children, ingesting food like other mortals? We vividly pictured their houses: a majestic hall, enormous maps lining the walls, framed portraits of great writers and explorers, shelves laden with books. They were omnipotent in our eyes and devoid of mercy. After all, they were the ones who could grant a matriculation diploma, with all its ribbons and seals, with the merest wave of a hand if they wished—or so we thought, anyway.

The examinations came and went. My brother, Benjamin, passed with flying colors, and I, too, did well enough, but that was not the case for most of the external students we knew. They failed the examinations, but not one of them commited suicide. As I walked along the shaded boulevards on the way to my students' houses, I would see them sitting on the park benches, whiling away the long hours in idle conversation or leafing through a newspaper. With bored, vacant eyes, they would follow the passersby, who were braying with laughter and chattering loudly about the pettiest details of their lives. One told me that he had received a postcard from his sister in the village, asking him when he intended to put an end to his misery and stop gallivanting about so far away from home; and the truth was that he was fairly sure, he said, that he had reached his limit, and he lacked the strength to keep trying to pass the examinations.

But to go back to the village? I asked, and he shrugged his shoulders glumly. There, far beyond the river and mountains, was the small town from which he had come, and in which his mother and married sister still lived, sending him a few rubles scraped together from their meager wages from time to time. And there, too, was the young woman with the morose face and slight frame, anxiously awaiting his return. But how was he supposed to go back there with no certificate? What was he to say when they asked him what he intended to do now?

So what finally happened to him? I asked.

He went on that way for another year or two. He never passed the examination—he wasted too much time and was paralyzed with despair. One summer he went off to a resort town and on a foggy morning, during his morning walk, he lost his footing. The hill was steep and there were boulders below, and he fell against them and smashed like a clay pot exploding into shards.

Was it an accident? I inquired.

Who knows? More than once, though, I heard him say he was tired of living.

The summers in the big city were so oppressive, so desolate! she hurriedly changed the subject. Everyone who could leave ran for their lives. The big stone houses emptied out and were bolted shut. Carriages jammed with furniture and kitchenware rolled toward the nearby forest where the summer houses were. Toward evening, people crowded along the shoreline, shoving their way onto the boats that would take them to the various resorts. When I first came to the city I went on an outing down the Neiman River with the Society of Hebrew-Speaking Women. I can still see that burning Kovno sun, the paved shoreline with its ragged porters, and the bridge where people strolled, hidden under colorful parasols; then, our boat bearing down on us with terrifying blasts of its whistle, we girls with our picnic baskets sailed off on our trip.

Later on, I spent long summers in the forest resorts. That was when I was tutoring the children of rich families, and I was brought to the resort along with the other servants. Far across the river a black forest of tall pines climbed the mountain slope, and it was toward this forest that we set our sights. Vacationers in their fresh white shirts, old and young, glittered in the sunlight there. Older gymnasium students played croquet along with the young governesses. And I, too, hiked at my students' sides, carrying my white parasol down the pine trails, which were always so pleasantly cool, so shady and still.

I could see it clearly. Dvora, the noble beauty, tall and black-haired, dressed in white from head to toe, strolling serenely alongside her young charges, speaking Hebrew with them. The man of the house and his wife walked a few steps behind, bursting with pride at hearing their little ones converse in the clearest, most mellifluous Hebrew with the fine young teacher they had hired. How could it be, I asked myself, that this picture was also part of that desperate world she had described?

Dvora, reading my thoughts again, continued her musical storytelling. But near our airy summer house, there was a poor neighborhood where the servants of the rich people lived, among which were some friends of mine, young women who gave private lessons. The houses there were cramped and dark, and the floors were as muddy underfoot as the village road after a rain. Some of the external students I knew also found their way to this neighborhood; and in the vibrant forest, they seemed even more listless and lost. There was a teacher there, a young woman with not an ounce of flesh on her bones and a despondent look; her roommate and friend, a nurse; and their friend the violinist, who would play, pale and emotional, by the moonlit window. Then, the elderly private teacher Rachel arrived, with her thinning hair always slipping out of a scanty bun. She carried a mathematics workbook wherever she went, asking ev-

eryone to help her solve some problem. They had all failed the examinations, and they were as miserable as the day is long. At night the girls
would scribble in their journals, sobbing unrestrainedly to the melancholy scrapings of the violin. Sometimes I would meet them along the
trails, and all they could talk about was how there was no hope that
anything would ever change, no hope at all.

But soon the summer will be over and we will all be back in the city,
I would say.

And what then? the elderly teacher would respond. More running our
feet off the livelong day from lesson to lesson, sloshing through the
muddy streets, with the key to that dreary room poking through the
holes in my pocket.

Listening to those people was like hearing the wind wail in the chimney, she continued, mourning a youth that had gone up in smoke. I
thought about Rachel getting older, everything she owned in this world
in one trunk: textbooks, pens, and notebooks, and a few pieces of lingerie
her mother had made for her many, many years ago.

But you weren't like them, I protested.

However hard it may be for you to accept this, she said, I worried
about ending up in their shoes, and I recognized their despair. Benjamin
and I treaded close enough to the humiliations of hunger; and even when
there was enough to eat, we did not always earn our bread with honor.
And then, of course, the questions continued to haunt me: Now that I
have left the world of arranged marriages, would I ever marry? Would I
find work I love? Will I ever finally reach my country, my homeland?

I didn't insist, but I had my doubts. After all, these were the years in
which she finished her education, supported herself, won a reputation as
a woman writer, and was adored by her fiancé and friends! On the debit
side, however, were her father's and sister's deaths, her brother's leaving
to study medicine in Germany, and the breakup of her engagement. Who
could do the math properly, with all these factors? Her letters from that
period complained of "ill health." Reverting to my professional persona,
I considered the term "endogenous depression" in all its ramifications:
feelings of despair and sorrow for no ascertainable reason. There were
people whose world went dark for entirely internal, psychological rea-

sons—even when the sun was shining outside. But these thoughts provided little in the way of a resolution.

In European cities at the turn of the century many people took their
own lives, Dvora Baron continued. You might say it was in fashion—
death had suddenly become attractive. Even in the shtetl I knew people
who killed themselves, mostly because of failed love affairs. Yes, she said
glancing at me, even in the shtetl, even among traditional Jews, those
sorts of things happened. They threw themselves into the river or slashed
their wrists, or even set themselves on fire. But in the cities there were
many, many more of them. In addition to those who committed suicide
because their hearts had been broken, I heard stories about people who
took their lives because they were in debt or had failed their exams.
There were many such stories.

Benjamin's good friend, she recalled, who traveled from town to town
speaking at Zionist clubs, once told us about something that had happened in one of the Jewish hostels he frequented. One autumn morning
a Jewish boy was found dead in his room. There was a rope around his
neck, and his heavy body dangled and twisted in midair. No one seemed
to know his name. The innkeeper's wife told our friend that she had
often heard him lumbering about his room like a caged beast. Once,
after she had asked him to stop his pacing, she heard him whimpering
softly in the stillness. And then one morning she found him hanging
from a rope in his room. She did not even know his name, Dvora repeated mournfully. There were some papers among his meager possessions, one of which testified to his broken heart. I will rip my heart from
my own chest, the young man had written, and I will mail it to her,
wounded and dripping with blood. Some scribbles and a dead body, that
was all he left behind.

That was how many of us lived, she concluded, cut off, anonymous,
alienated, as one would say today. And I, too, if I had suddenly taken ill
one night, who would know? Who would come to my rescue?

So did you, too, I ventured, consider suicide?

She reflected for a long time before she answered, her voice heavy:
there were thoughts, but after all, a long road separates thought from
deed. As the years went by, insipid and endless and gray, it sometimes

seemed to me that death would be a welcome respite. A nice long rest, the comforting sleep of someone who has finally found the answer to a vexing question.

And the question? I wondered.

Don't be so naive, she reproached me, but gently. We have been talking about these questions for many months, after all. The questions were: How to live? With whom to live? What to be? How to be? Are there more difficult questions than these for a twenty-year-old girl? I was at a crossroads in my personal life at the very time that our national fate, the fate of the entire world, in fact, hung in the balance. We were in deep mourning over the death of Herzl, on whom our fondest hopes had rested. Is it any wonder that the world appeared cruel and hopeless? And with a hopeless, dim voice, she continued, But why did I imagine I could make you hear what I was then?

Please, no, I answered urgently. It's my fault entirely if I can't hear you. Please don't give up on me. Don't go away.

Let us pause for a while and have a glass of tea, she said wearily. I got up and went into the small kitchen, boiled some water, and arranged a tray with two glasses of light tea and sugar cubes. I helped her sit up on the bed so she could drink, and was startled at how light she was in my arms, for all her height. The blanket slid down, revealing a shabby and wrinkled dress. Her bony hands gripped the thin glass, eyes fixed on her hands. Suddenly I realized how immensely frail she was. She handed me the empty glass and leaned back on the cushions I had arranged behind her head. And the real question, I thought, was this: What does a woman do in bed, shut up in her house for more than thirty years?

Strange winds were blowing among the young intellectuals in the city then, she began to weave her story again. The world was cruel and evil, but it was possible to repair it, we were told. Socialism could feed the hungry, free the masses. In my last years in the city my little sister Chana joined me; she was an impassioned Socialist and had all kinds of revolutionary friends. Late at night, they would meet in out-of-the-way apartments according to prearranged signals, arriving silently, one by one, weird, pale, underfed young people in search of redemption. Forbidden literature would pass from hand to hand, and weary eyes would study the cramped print.

One fine autumn night, however, the secret hideout would be surrounded by policemen. People would be led away, and the tenants of the courtyard roused from sleep. Unpronounceable Jewish names rolled mockingly from the prison warden's mouth as the iron gate locked behind their backs. What will be? What will be? The thought stunned the heart. And we, friends and relatives helplessly awaiting their release, would walk away from the fortified prisons, our heads bowed against the chilly wind.

I never saw myself as belonging to any political movement, she suddenly said in a completely different voice. I was not active in the Socialist movement in any of its forms, although I very much sympathized with its goals. Of course, I had a very strong connection to the Zionist movement, and even served as a Zionist youth leader from time to time; but from a very early age I avoided groups, preferring my room, my books, my desk. Even in Palestine Aharonovich and his friends could not recruit me to any camp, she said with a certain pride, but nevertheless, in my youth I thought long and hard about what was called "the class problem": the chasm between rich and poor. The longer I lived in the city, the greater my revulsion grew for the injustice I saw at every turn. I could also recall my hometown, where the same injustice prevailed among us Jews—things I had failed to notice as a child.

And these are the things you wrote about in your stories, after you left home?

Yes, she answered, there were poor families in the town, and, as in every society, there were the capitalists, the employers. On one side, the boss or landowner; and on the other, the miserable masses, workers who labored for a pittance in order to increase his fortune. In my childhood both these groups were Jewish, and in my innocence I had no notion of the exploitation of one class by another. I remember, for instance, Leibke the bricklayer, who made bricks like our forefathers in Egypt. You see, he was an older man, and far from small in stature, but they diminished him anyway with a nickname—"Little Leib Brick"—not from affection but to put him in his place.

And now we've begun to protest the exploitation of women by men, which is not so different, I burst in.

Dvora ignored me completely. Leibke would scurry around the lime pit, barefoot and shirtless, working with material he did not own, a hired hand of the furnace owner, Yechiel-Ber. Like our forefathers in Egypt, he would knead and tread the clay, and his boss tyrannized him: not with an outstretched rod but with a look. At noon, as the table in the boss's house was being elegantly set with appetizing dishes, the smell of which spread to the street outside, the boss would pass the pit on his way to lunch and fling a few words of rebuke at his worker below. Harsh was the lot of this Jew. His wife and all his children had died, and finally he, too, slipped and fell, never to arise again, as he climbed to shore up a pile of bricks. He died on the eve of the great fair, and people hurried to bury him early the next morning before the market square could be blocked with wagons and carts. And so, in the rush to their workshops or stalls, the man was immediately forgotten.

But the funeral of a rich man, how elegant that was! People streamed down the slopes of the hill under the midday sun with a mournful tread, looking gorgeous in their elegant black clothing, a train of empty, polished coaches following, among wreathes and flowing ribbons. Behind the coffin walked the widow in her long mourner's veil, supported by two daughters in simple black dresses and the cantor in his official skullcap, chanting Psalms to accompany the soul in its ascent.

That must have been in the city, I said, unable to reconcile this image with her descriptions of the shtetl.

Not in the city but in the resort towns of the rich, she answered, but so what? In the shtetl there were equally great class disparities. Take the porter, Nachum-Leib, for example, who was extraordinarily poor even for the gulch. He worked in a warehouse, unloading lead pipes from wagons, carrying sacks of flour to the bakery and salt and sugar to stores. But what a beautiful family life that poor man had. When he came home each evening to his shack, carrying the loaf of bread he had bought under his arm, he would be greeted by the cry "Daddy!" from behind the wooden fence, and that cry carried all the love in the world with it. He asked the children how school had gone, listened to his wife complain about the neighbors, and only then would he sit down to rest from the day's labors.

To make a little extra money to feed his children, he also worked for the old synagogue beadle, who had a reputation as a strict and stingy taskmaster. Stretching out in comfort on "Elijah's chair," the beadle would order the porter up a rickety stepladder to clean the windows beneath the rafters, and woe betide him if he left any streaks. Even his pitiful wages were not paid on time; and when the porter's underfed wife came to ask for some payment toward wages owed, she would be turned away. But there was one job they always set aside for the man: being called up to the Torah during the week the portion of Reprimands and Curses was read. And he, who never turned up his nose at an honest day's work, would go out and spend the money he had earned on a little cocoa for his children.

But that sort of thing can't have been so common in a community you described as being so united.

United up to a certain point, primarily against the gentile enemies, she said bitterly.

It's the same way here, I commented: A war starts, and we're all friends.

Evil was no stranger to town. I remember the hunchbacked tailor, whose friends at the shop were always mocking him, and the tailor who crawled on the ground like a snake, his feet raising a stink. They were Jews, and we, compassionate children of compassionate parents, did we lighten their burdens by a hair? At one end was the rich lumber merchant who lived in town and cozied up to the gentile; and at the other end was the poor tinker, whom the merchant evicted from his shabby house. While in the tinker's house his daughter lay dying with no medicine, the merchant's house rang with parties and late-night banquets. Once the merchant's workers cut down the oak tree that bordered the vegetable peddler's yard. The tree crashed to the ground, with its heavy fruit and birds' nests, while the woman was working at her meager business in the market. When she returned, she stood dumbstruck, as if the river had suddenly disappeared from beneath the bridge, the order of creation had been overturned. Her scream mingled with the shrieks of the birds who had lost their nests. "Where will we rest on Sabbath afternoons?" the women of the street keened. "How will we be shielded from the winter wind?"

And these events occurred in your childhood, in the same town you portrayed with such different colors earlier?

Certainly. You already know that I can see the town with the eyes of the rabbi's little daughter, with the eyes of the critical adolescent who intended to leave it, and also with the eyes of the young woman who can see things as they are. Is that so surprising? There were things in my childhood whose meaning became clear only much later. Under the influence of my new friends, my eyes were opened to the exploitation by the rich of the poor, even in my pious Jewish community. The symbol of all the downtrodden for me was Shifra, a poor young widow. One stormy day she froze to death walking back to town through the snow, after she had been forced to leave her infant son at her mother's and hire herself out as a nursemaid. She was subjected to such degradation—they scrubbed her down, milked her to check the flow—before they brought her a little creature, who fell upon her breast with the thirst of a bloodsucker. The rich have always sucked the poor down to the marrow.

From the time I arrived in the city, I was confronted with social injustice wherever I turned. I saw giant factories with their furnaces and chimneys, and the hundreds of workers swallowed up within it each day. It was in the city that I first became aware that sometimes it was the gentile who was the worker, and the tyrant was the Jew who oppressed him. There was an iron foundry near my house, on the mountain where all the poor people and laborers lived, which you reached by climbing a steep stairway. Every morning at the same hour the first whistle would spill over the top of the tin tower at one corner of the main building, calling the men to work: sharp and insistent, piercing through the early morning fog. The worker would arise in the still dark room, grope hurriedly for his clothes, and leave, on an empty stomach, bare feet trudging through yesterday's mud. In the factory building the deafening clang of iron against iron already filled the air, and a fire raged in the mouth of the enormous furnace. I would see the workers crouching, shivering in the morning chill, the reflection of the fire on their faces, as if they were worshiping some cruel god. Their steady movements continued the whole day long, to the beat of the hammer.

The exploiter, the owner of the factory, a Jew who had forgotten every word he had learned at his mother's breast, would arrive each morning at exactly ten o'clock to oversee his business. A comfortable coach brought him from his new home, which had been built at a suitable distance from the roar and noxious fumes of the factory. He was clean-shaven, spectacles attached to his waistcoat with a fine chain. The bareheaded manager appeared at the office door, smiling obsequiously, and the workers stood aside, making way for him in the middle.

Had she seen these things with her own eyes, I wondered to myself, or were we stitching together odd scraps of memory? Scenes from various films flashed before my eyes in the darkened room: *Metropolis, Modern Times.* Had she seen them too, I thought of asking. I strained to see her face, but there were only her words now, and the images she was painting.

During the meetings of our secret cell, we heard many stories about the exploitation of the workers and the need for change, for revolution. This was brought home to me when I worked for rich people. Their houses were so luxurious, compared to the poor hovels in which the workers lived. In the rich man's home the tile floor was polished daily, electric lamps cast a bright bluish light over the entire house. An expensive piano stood in the parlor and a rag was passed over its cool curves daily. In the study the shelves were laden with leather-bound books, protected by glass doors like a Torah scroll in the synagogue. Special cabinets held ledgers in which the numbers, black on white, showed the profits growing and multiplying from month to month. Heavy rugs covered the floors, and servants in soft-soled shoes gracefully brought dishes with French or English names to the table. Fruits imported from exotic regions, wrapped in special paper, were served for dessert, and wine was poured into the thinnest of goblets. While conversation circled around the fluctuations of the market and the weather, the parties that had been held and those that were coming up, servants glided noiselessly among their masters, ministering to their every desire.

Once something happened when I was working as a governess for the children of a warehouse owner. We were sitting in the dining room after the piano lessons of my two charges, sipping lemonade and nibbling freshly baked pastries. Their mother was crocheting and their father was enjoying a cigarette. Suddenly, the accountant came into the room, hesitated by the door, and dared to disturb the peaceful domestic scene by asking for an advance of a few rubles. It was a matter of life and death, he said, or he would not ask. He was a slight young man, poor and lacking in self-confidence, who toiled all day over the tiny, mute digits in the large ledgers. By comparison, the owner was sturdy and tall, and his gaze was powerful and penetrating through his gold spectacles. I could see how shocked our employer was by the incident: some minor employee coming to his home after work hours and ruining their pleasant evening with some trivial problem! His answer, in sharp tones, came soon enough, explaining to the worker that he never gave advances to anyone. It was his firm principle never to pay wages ahead of time, and he did not need to add that he had no interest in hearing his workers' difficulties—that was something that made his family very uncomfortable.

The young man left, bent in turmoil, and I remained alone with the children. All I was expected to do was to try to ameliorate the effects of the disturbing incident and find some reasonable responses to their questions. A few days later I heard that he had shot himself that night, taking his troubles to the grave.

There was beginning to be talk about a workers' war, about the strike as a weapon of the workers. My brother's friends, Jewish and gentile boys in simple cotton shirts with long hair and fiery eyes, would congregate in our room at night, whispering that the workers were threatening to strike at the foundry. Their leader, a tubercular young man with a scrawny neck who had never in his life not been hungry—Yashek he was called—was supposed to say his piece in a night or two. We gathered in a secret cellar, a rather sizable crowd, and heard from Yashek's own lips about the corruption of the social order. With great emotion—but also in the truest colors—he described the sufferings of the worker, who hired himself out to earn a morsel of bread for as long as he could shoulder the burden, but when his strength ran out he lay himself down to rot and die. He also talked about the troubles of the servants in their masters' houses: they came to their jobs fresh and eager, but when the hard work had worn them out, they were tossed away like yesterday's rubbish.

That was how Yashek spoke to us, a young gentile fighting a just war against his exploiter, the Jewish factory owner, she said with bitter sorrow. His life ended on a prison scaffold at the end of a rope, just like many other young people, innocent soldiers for a righteous cause. We saw them as seeds—seeds that would be buried underground after the earth was plowed, and would disappear; but in the end, they would strike root and send forth shoots.

All this must have created a revolution in your world, I said.

Certainly, a great revolution. My orderly world exploded like the reflection in a pond when the wind begins to blow. Not all Jews were good, not all gentiles were bad, we now knew. Sometimes the boundaries blurred and we fought together—young Jews and non-Jews—for the same cause; but it only took the slightest insinuation, a sudden grimace, a momentary sensitivity, and the chasm between us opened anew.

Can you tell me about that? I asked.

Not today, Amia, she said, practically whispering.

I have tired you out. I'm sorry.

Nonsense! she protested. I am tired of my life, not your presence. Very tired.

Shaken, I asked, Shall I call Tsipora?

In a minute. Let me stay here like this for another moment.

I don't know how long we sat together in the dark room. I don't know if she fell asleep, or was simply gazing into her internal kaleidoscope. For my part, I meditated on the great privilege that had come my way—to listen to Dvora at the end of her days—and hoped that nothing would stop her words now.

After a while she said to me in a stronger voice: Now call Tsipora and go on home; and henceforth I think we should meet twice a week. Tsipora will tell you which days would be most convenient.

tenth encounter

Two days later I presented myself again in Dvora's house. Dvora looked a little more rested, and a bouquet of white roses brightened the room.

Flowers? I pointed. If I thought you would have let me, I would have brought you flowers too.

Please, no. You must remember what I told you. I do not like cut flowers, but not all my visitors know that. Someone remembered my birthday, she said mischievously, and to avoid hurting his feelings I told Tsipora to put the flowers there. In any case, the damage had already been done.

I brought you something too, I said, handing her a gift-wrapped book. It's a collection of poetry by my friend Anat Ninio that has just been published. If you'd like, I could read you a poem or Tsipora could, after I leave, I stuttered, suddenly shy.

Read me your favorite poem, she said briskly, but first help me sit up in bed.

Friendship, I began.

> Look at the wisdom of old age, hard and so
> feminine: at the happiness of
> small ornamental stitches,
> nothing wild, the most delicate contact
> with other people's days, a few sentences
> here and there, wrinkles
> arousing tenderness at the corner of the mouth
> of another woman preserving sweetness,
> a new acquaintance, lost as are we all
> (rain in large drops fell on the desert,

and the children ran gaily about
in a spring picnic) the hard wisdom of old age
makes it possible for me to rejoice in our lot,
which has despite everything
some fragrance of remote blossoming citrus
that fizzes the blood, when the smiles are
sweet as honey, unbelievable.

I turned the page, and continued reading into the stillness, my voice trembling slightly:

We talk about the children
that is to say talk about love.
Our men flow from room to room
and sometimes one of them stays and he too speaks his piece.
Lightly, lightly we gather them onto our laps,
around the coffee table.[1]

You read beautifully, she said, and you chose your poem beautifully. "The wisdom of a hard old age makes it possible for me to rejoice in our lot?" she repeated as if asking a question. A good line. The description of the woman comes through beautifully. The children running about, the men flowing, and she remains fixed in her place, taking in the world, she said, smiling to herself.

Like you, I said.

True beauty is dew for the soul, she said with her mysterious smile, but I have already told you that, haven't I? I thank you for the book.

I had hoped to talk about the poem with her, to hear her comments on the subject of women's friendships; I had hoped to tell her that my birthday fell on the same day as hers, the eve of Chanuka; but I sensed that she was moving us toward her predetermined program. That's what old people are like, I thought, full of themselves. But Dvora's words immediately contradicted my ungenerous generalization.

I thought that this time I would ask you a few questions, she suddenly said. Will you answer them?

Certainly, I said, just as you answer mine.

1. Anat Ninio, *On the Edge of the Paved Pool* (Tel Aviv, 1989). In Hebrew.

Fine, she said. My first question is entirely outside the sphere of our conversations, she began. When you are bewildered, at a crossroads, for example, whose counsel do you seek?

That's a big question, I responded, groping. Every decision is different. Sometimes I talk with friends or my sister or experts.

Those people cannot tell you anything, she answered impatiently. After all those conversations and consultations you are left alone with a few phrases running together in your head. What then?

Perplexed about what she was driving at, I came up with no response. In the silence that followed I turned the question to myself; not to satisfy anyone's inquiries but just to look at the thing itself.

That was when the image of my grandmother Esther, my father's mother, floated into my mind: a tall woman, elderly, a broad-brimmed black hat on her head, sitting on a bench on the boulevard in the old neighborhood of Nachalat-Shiva, parceling out advice to the neighbors— old people like herself, some Sephardic, some Ashkenazic, who had come to ask her opinion. Did she resemble Dvora in any way? Of course she did. There was her height, her long face with its olive skin, the black hair gathered at her neck, her white lace collars, the darkness of her long, wide dresses.

I have a wise woman within, inside me, I answered slowly. I see her as a tiny replica of my grandmother, who is no longer alive, of course.

A miniature wise woman, she repeated after me, as if she already knew.

Maybe I'm not so unique, I thought aloud. Maybe the whole thing comes from a Gestalt group exercise; or did I make up that exercise because of the figure I carry around inside me? The truth is I don't remember anymore.

No matter, she prodded me.

Anyway, when things get rough, I find some quiet and take a private moment with the wise woman inside. I can raise her before my eyes as if she were sitting right across from me. What would you do? I ask. What should I do now? And she always answers. Sometimes I find it easier to talk to her when I write the questions and answers down on paper, but anyway that's how it goes.

And is her answer clear? Does she speak in riddles?

If I have enough peace and quiet—that is, if I am quiet enough—then her answer is clear.

Explain, she persisted.

I have no explanation. If I allow myself to enter into the silence, I find the wise woman and she gives me a straight answer, involuntarily, you might say.

That is what philosophers call "introspection," she surprised me by saying.

And in the East they call it "meditation," I suppose; and one Native American anthropologist calls it "finding one's way with heart."

We fell silent and I wondered, how had we come to talk about this, which I had never told another soul? Was it Anat's poem?

Fine, Dvora said after a moment. And now I have a different question for you, a continuation of our last conversation. When I tell you what happened to me, a Jewish woman living alone among gentiles, what comes to your mind as a native Israeli?

About myself among gentiles, I asked, feeling the miniature wise woman recede to her usual hiding place and Dvora swim into view. Smiling to myself at the quick transition, I searched for an appropriate response to this new question.

Dvora returned the smile and waited.

Obviously, as someone who grew up here, the relationship between Jews and gentiles never preoccupied me much. There were only Jews around, I rarely saw even Arabs, or maybe I just didn't feel their presence. When I was twenty-something I traveled to Europe for the first time, and even there what stood out for me was the diversity of nationalities, languages—in no way did I feel like a Jewish woman in the midst of non-Jews; that is, until I met my uncle who lived in Paris and stayed with him for a few days. Since he doesn't speak Hebrew, and my spoken French was far from fluent, the language we shared was Yiddish. So we wandered around the city with him showing me the sights in Yiddish, in a very loud voice, it seemed to me. Maybe I wouldn't have felt so embarrassed about the language we were speaking if, for our entire trip, on the tram and in the streets, he hadn't continually pointed out to me some man or another, saying, "That one, you see him? He's a Jew." And the same thing, over and over again.

What was the point of identifying every Jew we passed? I wondered. They weren't people he knew, just people he identified according to some private code. Were these possible safety zones in case of emergency? Or was he making a statement to me, the Israeli tourist in his country: You see, I'm not a member of some completely insignificant minority here.

It was clear to both of us that I couldn't distinguish a Jew from a gentile, not by the way they looked and not by how they spoke. My uncle laughed at such ignorance, trying to understand its Israeli roots, and hurried to give me a crash course in this vital categorization.

A good story, the writer said. But the ability to distinguish between groups is always the property of those who are familiar with the human landscape. We, too, when we first immigrated to Palestine, had difficulties identifying an Arab or Turk if they were not in their special garb or uniform; but we very quickly acquired the diagnostic sense.

What I was trying to say is that you're right, I continued; distinguishing between Jews and gentiles—even the word "gentile" is not part of my vocabulary—was entirely marginal to my life as an Israeli.

Yes, said Dvora, like a teacher finally satisfied with my answer, while for me, I never liked the ways of the gentiles. No matter how completely I rebelled against the ways of my parents, the gentiles were always a riddle to me. I remember the wedding of the daughter of the factory owner's driver and laundress to a boy who helped out in the cow shed. That day the factory bell whistled early in the afternoon, as if it were the eve of the Sabbath or a holiday. The workers, faces streaked with soot and their hair matted, streamed out en masse to wash off in the river. When they returned home, they prepared themselves and walked, again in a long row, to the ceremony, gazing affectionately at the groom, a sturdy, broad-shouldered boy who was a good foot taller than the rest of the workers in the neighborhood, and at the bright-haired bride in her red shoes.

But the bride had a young son, Mitke, she confided, who had been born out of wedlock three years before while she was serving in her master's house, a bachelor and engineer at the factory. As the musicians were sweetening the evening with their out-of-tune fiddles and drumming on a brass plate, suddenly all grew still. The engineer, father of the boy, lightly dismounted from his horse and greeted the people of the neighborhood. The dancing ceased and for a moment an unpleasant hush descended; but the engineer quickly left with a clattering of hooves, and the celebration gradually resumed its former strength. I happened to be there and was the only one who noticed the groom going out to the stable and flinging himself full-length on the ground, his body shaking on the bed of straw, trying without success to cry. Was he drunk, I wondered, or just newly conscious of how powerless he was? Everyone knew that—for all the dancing—his wife was not his wife, and even in matters between man and woman the master was still master: a worker had to accept his authority and no one protested.

Even then I realized, she added without pausing, that the exploitation of a woman by a man was very similar to the exploitation of workers by their employer; but I could not express these things to myself or to anyone else, and no one in the Socialist group had the slightest interest in this issue. I can still remember Hendze, the beautiful seamstress in my town, who went out one summer day with Yefis the soldier, who was home on leave. As I was passing by on my way to the meadow, I saw him pulling the girl toward a haystack. She protested and tried to turn toward home, but the soldier, who was stronger than she, blocked her path, and she did not even sigh. Covering her face with her hands, she took a few steps backward on the broken-up soil, falling back and rolling into the haystack, like a bolt of discarded cloth when the scissors cut it away.

Her voice was as rigid as metal; I thought about how much she sounded like a member of my own generation, how outside her own time she was. But I held my silence.

I came to know heartless rich Jews better and better as I continued to work in their homes. On summer vacations, which I spent in the forest with my students, I observed their habits up close, their fancy foods, their idle conversation. They would lie in hammocks until the day cooled down, and then they would go for a stroll. Sometimes one of the vacationers set up a gramophone and people would gather round; then the melody of "Blessing for the New Moon" or "Holiness" would drown out the sounds of the forest. Everything was so peaceful and serene for them in the summer months. But—I heard them say as they strolled on their walks—in the city there were many things that troubled them. Aside from family and business matters, there were also public issues, the neverending rattle of charity boxes, institutions and fundraisers and just plain poor folk and everyone with their hand out, robbing them of the peace they deserved.

Sometimes apoplexy would strike precisely there because of their indulgent habits. The gluttony I witnessed in their homes! At the very crack of dawn, farm women would appear from the villages with baskets of eggs, pitchers of milk and cream. In the morning they had cocoa and white bread with butter, to the sizzle of lunch frying in the kitchen. Although the house doctors warned them to stay away from heavy foods and liquor, and forbade them to put on weight, it was difficult, so difficult, to withstand temptation. And so, one of the neighbors dropped dead in the middle of a meal. The sobs I heard through their windows rang so disturbing and strange after the laughter and the tinkle of silverware that had emerged all spring and summer. A shudder passed through all the other potbellied men, and the doctor was called to advise and to explain that they must be vigilant.

The evil prosper while the just suffer, she said after a pause, and how shall we behold this and do nothing, we wondered in our youth. But as the years went by our dreams dissolved in the face of reality into nothing, nothing.

She sank into gloom, and I wondered whether I was hearing the disillusionment of youth or that of an old woman looking back at her life. But then a different train of thought occupied my mind.

I wanted to ask you something, I said, conscious of diverting the flow of conversation.

She turned a black look upon me and waited.

You were just emphasizing the bad eating habits of the rich as something you noticed when you were young. But you yourself are very careful about what you eat.

Tsipora is the same way, she said.

Yes, by your example, no doubt. In any case, when did you begin to be so careful about what you should or shouldn't eat? People say you practically mortify yourself.

When a person's health is weak, there is no choice, she replied with annoyance. I was a vegetarian from a young age because I loved animals; but most foods are harmful to me and that is why I refrain from eating them.

She seemed reluctant to go on—and I decided not to insist. And so, after a few moments of thought, she took up the thread of our previous conversation.

I saw how rich people lived and was greatly influenced by my revolutionary friends, but I also looked to Zionism for a solution to social problems. Instead of mending the old world, I thought along with many of my friends, we could build a new and more just world, a society of workers in the land of our forefathers. But only a few shared these views.

Most of the Jews, she added, those who had the means to immigrate to the Land of Israel in those days, refused to see the truth; others denied their origins. I recall the prosperous Jew who engaged me to prepare his children for the gymnasium. His house was not especially large, but it was freshly painted, with a balcony at each corner and a large porch held up by carved pillars. There was a garden outside and flowering fruit trees perfumed the air each evening. There was no serenity in that house, however, and it was some time before I understood the source of the tension.

The woman of the house would often sit on the porch and sing soft, sorrowful melodies. She would only laugh when her brother came to visit, picking out gay tunes on the piano and dancing with him. After a while I gathered that the brother had converted and married a Christian woman, and the woman herself had become estranged from Judaism. When her husband spoke to her in Yiddish, she pretended not to understand. When the conversation turned to Jewish matters, she would shut the windows and doors, pulling the shades and drawing the curtains. I once heard her argue that speaking Yiddish would make her children stammer. She forbade their father to speak Yiddish at home, lest it ruin the children's Russian accents and hold them up to scorn. I was instructed to teach them Hebrew no more than three hours a week and the rest of the time I taught them Russian, German, and French. But no matter how hard they tried to run from their Jewishness, when the pogrom came the rioters visited their house as well.

For Benjamin and me it was perfectly clear that we were Jews, and so our lives must lead to the Land of Israel. I was active in the Socialist movement, but I worked much harder for the Zionist idea. After I finished gymnasium, when I was living in Mariampol, I joined a group called the Speakers of Hebrew, a few dozen young boys and girls, and together we strove to revive the language. There was also a group of young people, raised in the best Lithuanian tradition of Torah and secular studies, who were studying Zionism and modern Hebrew literature together. Somehow they heard about me, and they gathered about me in the hopes that I would be their leader.

She smiled, the room lit up with her memory.

There was such hope and innocence in those young people. Although I was only a few years older than they, they admired my writing, I suppose, and showered me with love. Together we had wonderful conversations about Avraham Mapu's *Love of Zion* and *The Song of the Nightingale* by Buki Ben-Yagli, about Chayim-Nachman Bialik and Shaul Tschernichovski and others—the writers who had stormed their worlds. At the time I was living alone in a room in the house of a poor teacher and I became friendly with his daughter, who loved people more than anyone I have ever met. Very quickly she helped turn my room into a youth club, where twenty or thirty young people gathered at every opportunity. That was as sociable a period as I was ever to experience. But even then, you must understand, I was not acting under the sponsorship of any movement or institution. No one appointed me to the position, there was no training program I was required to complete; it grew of its own accord, from the enthusiasm of the young people and my own desire to help them develop. There was never another period like that one, she said meditatively.

I was once a youth leader, but I disliked it and never tried again.

Where was that, she asked with interest.

In my youth movement, in Tel Aviv. They sent me to a leadership seminar, and then when I was sixteen, they made me the leader of the eleven or twelve year olds, I don't remember which.

And why did you not enjoy it?

The girls were out of control; they just wanted to be wild. I was an industrious and introspective girl, and I might have been able to teach them something maybe, but I was definitely the wrong person to be leading social activities and sports.

Dvora smiled sympathetically.

I remember the group going for a Sabbath-afternoon walk along the Yarkon, which compared to the amazing rivers you've described was just a smelly little creek. All the girls rushed to hold my hand, and since I only have two hands, there was a constant state of war among them. They pushed and shoved and altogether made a nuisance of themselves. I was practically forced to set up turns and change handholders every five minutes. Only one thing saved me: the ability to tell a story. When I reached the end of my rope, I would sit down and ask: Anyone want to hear a story? Immediately the girls would take their places quietly and gaze at me, ready to listen.

And what would you tell them?

Anything that occurred to me—stories I had read and stories I made up about exotic lands or people I had never met—a complete mish-mash. But somehow I always managed to interest the girls in my stories and to carry over the plot from Sabbath to Sabbath. That's one of my favorite memories: sitting in the middle of a circle, spinning tales. If I lived in a primitive society, I would try to get the job of tribal storyteller.

You know, I did not tell the young boys stories, Dvora said. Rather than lecturing, I would draw them out so they could practice their Hebrew conversation. Each of them would prepare something to tell about himself in Hebrew, and if he could not invent something, he would bring a story or poem to read to us. The meetings that took place on Friday night, after the meal, were especially enjoyable. For lack of seats, I would usually sit on the bed, and everyone else would sit around me. On those evenings, my room would fill to bursting. The boys in their Sabbath clothes leaned against the walls, and one by one they would rise and

stand beside the glowing Sabbath candles to read something to the assembled group. Some could barely read, and others were graced with the
gift of self-expression and the Hebrew words flowed clearly from their
lips. I encouraged them all, to nurture their self-confidence.

If one of the pioneers from Palestine happened to be home visiting
his family, I would try to bring him to the group to talk about life in
the Land of Israel—so they should know that Zion was not just a land
of dreams—it was growing into a flesh-and-blood reality. And once a
friend arrived in Mariampol on a visit, a writer who had even published
some Hebrew verse. I assembled the group and warned them to pay close
attention to his talk, which would be given entirely in the Sephardic
pronunciation. How amazed they were to hear that Hebrew was spoken
in the Land of Israel with an accent different from the one they were
used to! I set to work teaching the boys the principles of the Sephardic
pronunciation. To my surprise they quickly accepted the whole matter:
how could it be otherwise? Was it possible that Jews in the Land of Israel
would speak just as in the Diaspora? Together we trained ourselves in
the "proper" accent, and talked long and hard about this new revelation.

Sometimes parents regarded our activities with suspicion, worried
that their children would be led astray and abandon the tradition, God
forbid; but as long as the activities did not take them away from their
regular schoolwork, the parents put up with us patiently. It may be that
my reputation, as a Hebrew writer and the daughter of a rabbi, protected
the honor of the group. The young people respected me too, and for my
birthday they brought me a large album, with slits in the pages for in-
serting postcards and colored pictures. I will never forget the Sabbath
they came to present their gift, inscribed with the dedication: "The leaders ceased in Mariampol, they ceased, until you arose, O Deborah." In
the difficult years when I was living alone, after Benjamin had gone off
to Germany, these boys became my new family.

In the meantime, however, great changes were taking place in my life,
and with them came the end of that chapter of my life.

Can you tell me about that? I asked, noticing the late hour.

Another evening would be better, she said pleasantly; the next chapter
in my life is not at all easy: a failed relationship with a man I thought

would be my friend for life, and a visit to my mother's house after my father's death—these are the things I will talk about when next we meet.

And I wanted to ask you something else, I added, hoping to contribute to her agenda: that is, how you became a Hebrew writer.

Dvora nodded. Then she shut her eyes, and I took that as a signal that our meeting was over. I left the book of poetry on the pile of newspapers beside her bed, said goodbye to the two women, and took my leave from the dark, close house. The pleasant fragrance of early winter greeted me with the evening chill and woke me to myself again. I hurried to start the car, eager to get to Jerusalem. How pleased I suddenly felt about my good health; my ability to get into a car and drive it wherever I wanted; my beautiful children, waiting for me in a well-lit, open home.

eleventh encounter

Since we had started meeting twice a week, I had begun to think of myself as one of Dvora's household. I no longer felt the anxiety mounting as I climbed the staircase, reaching its peak when I knocked on the door; I barely noticed the smell of the closed-in apartment; I had stopped worrying that I would knock on the door and no one would answer. Dvora and Tsipora had even started asking me for help now and then with various household matters, especially small errands to Jerusalem, and I was happy to agree.

I found Dvora on the red velvet-covered sofa as usual, her face the picture of gloom. The black circles around her eyes seemed darker than usual, and with her sunken eyes, she reminded me of some terrifying nocturnal bird.

We agreed that today I would tell you the final chapter in the story of my youth before I immigrated to Palestine, she began. Those were bleak years I spent in the Russian cities, desolate and lonely. We went hungry more than once, and we worked without respite. Our family was far away, and our friends were falling one by one into the arms of despair.

Despite myself, I was experiencing the old skepticism: Why was she presenting her life in such dismal terms? Was she concealing the true cause of her pain? Was it just the fashion of that generation, in those circles, to grasp hold of suffering and never let go? Did the roots of this depression lie in her personality? Was that why her life had been so hard, whatever the explanations she furnished for her misery?

This time Dvora did not read my thoughts and, lost in her own, she continued. On the worst of days I would be seized by the image of my father's house, and sometimes, in my despair, I would think: If only I could go back and see the house in which I was born—my troubles would be over. I dreamed of that house, leaning so humbly on its two supports. I dreamed that I climbed to the musty attic and found the yellowed Bible and my first Hebrew alphabet workbook hidden among the rafters. I even imagined I could smell those American potatoes with onions and pepper, roasting on a bed of pine chips at the front of the oven. Just a single taste, and I would die happy.

But there was nothing harder than going home after my father's death. Even before I reached the house, I could see how the town had fallen into disrepair. The mill with its wheel had sunk considerably into the slope of the mountain and the synagogue was still blackened from the big fire. The winter carriage stopped on the street before our house and my mother ran out to greet me. Her face told me just how cruelly God had dealt with her. Father's orphaned chair stood beside the dismal table. The potatoes Mother cooked, although they had been seasoned with onions and pepper, tasted as if they were missing a crucial ingredient. At nightfall, when the kerchief came off, strands of silver flickered in her hair. Again I lay awake listening to the familiar sounds: the rap-rap-rap of the night watchman's stick, the creak of the hoist of the well. The warmth from the stove dissipated as the night wore on, the cold reigned uncontested, and my father's bed stood empty and naked behind the partition. Father, Father! my heart wept within me, as I finally felt the sharp tooth of orphanhood.

Even though my mother died at a ripe old age, many years after I had left for Palestine, and even though I returned to the city after the mourning period and picked up my life where it had left off, I knew that nothing would ever be the same again. With my father dead and Benjamin gone to medical school, my loneliness grew. I stopped keeping even those religious observances I had kept at first. And in their place? What path would I find for myself in life? This question tormented me, as it did many of my peers. Sometimes I thought that I would find life's meaning in literature, and sometimes I wondered if I would be like all the girls and one day my true love would come and fill the black void inside me.

How strange, I said to Dvora. Although you were young at the beginning of the century, and I was young—oh, many years later, you grew up in a small town in Lithuania and I grew up in Jerusalem, no one could have expressed the central dilemma of my own life more clearly.

Tell me, she said.

Oh, I can't talk! I don't have your ability to express myself.

Nonsense, she declared forcefully. You told me yourself you were a born storyteller.

You know how it is. Today I don't feel that way. I'm no storyteller, and I'm no great psychologist, either, I said, surprising myself with my own words.

Nonsense, she repeated. What happened to you? Did someone hurt you? Tell!

I was taken aback by the ferocity in her words. To myself I thought, Yes, it's true, someone did hurt my feelings, and I didn't get the promotion I deserved at work. But I chose not to tell her about that world, which seemed so distant from her own.

I'll try to explain, I said hesitantly. When I was young it was all so simple. I loved the man who became my husband with all my heart and soul, and when we had our first son, the fruit of our love, I thought that my love for the two of them would fill what you call the "void" forever; but slowly it became clear to me that without creative work, without imagination, writing, the "pit"—that was what I called it—would open under my feet again and again. When that happened, my husband knew enough to give me the space I needed until I was ready to share my world with him. More than that, he took the burden of the family on his own shoulders when my own work consumed me. We were a good team, I said.

After he died, I continued, and I was left alone, the pit dropped wide open under my feet. Sometimes I would see myself groping my way around its slippery edges, expecting to fall in at any moment. It was only because my three children needed me, especially the youngest, that I resisted the impulse to give up and slide in. My relatives and friends all respected my ability to cope, my practicality, how well I functioned—I hated those artificial words—but they hadn't the faintest notion about the chasm yawning before my feet.

Very quickly after the tragedy I went back to writing, twice as energetically as before, sensing that this was the one thing that could save me. Now, however, in middle age, I'm in the same situation you were in when you were younger. Once again I ask myself what can fill the void. Love, which sometimes comes my way, seduces me with its promise to end my loneliness; but when I give myself over to a new relationship, my writing seems to suffer. Maybe it doesn't really, but there's no doubt that I have precious little time for myself, and I experience it as a sacrifice. And why should I sacrifice myself, really, for what?

I fell into a lost silence, and Dvora said quietly, Never sacrifice yourself for any man or woman, because you will only be disappointed. The only thing worth sacrificing your time for is children, your children; but raising children is, after all, a fairly short chapter in the life of a human being.

The most beautiful moments in my life, I said as if confessing a sin, have been when, after rereading something I wrote, I knew that a line in it, a paragraph if I was lucky, was the absolute truth. When that happens, sometimes I cry with gratitude.

Dvora stretched her bony hand from under the blanket toward me, and I took it in my own.

And now you tell me, I said, when the emotion had subsided.

In my years in the cities the need to write, and the sense of destiny that went with it, were already ripening within me, along with a deep suspiciousness about relations between men and women. These two things went together in my life. Even today I ask myself whether domestic life can be anything but slavery. And I wrote stories about this issue that were, to my surprise, accepted for publication, although they were full of bitter rage.

It's true, I said, I was really amazed when I discovered the early stories, the ones you concealed for so many years, which were published in Hebrew and Yiddish periodicals. They were full of social critique, either about the exploitation of women in the Jewish community, or about people mocking the poor beggars among them. I had two questions when I read them: Where did you get those ideas? And how did you dare to express them, once you had thought of them? You were just a young girl, fifteen years old, a rabbi's daughter, just starting out as a writer.

Look, she said, without a trace of pride, I was always an extraordinarily talented and unusual child. When I began to write—I was a little girl then—it was as a natural result of my Jewish education and knowledge of Hebrew language, as well as my exposure to the secular books my brother, Benjamin, gave me. When I was just seven years old I wrote a play in Yiddish, although I have forgotten what it was about, she smiled; but another memory has remained with me: I am standing barefoot by the well, washing the lunch dishes. A strange man comes up the street and asks me, "Little girl, where is the Baron house?" I point toward it. A few minutes later my brother excitedly calls, "Dvora'le, someone wants to see you!" And who was it? The famous writer Ben-Avigdor, who had made a special trip to Ouzda to meet the writer of the stories he had seen in *Hamelitz*. During those years, my sketches were readily accepted for publication, and letters arrived from editors asking me to send more essays, stories, and sketches in the same vein. We want everything you write, they told me, and there will be some money in it for you, too.

That could explain why your father let you leave home, I thought aloud. After all, you were already somebody even before you left your parents' house!

Yes, I was certainly a special girl, and not everyone loved me for it. Perhaps they were envious, she said sadly, although what was there, really, to envy? But let us not speak ill of the dead, she added cryptically.

We were talking about your stories, I reminded her.

Well, most of them were full of grief for the cruel and unjust world—my town, that is, which was the world in those days. Why did those particular things make such an impression on my young soul, rather than the warmth of my own home, which I only later described? You are the psychologist and will have to supply an explanation, she teased. Is it because negative things make a stronger impression on a young mind than positive ones? Or perhaps the consciousness wishes to eject from itself precisely the most distressing images and voices through writing them down?

I smiled and said: You know as much as I do.

Perhaps it is true that in my early work I put thoughts into the minds of children that would be unnatural for them to deal with at their age, she continued. But the fact is, those were mostly my own thoughts and I myself was only a young girl. Alongside tales about the yearning for redemption I satirically observed the ways of the Hasidim, the hypocrisy of traditional social conventions, and expressed this in my writing; but most of my stories of that period were depictions of family life. Some of my portraits were not particularly critical of social custom, for instance the story about a family that dreads the arrival of a visitor they do not like, but the instant he walks in, they greet him with pleasantries and beg him to stay. In the more critical sketches, most of which I did not republish because they were too one-sided, I observed the institution of marriage with an accusing eye—even then. For the most part, however, those were the stories I wrote after leaving my parents' house, she added.

But even so, you were not yet twenty and you were—if you don't mind my saying so—a pious young virgin.

Dvora smiled mysteriously and didn't try to dispel my amazement. Nevertheless, leaving home liberated my work from the critical scrutiny of the traditional Jewish community. I was greatly influenced by the freedom of city life and by the fascination with sexual matters in the European fiction I devoured. In my "brazen" writing, as some critics called it, I challenged the boundaries that had been firmly set in my father's home, and wrote about the same topics that concerned gentile writers, male writers, as these resonated in my own world.

That seems so extraordinarily daring, your shattering of conventions, all the while preserving your status as rabbi's daughter.

What choice did I have? It was my natural development and I do not remember thinking that I was a particularly daring person, she said impatiently.

So you wrote about a husband having a nice drink when his wife dies; or about another husband who lusts insanely after his wife and beats her when he can't have sex with her. Or about the woman whose husband wants nothing but her body. The house was full of little boys and girls, a crowded room on a wintry night, and after he had sent her, of course, to take a dip in the ritual bath, he laid their little son on the cold floor to make room for himself in the mother's bed. The rage in these stories, the hatred against men!

The men were also pitiful in those early stories, she said in weak protest. You remember Akiva the beggar, who crawled on his belly like a snake, whom people avoid because he stank of rotting flesh? Or the poor devil who was nicknamed "Murderer," because he had been forced to kill his horse and sell her hide for a few pennies to buy wine for his wife who was in labor and wood to warm their houseful of babies? The protagonists of these stories, she repeated, men as well as women, were wretched and oppressed. Think of the consumptive little girl who tried with all her might to restrain her cough so her widowed mother would not lose her job as nursemaid to a rich man's son. Misery was everywhere in world literature at the time, too. I remember a short parable I wrote in that period, in which I stood in the heart of an ancient forest where the trees had lost their leaves and a chill wind always blew. She dropped her voice in self-mocking solemnity: "I asked the trees: 'And man, where is he?' And the ancient forest answered: 'Nowhere.' " Despair and desolation were just the topics of the day, she laughed.

But in your stories, the women are more miserable than the men, I insisted. If not, they're empty and frivolous, thinking only about dresses and men; but when they marry, their husbands use their bodies without their deriving the slightest pleasure from the act.

What women knew about sexual pleasure in those days? she asked.

Did you know? I asked. How did you know enough to protest?

She shrugged. For all my daring, as you call it, she finally said, sometimes I chose to express myself in parables. So I wrote about Liska, the Jewish dog, who went astray when she sought carnal pleasure among the gentile dogs.

You didn't answer my question, I thought, but respected her silence.

How were those pieces received? I asked aloud.

Initially, I was accepted into the world of young Jewish writers, and the editors knew my work and were happy to publish it. Brenner, Klausner, Kaback, Shoffman, and Weinberg were among those writers who wrote to me in response to my early stories, which had appeared in Jewish periodicals in both Hebrew and Yiddish. They addressed me in their letters as "honored author" and that was how I often felt, although I was still just a struggling external student. From the comments of writers and editors, I understood that most had no idea that I was a young girl, for how could a young girl write such things? Others wrote to me directly about how shocked they were that I dared to deal with erotic issues or the connections between the sexual and death drives. It was clear that my position as a woman writer, a rabbi's daughter, gave rise to certain expectations about my work, and that I was shattering these stereotypes in my writing. Some editors praised me to high heavens for the delicacy of my descriptions, the clarity of my prose, the innocence and beauty of the town I described; but others considered it chutzpah, she said with a mischievous smile. Some asked me explicitly how a nice Jewish girl could write about men in the bathhouse or about what some man did with his best friend's wife. But they were also fascinated with the novelty of it, it seemed to me. Despite the fuss, she leaned forward urgently, I must tell you that I continued to appear and to be a decent Jewish girl with a modest demeanor. In my first years in the big city I was protected by my brother's shadow, and after that, by the respectable Jewish families in whose homes I worked.

So there was a big gap between the world of your literary imagination and your actual way of life?

Exactly, she said, satisfied that I understood, but the apparent audacity of my stories seems to have planted false notions among some of my readers. That was part of the reason my relationship with Moshe Ben-Eliezer soured—a hidden chapter of my life I have never discussed with anyone before.

My heart beat with anticipation, but she turned to me and said, Before we discuss that, however, I wanted to tell you something about the enormous difficulty we faced, all the Hebrew writers. You are a native Israeli, and Hebrew is a living language now, your mother tongue, so you will never know how we suffered in our first attempts at writing Hebrew.

Many of the writers did not know Hebrew at all, so they were literally writing in a foreign language. Fortunately, I was not among these, although the Hebrew of my father's house, of the study hall, was the Holy Tongue. And here were we, young writers, clearing a path through this sanctified territory for a secular literature, for mundane matters, for our own lives. None of us spoke Hebrew naturally; that we did in Yiddish in our youth, and the characters we wrote about were also Yiddish speakers. Now, I wanted to write conversations in Hebrew! There are no words to describe the agonies that accompanied each and every line I wrote. For all my knowledge of the Bible and Hebrew sources, she said and stopped, as if astonished by her own words, there still has not been a proper appreciation of the tortuous path of my generation, writers in a literature with no land and no vernacular.

I think I felt some small fraction of the difficulties you're describing when I started writing in English, I said.

No comparison, she said scornfully. English has a vocabulary and all you had to do was learn it. But the Hebrew of my youth lacked the very words I needed to write my stories, the idioms my characters would use. Every so often I look over those early writings, and I remember the frustration I felt until something came to mind that could express some small part of what I was trying to say, and the results—how inarticulate they seem to me now. When Hebrew literature migrated to the Land of Israel and began to strike roots there, everything changed. The language left the book and returned to the people, and we, the creators, slowly began to write for readers who actually conversed in the language of our stories. Hebrew literature was a natural part of life in the Land of Israel, but in my youth it was the hothouse literature of a ghetto culture, with no ground beneath to sustain it.

It's true that the Hebrew you used seemed difficult and lofty when I started reading your stories, even the later ones from the collections, I said. But I got used to your style and it started sounding fluent and free to me, even though it's very different from the language we speak today. What's so beautiful, I added, is that even the way you speak now, especially when you tell me your memories, still has some of that style.

When I first came to this country I would address people in the third person, carrying on entire conversation with "Mr. this" or "Mrs. that." Even then, the pioneers spoke in a more lively and informal fashion, but I, with the heavy load of ancient Hebrew I still carried from my studies with my father, years passed before I could speak with their lightness and ease. However natural a tongue Hebrew became in the course of the years, I never had a light pen, and every line that emerged went through endless drafts and revisions until it sounded right. But who knows, perhaps I would have struggled just as much had I written in another language.

They say that there are no superfluous words in your stories, that your style is as clear as fine wine.

She bent her head and ignored my compliment.

Well, she said, in the tone of someone finally getting down to an unpleasant task, it is time for me to tell you about my relations with Ben-Eliezer, that long-forgotten story. I was seventeen when I met Moshe Ben-Eliezer in Kovno, when Benjamin and I were still together. Ben-Eliezer was living in Vilna, but he had come to Kovno to visit his sick brother. He became friendly with my brother, and that was when our own relationship began to take shape. He was older than I, a young writer who published his work under numerous pseudonyms. I will not go into details, because much has been forgotten and in general the matter is distasteful to me. At one time, there were strong feelings between us, she continued calmly, and we were even considered a betrothed couple, but it may as well have never happened. When our engagement was broken after approximately five years, I immigrated to Palestine and eventually married Yosef. Ben-Eliezer also married, immigrating to Palestine with his wife a few years later. We never renewed our friendship, and I see no point in fussing over the matter.

Still, I coaxed, tell me a little more.

We had a complicated relationship. There was mutual affection from the very beginning, but at the same time we never truly understood each other. We spent relatively little time together, for the chaos of the world and our own quests conspired to keep us apart—he traveled to France, England, and America, working as a journalist—and I went to school and then moved from house to house, earning my bread.

So that was why things didn't work out between the two of you? I asked.

In part, she said, searching for the right words, but I have already said that there were gaps in our understandings of each other. He had never known a woman before me and was often ambivalent about his feelings and skeptical of the very possibility of love. He concluded from reading my stories that I had more experience than he did, and he would not see me for what I was: an innocent, decent woman, who spun tales by the light of her imagination. Benjamin's jealousy and protectiveness did not help matters. I was the one who laid the ground for our closeness, inviting him to my older sister's house to meet the family, but later I heard through my friends that my attitude toward him had distressed him. The truth is that I never got to the bottom of his disappointment. I think that the gossip about me spoiled things for him, while I—but I already explained all that to you: this was the first crossroad of my life.

What do you mean?

I told you, she sighed, as if my pestering was exhausting her. With Ben-Eliezer I first felt in my own life—not as an observer of other people's lives—how heavy a price I would have to pay for a family. Perhaps, if I had loved him a little more, I would have been prepared to pay it; but it was not that way. I was unable to return the affection, the passion, he felt for me. It seems that I had always imagined a different sort of mate, a man of valor—childish fantasies, she said dismissively.

In any case, she continued, I remember Ben-Eliezer's terse remarks, attempting to direct my life in ways I was unprepared to accept. Not only did he have suggestions for what I should write and how to publish—that sort of advice was taken for granted among us, the young writers—but he also asked, for example, why I did not want to live in Ouzda, where I had such a nice family. I could sense his paranoia, his tendency to see rivals in every shadow. When you add my brother's jealousy, which was also flaring up then—perhaps Benjamin, too, was disturbed by my independence, by the boldness of my stories—it was more than I could bear. After all, I was my own person, I was surrounded by friends, I was finally about to enter the gymnasium—why should I give all that up? And what would become of my writing? Then, there was the enormous geographical distance that separated Ben-Eliezer and me, and the long durations that passed between our encounters. When we met again, he seemed a stranger to me, and I, too, had changed.

That was how it happened, she sighed, that when Ben-Eliezer came back from New York especially to see me, he said that he could no longer be left hanging in midair, he wanted to marry me and take me back to America. I responded that I could not give him an answer for another five years, and since he was unwilling to wait another day, our relationship came to an end.

Both of us were very upset about it, she said, although I can barely remember that now; unlike other events from that period, this episode has been erased as completely as if it had never happened.

That may be the proof of how important it was, I thought as a psychologist. Would she read my mind again, I wondered, and was relieved to sense that she was lost in her own thoughts.

Some people saw it as a tragedy, and Benjamin felt that I had been jilted. We were engaged, and he had discussed our relationship with mutual friends and dedicated a story to me in *Haolam*—a periodical that frequently published my own stories. But now, after all these years, the point of the story is the lesson I learned from it—or perhaps did not learn so completely—about the danger of the enslavement of a woman's creative spirit to her spouse, her "master," as a husband is called in our language, even if he is enlightened and honest and has the best of intentions.

Is that what happened to you later on? I boldly asked.

We have not yet arrived at that chapter, she said. I could see how exhausted she was. Perhaps you will answer that question yourself.

What can I add to what I've already told you? Here I am, an adult woman with her own children and her own life. It's far too late for me to let any man be the master of my spirit.

Then we are exactly the same, she muttered.

twelfth encounter

Finally I left the Diaspora, never to return, Dvora began after I had taken my regular place by her bed. Her face seemed more drawn than usual, her cheeks sunken and pale. The gaunt face, the melodic voice, were becoming more and more captivating.

So, in my quest for a new homeland, to which I had dedicated myself since childhood, I left my old home; but I did not know that I would never see it again, nor that I would be forced into a different exile once more.

Over the years, I gradually saved enough money for my journey. With heartfelt generosity, the industrialist family in whose home I worked at my last position agreed to help with my expenses. I had already completed my studies, and my ties with Ben-Eliezer had dissolved into nothing. My family—although they were very precious to me—no longer posed an obstacle to my departure. Benjamin, with whom I was closest, promised that he, too, would follow me to Palestine as soon as he completed his medical degree. When the preparations had been made, nothing remained to be done but to secure myself a position in Palestine so I would not be dependent on strangers. Benjamin worried about my health, which had not been very good, and was afraid that I would make the trip before I had found myself a source of livelihood; so he himself turned to some acquaintances who had already emigrated whom he hoped could help me find work.

In the two years prior to my departure I received numerous offers of work in the Diaspora. I was invited to teach in various Jewish schools throughout the country, and they even tried to persuade me to be the

principal of a girls' school. But I had no great interest in standing before
large groups of students, and had found that home-teaching was better
suited to my temperament and left me more time to read and write; I
also turned down these generous offers because I feared that the arrangements involved might actually postpone my emigration, and I was impatient to take the step that had been so long in the planning.

We sent off dozens of letters, my brother and I, to Palestine, without
success. We were told that it was not easy securing a position for someone
that had not yet arrived in Palestine; moreover, the Teachers' Board
required that candidates for a teaching position in Palestine be examined
by teaching a model class. Some people wrote that Palestine was full of
teachers who had arrived from Russia before me—some of them even
had university degrees—and who had not yet found work. One person
suggested I study to be a nursery school teacher, since it was easier to
find work in that field. Others assured me that I would certainly have
found a position already if I were there. In the course of three years of
correspondence, which traveled by the slow rhythms of overseas mail, it
was impossible to settle the matter, although I received many words of
encouragement in response to my queries.

When it became clear that I would be emigrating, whatever happened,
writers and editors with roots in the Diaspora made me swear that I
would record my impressions of Palestine for their periodicals. These requests made me feel as if I were a scout bravely preceding my comrades,
but there were also a few of our group of young writers who had already
made the trip to Palestine and who sent news about what was happening
there. I remember, for example, Zrubavel's letter, rhapsodizing in Yiddish
about the pure blue skies of our land, although he confessed that he
missed the Jewish life of the Jewish streets. "The torments of the Land
of Israel" or "a cultural wasteland" we called that feeling later. Kaback,
by contrast, simply wrote from Jaffa that he had already rented a room
for me, and now he was impatiently awaiting my arrival—so I went.

An expectant silence filled the room. The ruddy light of the stove, lit
this evening for the first time, flung perturbed shadows against the wall.

How can I describe my final leave-taking from my mother and my
town? Or that magical journey to the Holy Land at the beginning of the

century, she said, transforming before my eyes. Her face was lit from within, her voice emerging from the depths of a dream. What is the truth and what is just longing, what is reality, imagination, dream—all of these combine into one fluid image.

I didn't come here to get the facts straight, you know, I said to the radiant face before me. Tell me what you see in your mind's eye now.

As one woman storyteller to another, she responded.

One morning, after the necessary documents had been drawn up, I traveled to my mother and oldest sister's house for the last time. A large trunk had been taken down from the attic and stood open in the center of the room, and the two of them were filling it with anything they thought I might need on my journey. I have not danced at your wedding, said my mother, lovingly folding dresses, a new winter coat, the embroidered linens, sheets, and towels she had accumulated over the years for my dowry, but may God's will bring the matter to pass in the Holy Land at the propitious moment.

Relatives from all the surrounding villages gathered to say farewell to me. I showered my little nieces and nephews with love and fiercely embraced them, regretful that I had chosen my own life and missed so much of theirs. And when would this happen again, I thought through my tears. When next would I hug and kiss the little boy with soft hair and an innocent smell who called me Aunt Dvora? And my good mother—when would I see her again?

All that night I wiped away tears, and I could hear my mother trying in vain to stifle her sobs. Early the next morning I slipped away to the cemetery, to the graves of my father and relatives. Many gravestones had been raised since I had been here last, after my father's death. A stone had been added to the row of priestly gravestones, the town bakers (who were also priests), on which two carved hands were raised in the priestly blessing. I went to the grave of my father in the shadow of his ancestors and relatives and I sat there, my heart beating to the mysterious rustle of the ancient trees, and within the mourning in my heart stirred a trace of envy, envy for those around me who had never wandered on lonely journeys to distant places and who now rested peacefully in the lap of their family.

But when I went back to see my mother, my mind clearer after my cry, I understood that her sorrow was greater than my own. After all, I was following my star. I could read the thoughts of this Jewish mother, who had passed her fiftieth year: Was this to be our final meeting in this world? Although she had sewn my traveling clothes and blessed my journey, it was with the feeling that what she was sewing was my shroud, God forbid.

Have no fear, I said to them all, many have gone before me on this journey, and the way is open for all who seek it. I can help you follow. To my mother I said, There are many parents who follow their children to a foreign land, and this is no foreign land but the land many of our people come to, if only to be buried in its soil. And to the young ones I said, And you, study hard, and when you are older you too will be a pioneer and build the land; and I, Aunt Dvora, will already be there to prepare the way.

When one or two of the little ones clutched me, I sat them on my lap and told them a fairytale: Once there was a Jewish family that left for the Holy Land, with its old and its young. They brought an enormous trunk down from the attic, just like the one you see before you, and put all their possessions inside. All the relatives came to see them off, and cried and cried. As they passed through the outskirts of town in their loaded wagon, all the dogs came from all the yards to bark at them, and the hoodlums threw rocks; but they drove courageously on until they came to the big port city and went up on the boat. And then, I went on in a whisper as all my relatives gathered round to listen, one Sabbath eve the sea was very stormy and it looked as if the boat was going to break into tiny bits. The father said to his wife: "It is time to light the Sabbath candles." The mother took her silver candlesticks from the trunk and the candles from her basket and the father made a kind of tent around them with a few boxes, and she lit the candles and made the blessing. To the great surprise of the gentile sailors the candles stood in a straight line and the wicks caught fire: the sea was appeased from its rage and became still as a pond, and even the flames did not flicker. By the merit of these candles they all arrived in peace at the place for which they had yearned.

As if I had cast a magic spell on the members of my family, old and young alike, they smiled and waved to me in the certainty that we would meet again. My mother brought the town rabbi from up the street, and he placed his hands on my head and blessed my journey. And so I climbed up on the carriage with my traveling trunk and a jar of stewed cherries, a thread carefully and devotedly securing its paper cover, my mother's final gift, which I cradled gently in my hands.

At the port city, in the noise and confusion of travelers, porters, and government officials, I tore myself away from Benjamin's arms. I can still see him waving to me from the dock and I, returning his wave with a white handkerchief, until he vanished from view.

A heavy silence hung in the room.

You loved him very much, I whispered.

As the love of David for Jonathan, she replied. Wonderful was your love for me, surpassing all others. Did you know, she added conversationally after a few minutes, that from the day I heard that my brother, Benjamin, had died, I did not cross the threshold of my house?

So shutting yourself in your house was your way of mourning Benjamin?

Her gaze turned inward. That is one face of the truth, she finally said.

It was not clear to me whether she was mocking me. Do you want to tell me the rest of Benjamin's story today—or some other time?

Why not today? she said, with the same hard expression. It is a short enough story. Benjamin had one more year of medical studies in Germany when the Great War broke out, and he was drafted into the Russian army as a medic. He moved from one army camp to another, rising in the ranks, and visiting our family from time to time when he was in the region. He looked wonderfully handsome and tall in his officer's uniform, my oldest sister Chaya-Rifka and her children recalled, and that was the last report they had of him after they had immigrated to Palestine. And Benjamin continued to plan for his own emigration after the war. Well, he survived that bloody war, and then he went back to the university in Russia to complete his medical degree; but in tending to the sick in the Russian tundra he contracted typhoid, the disease that killed him. News of his death reached us only much later, when we had returned from our exile in Egypt, and I never even learned the day of his death. He was about thirty-six when he died. They told me that shortly before his death he married a Jewish woman, but she disappeared into the plains of Russia and no one seems to know anything about her. There was no child.

But we were talking about my journey to the Land of Israel, she said. Tell me, then, about the journey, I said.

In October of 1910, after the High Holy Days, we departed; the sea was not stormy and we needed no miracles to appease it. On boarding the ship in Odessa, I met groups of young people who were also on their way to Palestine. They would congregate on deck and sing Zionist songs and read Hebrew poetry. The medieval poet Yehuda Halevi seemed especially able to express our feelings. We sorely missed those we had left behind, but our hearts were already in the distant Orient.

Along the way we stopped for short tours of the Turkish ports. I remember our ship entering the waters of the Bosporus early one daybreak, and around us opened up—at the height of autumn—clear blue skies and green-daubed mountain slopes, gazing at their own reflections in the gulf waters, crouching calm and confident in their own beauty in the rays of the rising sun. I also remember the noisy band of sailors—the first Turks I had ever seen—climbing from their dinghies up the ladders of our ship. A wonderful fragrance wafted from the port waters, and from the kitchen came the rich steam of coffee, which was now being prepared in special little pots, black and dense, according to the custom of the place. At its sharp and intoxicating smell we immediately relinquished all our loyalties to the thin, lackluster Russian tea. When darkness finally filled the void, a melancholy moon rose in the sky with the kind face I remembered from childhood, and my heart filled with hope.

Then, day finally dawned and the shore toward which we were sailing appeared, illuminated, in fact, by the very light I had always pictured. This was the final shore, the immutable shore, the shore of my homeland, she said in a blaze of enthusiasm. Clear and sundrenched it appeared before our eyes, with sandy beaches, pure and blindingly white, stretched out extravagantly along its length; while "there" even just a pinch of this holy soil could protect a pious person from worms in the grave. I immediately set my feet firmly on the ground from the very first step, although my body still trembled with the echoed motions of the journey.

My friends, who knew I was due to arrive, were joyfully waiting for me at the Jaffa harbor. They held a telegram from *Haolam*—the journal to which I felt closest—which said only: "Welcome to the Land of Israel," signed by my friends who had stayed behind in Vilna. I wordlessly hugged the people who had come to greet me, tears of gratitude streaming down my face. As soon as my packages had been unloaded I was taken to the roof of a hotel, from which one could see the entire city and its environs in a single glance. How familiar were the furrows that crouched there, between the boundaries of the fields, young, their rows straight, the smile of creation between their folds. I saw a dying bonfire at the edge of a field and someone, some wonderful, invisible person, was playing a flute beside it; and beyond, on the slope of one of the hills, a flock of goats slowly flowed down the slope, a childhood lesson come to life.

I could not get my fill of all I saw. How sweet was the taste of the first orange I peeled with still-clumsy hands as I walked down the path between the Ekron orchards that evening. The sight of tanned and muscular young men plowing the furrows immediately brought to mind the image of Rabbi Eliezer ben Horkenos in his youth, before he answered the call of Torah. I was filled with pity for the schoolteacher who still sat in my hometown, calculating the messianic era, while here they were making a start of it! Even as I stood among the ruins of the fortress, atop its broken walls, eroded by weapons and dust, not a trace of sorrow stirred my heart; on the contrary: against the old, I felt the fresh scent of blossoming more powerfully. I passed through thousands of years, from ancient ruins to budding wheat fields, in the course of a few hours' hike.

I walked spellbound all the way to the hills of Jerusalem, greeting the land of my fathers. At nightfall we arrived in the holy city, toward which I had directed all my childhood prayers. When I awoke the next morning in an old hotel near the city walls, I saw a fat sun settled atop a hill across from me. It was so close, I could practically reach out my hand to caress it. The windows were aglow in all the surrounding houses, as if the sun lived in each of them, too. That was how the holy city welcomed me, she said dreamily. Through the mist I could see the Dead Sea drowsing and I thought: a two thousand-year exile is not so much, as long as one comes home again. Until now I have been cut off, suspended in midair, and now I am rooted on a piece of land with its own place on the globe and its own square of sky spread eternally above it.

I was not in the least bit tired as I traveled around the country. In one of the settlements I saw trees I had never seen before: "These are lemons, and those are oranges," my hosts told me. "Here, try it," they said, handing me a ripe fruit. In the courtyard I was greeted by friends from my city. The carpenter's wife set up a table outside, and on it were a basket of peanuts and a pitcher of pomegranate juice. Chirping birds circled us and scratched in the grass, and beyond, at the crossroads, rustled a grove of olive trees. I saw what just a short time ago seemed a mirage: young Jews on Jewish land. Two thousand years of Diaspora seemed to collapse upon itself, present and past becoming one. Then as now the olive trees rustled, and people sat in their shade and sipped pomegranate juice. I could feel my health returning with every sip.

A few days after my arrival I was brought to visit Gitl, my childhood friend, who was living on a farm in one of the settlements. Gitl, who had become a beauty in this country, walking around free as a bird in her simple colored headkerchief, showed me her house and her children and the farm they had built with their bare hands. They had been tilling the soil for ten years by then and were like natives, swarthy and tough. Sitting on the grass in the shade of the apple tree before her house, Gitl told me everything: how they had disembarked and seen the sunlight just as they had always envisioned it; how their friend from youth, from our hometown, took them straight to the plot of land he had acquired for them to build their home; and how they immediately began working the place, at first using tools borrowed from wherever they could find them. They sectioned off a plot for a vegetable garden in front of the house and behind, for saplings; exactly as when we played among the wooden boxes in her father's house, we remembered. The farm buildings arose slowly along the side and all around, like a frame encircling a picture, leafy hedgerows.

She excitedly told me about the first seedlings they had planted in holes they had dug, each with its own kind, until they filled up the plot. The seedlings were too weak even to drink from the soil, my friend told me; they had problems acclimatizing themselves, as we did. After only a few weeks had gone by, however, the vegetables had already begun to send forth shoots. Frail, but rooted and standing on their own power and shivering with life whenever the wind touched them, exactly as we had dreamed, I said in amazement, looking at the garden blossoming around us. I tore up every weed furiously, Gitl said, as if it was my own life it was threatening to destroy. And all we were eating then were marinated olives, scallions, or radishes with a loaf of bread, and on holidays, a few hardboiled eggs. But their hard work paid off, and they struck roots in that place. For added safety they raised the fence higher, and so they could leave their windows unshuttered; that way nothing came between them and their land, even at night.

Once, Gitl told me emotionally, it rained locusts and the horizons darkened as if the clouds were gathering; but they covered the vegetable beds with blankets from their mothers' house, drummed on sheet metal against the destroyers, and covered the small shoots with pots, saving their garden.

Together we strolled over to see the cows in the shed, the vegetable garden, and the vineyard, and from afar, the settlement fields. Toward evening we made our way back to the house. Gitl's husband returned from the field in a wagon drawn by two mules, dressed in pioneer style— a cotton shirt with sleeves rolled up. "Reuven," Gitl called him now, his name accented on the last syllable according to the Sephardic pronunciation. He said to her, "Good evening, Tova," as if those had been their names from the day they were born. After serving me roasted pumpkin seeds and orange juice, Gitl cooked her family dinner from the fruits of her garden on a Primus stove, which spread a bluish light in the kitchen. The one-room house was freshly painted, and through the windows the houses of the village stretched like cubes set in rows, and over them the sky was grayish-pink in the sunset.

I took many trips in the first few years I was in the Land of Israel, she said wistfully. I was thirsty for the landscape and the historic sights;

I traveled to the heights of Mount Hermon, I saw the "Stove" with its beautiful waters and the fortress ruins. My friends on the farm often tried to persuade me to come and live with them. My heart was with them, and I admired the beauty and cleanliness of their healthy world, but I did not see my place among them. I had never been physically strong. I was hoping to find a position in the city, either in some literary field or in teaching. That was where the people to whom I felt closest lived, and that was where I hoped to make my start. Jaffa was my first stop.

What was Jaffa like in those days? I asked after a long silence had descended upon the room.

Crooked alleyways, where the braying of donkeys echoed like a trumpet call, she said somewhat sadly. Sidewalks strewn with banana peels, and the burning gaze of the natives, penetrating like sharp skewers from the dark shops. In the hotel in which I first lived the rooms reeked of mothballs, and the beds were draped with flimsy netting and were so big, they left me with a heavy feeling. The mosquitoes broke through the folds of the net anyway, murderously attacking my face and hands.

My first room was in one of those alleyways. It was an old neighborhood, with many Jews. On Sabbath you could see the women carrying their Sabbath stews from the baker's shack, where they had been left on the stove the day before, just as in my hometown, she said smiling. The smell of laundry and fried onions wafted from every courtyard. But for all the similarities I saw between my town and this neighborhood, it was still a strange and alien place to me. Sometimes camels would saunter down the alleys, and at dawn an Arab would bring his goat into the courtyard and milk her directly into the women's bowls. A Jewish neighborhood without a yoke and water buckets; instead of wood for heating, coals; and instead of potatoes, olives. It was there that I saw my first tomato, squash, and eggplant, and learned to make cutlets and soups from them. When summer arrived, the irrigation machines in the orchards sent their sharp, short squeals into the night. The sea roared beneath, terrifyingly close, until it seemed to me that it was licking at my walls. It was hot, hot. To escape from the choking streets I would sometimes go down to the shore, walking along the barren sands and eating black muscat grapes that tasted like nothing I had ever eaten before.

How strange, I said. It's hard for me to picture Jaffa at the turn of the century, even though I've read about it in S. Y. Agnon, maybe because everything has changed so much since then. Jaffa, which was a big city to you, is just a tiny appendage of Tel Aviv to me, an exotic place you show tourists, with a few Jews living there who have unusual taste. The harbor where you all landed is just a little fishing port with a remodeled lighthouse, where newlyweds come every Tuesday to eternalize their day of happiness in snapshots.

I have not seen it for many years, she said wistfully.

I could take you, I burst out, I could get a wheelchair, you could see Jaffa, smell the orchards again. We would be very careful, Tsipora and I, we would carry you, nothing would happen to you, I promise.

I have no interest in leaving the house, she said more coldly than I had ever heard her speak, and I immediately regretted my impulsive invitation. Only much later, as I was driving home, did I realize that I had been too confused and embarrassed to ask her why she has no interest in leaving the house. I felt that I had missed an important opportunity.

For some time she lay in stubborn silence, her face turned toward the ceiling, her hands crisscrossed over her eyes. I tried to divert her attention.

When I was a little girl during the War of Independence, I told her, we lived in Tel Aviv. I remember enemy Jaffa as a shadow that clouded our lives, peeping from the southern ends of streets. "Don't walk down those streets out in the open," my mother warned me, "the snipers could aim at you." I imagined them standing on the minarets of their mosques, sighting us in their cross hairs, little children scurrying off to school. Every morning we would collect exploded shells from the streets, and some of us would boastfully point at the pocks in the walls of their houses where the bullet had just missed them.

I still remember, I continued, after the war, when the great waves of new immigrants came to Israel and there was nowhere for them to live, many of them were put into abandoned houses in Jaffa. One day my mother took me to visit her friend, a schoolmate, who had arrived with her elderly father, after they had survived the rest of their family. Jaffa was completely destroyed, and between the piles of rock there were a few tall, charred buildings, proud, it seemed to me, of having been left intact. I walked in my sandals between the ruins, clutching my mother's warm hand, to the entrance of one such peculiar building, suspended over the void. We slowly climbed the dark stairs to the fifth floor, and in a strange apartment shared by a few families, a light-haired woman fell into my mother's arms. "This is my friend from school," my mother said, her eyes streaming tears. "Say hello to her, Amia, she'll understand; in school in Poland we learned Hebrew together, she and I, together with your father." An old man with a white goatee poked his head out from the kitchen and then came to hug my mother too, and I, embarrassed by this sudden display of emotion, bewildered and left out by the Polish conversation, wandered down the long hallway to the broken window and looked out at the sea, so calm and beneficent from this height.

While I was glimpsing the Jaffa seascape of my distant childhood, the view was transformed into the one from the courtyard of my friend who lived in Jaffa, and my heart grew warm remembering our love. But I won't tell you about that, Dvora, I said to myself.

Well, you are a born storyteller, Amia, Dvora said affectionately, and I knew she had forgiven me for my attempt, which must have resembled other people's attempts, to revoke the decree she had passed on herself. If I wanted Dvora to leave this room with me, I thought, it would only be on the tape recorder.

thirteenth encounter

The next week I awoke on the day we were supposed to meet with a terrible cold. I telephoned Tsipora and asked her if she thought it would be a good idea to cancel, so as not to pass anything along to Dvora, whose health was so fragile.

Of course, Tsipora answered brusquely. She didn't ask how I was feeling or thank me for my consideration. Clearly this strange woman, who as far as I could tell lived only for her mother's sake, was also jealous of me on her mother's account. When I came to visit, Dvora, herself a reserved person, would welcome me warmly, while Tsipora could barely suppress her rage at the sight of me, as if I were stealing something by tape-recording her mother, or maybe robbing them of their precious time together. It was true, though, that she sometimes permitted herself to ask for my help and used my visits to run errands or shop for things they needed, which were often so unusual they required a lengthy search or special orders; sometimes she allowed herself to go out for no particular reason, to "get some air" in a café with a novel or notebook. Only once so far had she stood in the corner of the room, like a silent shadow, listening to her mother's story. Should I ask her for an interview too? I wondered. Is her story part of what I'm looking for?

And what exactly was I looking for? I thought, lying in my warm bed in Jerusalem. A Brahms requiem filled the house, and I felt myself dissolving within it in a kind of feverish delirium. Some people travel to distant regions, trek the Himalayas and Amazon, while I—I explore people. Dvora too, I realized with a start, shuts her door against the world and spends her days wandering through internal landscapes. Are we really so similar, then? I would have to make sure we didn't become a little too similar, I thought, picking up the phone to invite a few friends to visit me that afternoon, the very time of my appointment in Tel Aviv.

The next week I stood again before the door of the house on Oliphant Street in Tel Aviv. I carried a package of homemade, all-natural cookies in my hand. Maybe they'll put something in their mouths, those two, I thought, and if not—at least they'll have something to serve company.

After our break, the oppressive atmosphere of the house weighed particularly heavily. Dvora inquired after my health and told me that, in my absence, she had sorted out her papers with Tsipora's help, discovered some letters from those early days in Palestine, and read through some of them.

I'm touched that you prepare for our meetings, I said, but your memory is excellent even without that. I brought you a new book I found, I said, hurrying to slip it in before our "work" started. It has some wonderful things in it about remembering the past. Can I read you some passages?

Certainly, said Dvora.

The book is called *Invisible Cities,* and it was written by Italo Calvino. It's a collection of stories about Marco Polo's travels, as though he were telling them to Kublai Khan. The stories—a mixture of biography and fantasy—are like parables with a philosophical moral, like the title, invisible cities, which you can't find on any map. This is the passage I picked out for you. It's called "Cities and Memories 2":

> When a man rides a long time through wild regions he feels the desire for a city. Finally he comes to Isidora, a city where the buildings have spiral staircases encrusted with spiral seashells, where perfect telescopes and violins are made, where the foreigner hesitating between two women always encounters a third, where cockfights degenerate into bloody brawls among the bettors. He was thinking of all these things when he desired a city. Isidora, therefore, is the city of his dreams: with one difference. The dreamed-of city contained him as a young man; he arrives at Isidora in his old age. In the square there is the wall where the old men sit and watch the young go by; he is seated in a row with them. Desires are already memories.[1]

1. Italo Calvino, *Invisible Cities,* trans. William Weaver (Torino, 1972; reprint, New York, 1974), p. 8.

There are people, she said after a thoughtful silence, whose memory is their curse.

How can you talk like that? Without your memory you couldn't have written such important stories.

You think they're important, she said desolately, but others did not share that view. I practically had to beg to get a volume of my stories published or a new edition released. And how much of it is available now in the bookstores?

Oh, I don't agree, I said weakly, knowing there was some truth in what she was saying. If I remember right, you won three major awards for your stories: the Bialik Prize for the collection *Little Things*, the Ruppin Prize for *For the Time Being*, and the Brenner Prize for *Chapters*. Am I right? And last week I heard that a young instructor at Hebrew University had done a close reading of your story "A Thorny Path." I was sorry I didn't know about it ahead of time or I would have gone to the lecture.

When I saw that she was smiling, somewhat pacified, I said, But let's leave that and get back to your story. You said that you were preparing to tell me about the beginning of your life here.

Yes. After a few moments she continued: My first years in the Land of Israel were wonderful. I worked, married, set up house, I made many friends, I gave birth to a daughter. Only a few people noticed my deteriorating health and my despair, buried deep beneath the daily worries and small successes. It was Brenner, with his rare sensitivity, or perhaps because his own soul was so dark, who wrote to one of our common friends in Russia who had asked how I was getting along in my new country that I was miserable, like everyone else. But I am convinced that most of my acquaintances saw me differently in those days.

After a few trips, in which I spied out the land and everything in it, from Rechovot and Rishon Le-Zion in the south to Metullah in the north, cooperative villages and workers' communes, I made my first home in Neveh Tsedek on the edge of Jaffa, across an expanse of white dunes from Tel Aviv, which was rising from the sands.

It soon became clear that my name had preceded me. I was known in the literary circles of the country, and was immediately recruited for the struggle to create an original literature in the Land of Israel. My plans for becoming a teacher never came to pass, since I was drafted into serving as literary editor at the *Young Worker*, a journal in which some of my stories had already appeared. The truth is that I was not surprised, since I had received encouraging letters from the editors of the weekly while I was still in Russia, and had even used their office as my forwarding address with a few friends before I left.

I began wearing my hair in two long braids down my back, Palestinian style, and each morning I would walk from my room down Herzl Street to the editorial office. Seedlings were being planted along the sidewalks, and I would follow their progress as I passed. I worried for them, for despite the care they received from the punctilious German gardener, it seemed to me that they were not thriving. We were all in that delicate process of blooming when the danger of wilting is greatest: the trees, the journal, the new city, and I as well.

I was thrown into a period of frenetic activity and hard work in the newborn society, she said, still awed by the memory. I traveled everywhere under the wing of my new friend Yosef Aharonovich, editor of the *Young Worker* and a respected leader in those days. There were celebrations for the founding of new settlements and new factories, and on my first Passover, there was the anniversity celebration for the city of Rechovot, which was a major event, with a parade and marching band and agricultural exhibitions. It was not just because of Aharonovich, she hurried to add; I, too, was accepted everywhere, especially among the young writers who lived in Palestine. Those days were a continuation of the period when I was active in Russia, in the city, before I emigrated— although it was certainly a brand new era, full of hope.

She sank into a dreamy silence, and I imagined she was seeing in her mind's eye her new love for Yosef, her hopes for a family of her own in place of the one she had left so far behind; but she suddenly began a new train of thought that surprised me.

Only much later, and gradually, she said, did I sense the ugliness of public life, the petty rivalries and hateful gossip that were part of the struggle; ever since then, I have retreated to my own four walls. I went

back to my old ways, refraining from public activity and expressing myself solely through writing and editing.

But you withdrew into your house much later, I commented, after you
quit the journal.

Of course, I am not referring to my illness, she said impatiently, or to
the fact that I am shut in my own home. I see the process of gathering
myself inward—or more precisely, of distancing myself from public life
in Palestine—beginning much sooner, after I married Aharonovich. Although I continued to appear at the offices of the *Young Worker* every
morning and to host many of its writers at our house, I refrained from
expressing an opinion on matters of fierce public debate—things Yosef
took very seriously. While he was at the center of the struggle, I tried to
avoid the turbulence that raged around every issue, whether practical,
spiritual, or communal in nature.

What sort of journal was it? I asked.

The Young Worker, you see, was first and foremost the title of a po-
litical party, the Zionist Workers Party of Palestine. It was established in
Petach Tikva in 1905, and Aharonovich was among the founders. Its
guiding principle was the sanctity of labor, the hard physical labor of the
Hebrew worker in the Land of Israel. It was a rival of the Workers of
Zion Party, she sighed, but who can remember the splinters and the
splinters of splinters that seemed so crucial then? In any case, the Young
Worker established the first publication of the workers' movement in Palestine and named it after the party. That was in 1906 or 1907, I think,
and just imagine: it's still published today. It brought the news to the
workers and the rest of the Jewish settlement in Palestine, and of course
it was also distributed in the Diaspora, and in that framework the journal
brought together the best Hebrew writers and poets. It wouldn't hurt you
to leaf through it once, she said. You must have it in that university library of yours.

But the work was not easy. It was an endless story of persuading and
prodding the writers and poets to submit something, an unbearably tiresome job. How can I explain to you, she asked wearily, how hard everything was in those days? No doubt you think of prestatehood Israel as

the "spiritual center" of the Jewish people, the way it truly has been since your childhood; but we, who came to Palestine during the Second Aliya, found a cultural wasteland here. It was as if we had been cut off from the soil that nourished us—from the great cities of Lithuania, Russia, and Poland, where we lived and breathed Jewish culture, literature, poetry, theater. The question of how we could transplant ourselves to this wasteland and continue to create tormented those who immigrated and those who stayed behind, for the time being, in the Diaspora. What would happen to the language? Where would we find material, inspiration? We continually examined ourselves and our peers; whose fountain had gone dry here in this land? Whose was flowing with new vigor? All these struggles took an extraordinary amount of time and effort.

How little I had understood the period in which she immigrated to Palestine, I thought. The first pioneers had seemed like giants, each with their own eccentricity. But how many of them had made it? In the course of the struggle, how many fell by the wayside, crawled back home with their tail between their legs, became ill, died young, committed suicide? And among them was Dvora Baron, certainly another strange one, a solitary bird—and for all that she survived. She never left the land once she had set foot on it, except when forced into exile; and despite her obscure illnesses she lived many long years and continued to write. She suddenly seemed immensely admirable. But as I searched for the words to express my regard, Dvora—as it often happened—had already long overtaken me.

Sometimes I was reined into helping Aharonovich edit other sections of the journal, informative topics not at all to my taste. Although I was complimented on my editing, I felt that the work was draining what little energy I had, leaving me nothing for my own writing.

But you also published quite a bit in the *Young Worker*, no?

I helped fill space when we were short, although I always preferred to make room for other writers, young people or new immigrants. But that is anticipating later stages of my story.

Let's go back, then, to the beginning, I suggested.

Yes, she said, drawing out the tangled thread of her thoughts as the darkness began to fill the space between us.

Not a year had gone by since my arrival in Palestine when Yosef Aharonovich and I married, in October of 1911, and set up house. I met Aharonovich, who was ten years my senior, through our work together, and found in him an honesty, modesty, idealism, and responsibility that spoke to my heart.

Tell me a little more, I asked when she fell silent.

Look, Amia, I was young and lonely, and wanted to join my life with someone and start a family. To the outside world, Aharonovich was known as a leader of the Jewish community in Palestine, and marrying him was like choosing a fairytale prince as groom. The writer and the leader—a Hebrew match of all matches! she said bitterly. But as always, in private chambers things looked different.

After a pause she continued: Today I think that in building a home with Aharonovich I could trust that I would not be forced to give up my writing, as women are, since our relationship arose and blossomed in the course of our shared work on the paper; and perhaps there was something else, she said, and sank into her thoughts.

What do you mean?

I knew that Aharonovich would not tamper with the independence I had won with such effort, first by leaving my parents' home and later by removing myself from Benjamin's watchful eye. I knew from my experience with Ben-Eliezer and others, and by noticing how different I was from my sisters, that I could never live with a man who restricted my movements. All this was far from clear to me, and in those days the subject was rarely discussed. On the farms, there were pioneer women who demanded the right to work and to carry the burden just like men— but they lacked the strength to achieve those objectives. And in the city? We were young, we had left the ways of our mothers far behind in the Diaspora and could not see a new road before us.

Who's "we"?

I had a few women friends, Rachel Katzenelson and others, but we did not speak much amongst ourselves. Today it seems to me that Yosef's generosity and his complete immersion in his own world allowed me to hope that we could live together as a couple. I remember, for instance, she smiled triumphantly, that I had two close friends in the Vilna circle of writers, and we swore we would meet in Paris on July 14, 1912. And here I was a married woman, but I wrote to my friends anyway to suggest we keep our promise. I would have traveled to Paris from Palestine if the two young men had not found various excuses for backing out.

Well, that would be unusual even in our own time.

Aharonovich, like myself, was the son of a rabbi, Dvora continued with closed eyes, and in his childhood he had lived like a country child in the lap of nature. He loved people who earned a living by the sweat of their brow and saw the simple life as the greatest good. Like myself he was a very educated man, both in Jewish and secular studies, but he had no desire for further education, seeing agriculture as the sole basis for the revival of the Jewish people in Zion. When he immigrated to Palestine at the beginning of the century, he went straight to the agricultural colonies, working in the orchards of Rechovot and Nes Tsiyona, doing guard duty in the vineyards, and even cooking in the workers' kitchen, when no one else wanted the job. He still had many friends from his life as a pioneer and worker, but his party called on him to trade in his hoe for the editor's pen. That was how he was when I met him—a man with original ideas, willing to educate others and fight energetically for what he believed. He was not blessed with the best of health and suffered from chronic stomach problems, the result of his poor eating habits. Even in this I may have seen him as company for my misery. But at other times I found in him the assurance of my rabbi father, she said; he was a confident man who knew the correct path. That attracted me, I suppose, as someone who was filled with desperate fears and doubts.

And were you disappointed in the end? I dared to ask.

That is what they told you, she said dismissively. And who is not disappointed in marriage? He, too, was certainly disappointed. Some of his friends said that I ruined his life, his chances for advancement in the public realm, because he was always occupied with female troubles at home—my own health and that of Tsipora. We had a hard life; it was not a home like other homes, but he remained my main source of support as long as he lived. With his common sense, he was often consulted when it came to establishing settlements and institutions, and he was always ready to lend a hand, becoming increasingly weighed down with various projects. So Tsipora and I were left to fend for ourselves, she said wearily, but again I am putting the cart before the horse.

There were many questions that troubled me about this marriage, but I sensed they would be cleared up in the course of time, and there was no point in trying to expose what she was determined to conceal for now. I poured Dvora some tea from the thermos that stood on the small table beside the sofa, and rearranged the pillows behind her back. She looked at me gratefully and continued.

Rav Kook, the chief rabbi of Jaffa, conducted the wedding ceremony. Not a single member of our families was there—many of us had left our relatives behind, she said in a hard voice. The wedding party was organized by our acquaintances in Jaffa and Rechovot, where Yosef had lived in his early years in Palestine. After our lives were linked, we spent every day together absorbed in the editorial work, and the evening was spent at our small house in Neveh Tsedek, among the circle of friends who would congregate on our porch each night.

You described the chapter of your coming together so briefly, I said, despite all my intentions to hold my tongue. After all, that's a very important phase in a person's life—finding a partner for life. And in my heart I thought, she hasn't said a word about love.

But Dvora was staring at the ceiling with a dull gaze, and I imagined I saw the shadow of a mocking smile on the corners of her lips. Those were different times, she said, seeing straight through me. In the tiny Zionist community in Palestine personal matters and one's private life were of little import compared with praxis—the daily work that went into the national revival. A wedding took place and the couple would go right back to work as usual. Our heroes in those days were bitter and despairing people, and their lives as Jews seemed a labyrinth with no exit. To be happy with one's lot was not at all the norm among us, and may have even been considered a vice. And most importantly, we lived under a cloud of fear, worry, and homesickness for the families we had left behind.

Yet there was a closeness and warmth in the circle of friends whom I regularly saw. On the porch of my first home with Aharonovich, the gate of which had sunk into a sand dune, we talked about anything and everything. We had a single room, in its center a table and a lamp with a green shade that suffused the room with radiance. Many came for a mere visit and left fast friends: Brenner, Shimoni, Rabinovitsh, Ben-Tsiyon, Agnon, and others, no less important in my eyes. We spoke Hebrew, although a Russian word or a Yiddish expression would sometimes fill in the gaps of a hesitant sentence. Did you know that we would address each other in the third person? she laughed, and only after a long acquaintance did we dare to address one another as "you," as in European languages. Sometimes I joined in the conversation, sometimes I embroidered and listened, sitting on the steps. Aharonovich would serve tea and the conversation would continue until all hours of the night. Sometimes friends from the villages would stay over, and I was happy to see them.

When my first stories published in Palestine continued to deal with our sad lives in the Diaspora without the faintest flavor of the Land of Israel in them, the response was far from enthusiastic. That was just the beginning of a path on which I stubbornly chose to remain, she smiled bitterly, avoiding the high road of the new Hebrew literature. Like the others I struggled mightily with Hebrew, in the endless effort to make it serve as a living language, but it was said that one could not distinguish between those of my stories written while I was still in the Diaspora and the stories from the Land of Israel, she smiled in recollection. At least my fountain had not run dry, as it did for some of my friends.

I also continued writing angry stories about the injustices in the town of my childhood, where poor people existed only to serve the needs of the rich. But the tone was somewhat more mature, more accepting of fate, in these stories. After all, in the final analysis, that was the way things had been in the world from time immemorial. Exactly as if I had not left "there" at all or did not believe that here, in the Land of Israel, a new world was being created free of injustice, a world in which there were no differences between rich and poor, man and woman. I paid no attention to criticism or the advice of friends who demanded "Zionist topics" from me. The chaos at the editorial office also irritated me, and I limited my time there to dealing with people. For my own writing or editing, I worked best when I was shut in my room, alone with my pen and my thoughts.

You know, I said hesitantly, seeing that she needed a rest, in this chapter, too, I find some echoes of my own life. I also met my husband when we were working together at the university. We married with the understanding that we would both continue at the jobs we had been offered at the institute. Each morning we would leave together for our offices in the same building, and we often met, by chance or design, in the course of the day, so that our worlds were exposed to each other's view. As with Yosef at the paper, there were years when my husband was a sort of "boss" to me, when he was head of our department, and later these positions were reversed.

Was it good that way? she asked.

Many people asked me that, and I always answered: I don't have anything to compare it with. We certainly helped each other out; but maybe we also closed some things off. I thought about these things much more after his death, but when he was alive I wouldn't have changed a thing.

Tell me, she said, and I could feel her eyes observing me and I knew I could not hide.

I'm thinking about the fact that since he died I have written so much. Would this have happened anyway and maybe the time was just ripe? Maybe it was my way of burying the pain and filling the space left by his death? But maybe I couldn't have done it as long as I was somebody's wife, who was somehow supposed to live in the shadow of her husband?

You? she asked in surprise.

Yes, me too, like you, like all of us. Maybe there was some desire transmitted to me subterraneously, without his even knowing it, that I should be small and pretty and nothing more? I asked hesitantly and continued, stammering. Or not expose myself too much so that I wouldn't expose him too? I groped for words. My poet friend told me how hard it was for her to write love poetry because her husband got jealous, and she tried to explain that it had nothing to do with her personal life.

And did she succeed in the end, she asked, almost smiling.

In the end she got divorced, I said.

I will speak again about marriage, she promised, but not today. Although I was not so innocent when I married Aharonovich, I did not, of course, see things as I do today.

And where do we go from here? I asked, lost in the maze of our stories.

I thought I would tell you about being cut off from our families and origins, about how much we worried about them.

And will you tell me about Tsipora's birth after that? I added.

She nodded and began to weave her story again. This period of my life lasted only approximately five years: my arrival in Palestine, my work at the *Young Worker*, my marriage to Aharonovich, and Tsipora's birth—and then the chapter ends in our exile to Egypt during the First World War. An eventful existence, cut off in the blink of an eye.

But what stands out in my innermost memories of those years, when I was still healthy enough and came and went among people, is how I feared for those who had remained abroad, my brother, Benjamin, and the members of my family who had remained in the shtetl. I had the sense that somewhere in the distance stormy winds were blowing, and our correspondence became more and more sporadic until it practically stopped. In our free time we would pore over old letters and write open letters, bulletins that we would post into the void: "We are fine," we announced. "How is it there with you?"

Not a night went by that I did not dream of my father, she said softly, and about the town that floated like a lost speck in the vastness of space and time. I carried the memory of my native town like a talisman. In my dreams, in my homesickness, I believed that it was there that the skies had first been spread over the formless void, that there, at the entrance to the gulch, was the grove of trees that first stretched limbs at a word dropped from God's lips. Aware as I was of living in the Holy Land, and hopefully as I clung to my new life, everything roiled about me, leaving me prey to the darkest of fears. Whither led the path I had chosen? At those times I felt that only there, in my town, was there any permanence. The houses, for all the expectations that the Messiah would not tarry, had been built on sturdy foundations, cemented with the power of faith. There was a mezuzah on each doorpost and confidence in every heart. Of course the gentiles teemed all around, rising up from time to time to riot; but then the Jews would come from Chmilovka and Tokhanovka and shore up the ruins and seal the breaches, and everything would go back to the way it had been. For was it not there, one cloudy day when a rainbow had broken through, that I seemed to hear the words of the oath that "for all the days of the earth sowing and reaping, winter and summer, day and night shall not cease." I tried to grasp this, across the distances, like a sturdy crutch. But my terror knew what it knew.

When I received no news from my family, I told myself that it was impossible that ruin and devastation should have overtaken them. The One who protected the sprout of wheat under the snow and the seedling during a storm—He would guard the remnants of the town; but that was not the way it was to be.

She spoke as a prophetess must speak, declaiming as if she had forgotten my presence, as if she were dictating the book of books. And then a day came, when I understood that the pillars of the universe had shaken and everything around me began to spin. It was like the assault of a raging storm, and I, who had tried to take shelter, when I looked out as the storm abated—everything had been destroyed and all creation erased, torn out by the very roots. The rainbow had been swallowed by a cloud, the oath annulled, everything returned to formless void. And only I was still carrying with me the reflection of the river and the sweetness of the well-water, the fragrance of the holidays and the echo of old men praying at dawn, and the call of children in the houses of their teachers.

Do you mean the Holocaust? I asked, almost to myself.

No, she said, annoyed, there were pogroms, the Revolution of 1905, and then again pogroms, the First World War, the Bolshevik Revolution; my town was destroyed even before what you call the "Holocaust." They took old people from their tables in middle of the meal, and the children who clung to them were taken as well. They gathered the barefoot men in the forest and murdered them, and then gangs of looters from the surrounding villages rioted their way through town. Those who escaped returned to find nothing but a mound of dust, the hoist of the well protruding above the ruins, and only the graveyard left untouched.

Caught up in her lamentation, I refrained from asking for the chronology of her story. Dvora Baron, I understood, abandoned her old world the way Lot had left Sodom, the heat of the conflagration at her back. And there was no return, I mourned with her.

And the home you made in the Land of Israel? I asked.

By daylight I would see it standing on its hill with me in it, my small family, Aharonovich and our Tsipora, our friends, my stories; but every night I would return and see my vanished father, the ruins. I am not yet finished mourning.

How extreme she is, I thought. If she mourns, it is until the end of her time, barely eating and never walking among people. Nothing will persuade her to change her ways. Like a monk, an ascetic, a fundamentalist with no religion, she spoke, her eyes burning. In her childhood she was the learned daughter of a rabbi, observing Jewish law to the hair. For a time, in her youth, she gave up her faith; and now, once again, she observes the commandments—her own strange commandments—with the fanaticism of a monk.

Shall we go on? I hesitantly asked, after we had been silent for a while. It had been dark in the room for a long time, and only the light of the streetlamps penetrating the curtain allowed me to trace her dark silhouette on the sofa, wrapped in a sweater and a few shabby blankets.

No, leave me be, she said in a voice full of despair. I took my leave with a light caress on her shoulder, and I didn't know if she smiled as I left, as she usually did.

How heavy the last few visits have been, I thought as I put my coat on, but I didn't know if it had really been that way.

I made my way out by the light of the streetlamps, impelled by a powerful force. In a café on Sheinkin Street I listened to passages of the tape recording, sipping strong coffee, the kind that never crossed the threshold of Dvora Baron. At least I have all the material with me, on the tape. But what would I do with it? Two young men dressed in black smoked at the next table. One wore a single earring. A thin woman joined them, laughing and flinging her blond hair. How odd I felt beside these creatures, carrying the heavy voice, the vanished world, the sorrowful smell of Dvora Baron within me. Had these people ever heard of Dvora Baron? And if she is forgotten—so what? Which of us lives forever? I would have to shake off this untimely sadness before I got on the road toward home, to Jerusalem.

fourteenth encounter

Only two days passed before our next meeting at Dvora's house. An ugly rain was falling over Tel Aviv and an early evening shrouded Oliphant Street. In the quiet stairwell piano music could be heard coming from Dvora's apartment—Chopin, I think. When I rang the doorbell, there was a clatter inside the apartment, and after a long while, after the light had already automatically shut off on the stairs, the door suddenly opened and Dvora herself stood at the door. She stood tall and erect in her long brown dress, wrapped in a dark woolen scarf, her penetrating eyes blacker than black. I put out my hand instinctively, as if afraid she would collapse at my feet. But Dvora turned her back to me and, leaning on a stick, walked with very slow steps to the unmade sofa, beside which glowed the antique brass lamp.

You got up yourself to open the door for me! I said. Are you alone?

Yes, after too many keepers. The first rain descends and no one arrives. Tsipora had to go to the hospital to get the results of a test. She suggested that we leave you a note on the door, but I promised her that I could get up today. I did not wish to cancel our meeting, she said, and lowered herself onto the sofa, panting.

Moved, I approached her and supporting her thin body, cleared the cushions still warm from her body and the many blankets off the sofa and, when she had lain down again, covered her tenderly. I caught a glimpse of her frail legs, shockingly long and thin. How could such toothpicks carry the weight of such a tall body, I thought. Watching the effort visible on her pale face, I felt a surge of anger at Tsipora. But maybe it was better for her to get up a little, I thought; and she, the mind-reader, said to me with a caressing glance, but a voice made weak by strain:

Today I am filled with regret that I took to my bed so very long ago. Over the years my muscles have weakened, and I recently discovered that even when I feel well enough to walk, my legs will no longer carry me.

But you're not that old. If you keep trying, you can walk again, I said fervently.

She shook her head and sighed, Too late, I fear.

While she caught her breath, I watched the blood coming back to her cheeks and thought, You are a beautiful woman, even now, just as the poet Rachel used to say about you. And she said aloud, How happy I was when I gave birth to her! What a beautiful baby she was, a beautiful girl. I called her Tsipora after my younger sister, the one who drowned.

A shiver ran up my spine. Dvora had spoken the very phrase that had passed through my mind a moment earlier. But Dvora did not notice my emotion and continued.

It was the 26th of Teveth, 1914. I worked and wrote all through my pregnancy, perhaps to escape from my growing anxieties, for my heart was always prophesying the worst. But the baby was born healthy and perfect, and I continued to work as an editor while caring for her in our house in Jaffa. Aharonovich was a great help with the baby; that was not so usual in those days. I remember how surprised our writer friends were when they found him heating milk for the baby or serving our guests tea. When he was home he always noticed my weakness, and he would gently try to help even if I had not asked him for anything. Sometimes I grieved to see him exerting himself for us and worried that I was an inadequate mother; but in those first days our love and concern for Tsipora drew us closer together. For she was a child of the Land of Israel, and Hebrew, Sephardic Hebrew, would be her native tongue! It was as if everything we had inherited from our parents, everything we had left behind—we did not know then that it was gone forever—broke through to stream into the soul of this girl, a first fruit of the revival.

And so, while I was getting back on my feet after the birth—immersed in the *Young Worker* and in caring for the child—the war began to rage around us. Tsipora was only a year old when my world shattered beyond repair. I would never be whole again.

Again she's being dramatic, I thought, shifting uncomfortably on my chair in embarrassment.

I do not know how to go on from here, Dvora said suddenly. I could tell you about Tsipora, or about our descent to Egypt, into exile. The two stories are intertwined.

Tell me first about Tsipora, I answered, grateful for whatever had taken Tsipora out of the house this evening.

More is hidden than revealed when it comes to Tsipora, she said unhesitatingly, as if she had been waiting for an opportunity to set the record straight. I knew how they spoke of me as a mother, but I held my tongue.

Here's your chance to turn the tables, I smiled; but seeing her hard expression, I stopped immediately.

Tell me, she said, you are a psychologist, after all. When a person lives in the shadow of fear—that is, when they carry within themselves a sense of impending disaster, for themselves and those they love—what would you say about that?

I was taken aback by her question, unsure of whether she was mocking me, since she had never expressed the slightest respect for those who made the human soul their profession. I kept silent, searching for an appropriate response.

I don't know, I finally said.

Nonsense! she said forcefully. What are you trying to hide from me? I am not afraid of diagnoses of that sort anyway.

So why do you want me to give you one? I protested.

Nevertheless, she pressed, and I felt the force of her character yet again.

I would think that such dark prophecies might torment a person whose confidence had been wounded. The phenomenon appears in various manifestations, I stammered, but, in each case, the trust that connects an individual and the world is violated; and if this trust is utterly destroyed, there is a significant likelihood that this person would be vulnerable in the manner you described.

Something utterly destroyed this trust? And when does that not happen? Once, in my childhood, she sank into remembrance, my mother promised that I could get the girl's haircut I had chosen—a "Polish" haircut, we called it in Yiddish; and instead she instructed the barber to give me a boy's crewcut, while she diverted my attention by presenting me a poppyseed cake with her beautiful hand. When I went outside, the neighbors called out, "Hey boy!" and rubbing my palm against my clean-shaven scalp, I felt the humiliation of this shameful haircut, which was given only to children with lice.

Is that what you mean by a violation of trust? she challenged me, and seeing my skeptical expression, she continued, No, do not make light of this memory. I later saw it as the basis of all the tricks life played on me, and that dulled their sting.

We're not talking about a single incident, I said, unless it was much more serious—a child being taken from his parents, who died or gave him up to strangers. I was having a hard time expressing myself, and altogether I was not enjoying playing psychologist before the sharp eyes of Dvora Baron. I stumbled on. Or if a child's trust is repeatedly violated, even in an apparently stable home, that can certainly be as damaging as a sudden trauma—for example, if parents punish a child without reason and then shower him with love—things like that.

Dvora smiled tolerantly and shook her head. What you describe is very far from my childhood experience. There was our mistrust of the world that surrounded us, the gentile world that could explode at any moment in all its fury; but all of us felt that.

True, but if someone were especially sensitive, she might be more effected by experiences like these.

So people are born with greater or lesser sensitivities. Then inheritance is the determining factor?

Feeling helpless and attacked again, I kept silent.

Or perhaps, she continued, the matter is rooted in that early experience I told you about during one of our first meetings, when I was a baby.

And as she spoke, repeating the things she had told me virtually verbatim, the mockery dissolved completely. Relieved that the danger had passed, I listened as if hypnotized.

I was told that when I was still an infant I would suddenly fling myself down on the floor and cry wildly and bitterly for no apparent reason. In the beginning they would try to calm me down, but when that had no effect, they would just leave the room and let me sob my eyes out. How could they treat a tender and helpless creature like that? she wondered, with no trace of anger. And the truth is that I am sure I was not crying that way from some childish lunacy but from foresight, from a prophetic feeling about what was approaching in the course of time—a kind of forecry, which however great it was, still did not begin to grieve for all that was coming. If my mother had guessed this, instead of punishing me, she would have showered me with the compassion and love that might have inoculated me against the pain that was to follow; and the fears themselves, she concluded with assurance, justified their own existence in the light of reality, and they accompanied me through the course of my life.

A prolonged silence fell on the room. The record had long since ended, and the rain could be heard drumming on the windowpanes.

We were talking about Tsipora's birth, I finally said.

Well, that was how it was. The birth of a child from my womb was a matter of enormous concern.

During my pregnancy a cloud hung over the house, and at night my sleep was plagued by nightmares. Once I dreamed of a bride, all dressed in white, who boarded a train immediately after the wedding, and then a storm broke out and the train was derailed and she was killed. When I woke up from these dreams into the stillness of dawn, I felt with prophetic certainty that the child who was to be born to me would not be mine, because some disaster would overtake her sooner or later. Perhaps I was dreaming of my beautiful sister Tsipora, who drowned after her wedding, she said thoughtfully. I did not know when or where disaster would strike, she continued, but it was certain that it waited somewhere, biding its time. My child would be blond and blue-eyed, an angel, I dreamed, and she was fated to die, as if a great curse ruled our destiny.

Like a fairytale, I whispered.

Then I remembered other women I knew, from my town, who had visions exactly as I did, and how greatly they suffered! One of these was my mother's servant girl, Basya, who lived in fear from the day her father was attacked in a pogrom when she was still a child until long after her husband was murdered by gentiles. She would count her children each time they left the house and each time they returned, as if she would never see them again. Some thought it madness, but others were convinced that it was a form of prophecy, a prescience for what indeed was to follow.

For a moment, fear pervaded the dark room, spirits of the dead rustled in the shadowy corners, and a chill stole in through the window. I shuddered. Then why did she name her child Tsipora, if those were her fears? I thought. Did the custom of carrying on family names prevail over her prophetic heart? Trying to combat my dread with rationality, I commented: But it was different in Basya's case: she was afraid of the gentiles. But when you were pregnant with Tsipora, you were already in Palestine.

Nevertheless, we had our gentiles, the Turks, plotting against us and expelling us from our homes. But I do not know if that is the explanation, she said impatiently. The terror was within me and I lived in its shadow. And in fact disasters did rain down on our heads: first, the exile to Egypt, and not long after, the appearance of the disease.

Dvora breathed heavily, and she looked pale.

I have never spoken about this with anyone before you, she said, as if she still doubted my seriousness.

There was ecstasy in our home when Tsipora was born; I have already mentioned that, no? She was not blue-eyed and blond-haired, of course, from whom would she have inherited that? But she was a beautiful and intelligent child. Yosef and I drew close around her and we became a family. From the day of her birth we had Sabbath meals in the house, with wine and candles, so she would know a little something about what it meant that she was Jewish. We told her stories about the rabbis, we sang for her the melodies of our parents' homes. In the new Zionist community there were not many secular Jews who did as we did; Jewish customs were absurd and loathsome to the young workers of the land. If any of our writer friends happened to witness such a festive meal at our house, they would stare in amazement.

But not long after Tsipora was born, the First World War broke out.

The Zionist settlement in Palestine, impoverished and starving, was caught between the Turkish occupiers, whom we hated, and the British, whom we saw as our saviors. We lost contact with the rest of the world, with our families and our cultural roots. But the hardest to bear was the fury of the Turks against the Jewish population of Palestine. Whoever was a Turkish citizen, an "Ottoman Jew," was required to serve in the Turkish army, and whoever was a citizen of another country had all sorts of punishments heaped on him until they came up with a permanent solution: exile. Mortal danger stalked us all.

Aharonovich, it is true, had obtained his Turkish citizenship, she continued; but far from helping him, it turned him into a servant of those brutal masters, who tormented him as they did all the community leaders. A notice that appeared in the *Young Worker* drew their fury, and they brought him in for brutal interrogations and charged him with revealing state secrets. He went into hiding to avoid another interrogation, and I was left alone in the house with a small baby. Several times they came to search the house and I was sick with worry about his safety. I loathed the Turkish police, the strange commissar and his henchmen. They had heavy jowls, the ponderous Tatars, frozen expressions on blunt faces. It was the fear and the rage, more than the hunger, that damaged my already weak health in that period. Finally, Pasha Jamal issued an expulsion order for all the inhabitants of Tel Aviv, and we were exiled alongside thousands of others. I had just begun to strike roots there, and being wrenched from my home again broke my spirit. And Tsipora was with me.

I will speak of the exile soon, she said, trying to make some order in her thoughts; but in terms of Tsipora, suddenly the thread that bound us into a family tore. I was left with the infant in our poor quarters in Alexandria, while Aharonovich was called into service by the exile community. I became ill and felt weak, and the little girl who had been a ray of light now became a great burden. Then, her illness was discovered.

What illness? I asked.

Epilepsy—a terrible illness. She would fall, go into convulsions, lose consciousness, and I could do nothing to help. Exactly as I had dreamed in my pregnancy: an incurable disease. And worst of all, she continued in a whisper, we did not tell a soul. We ourselves and a handful of doctors we consulted locked this knowledge deep in our hearts, like a wound that grows in secret places.

But why?

Because of the shame, she said hesitantly, so they would not mock the child, or consider her mentally ill, or pity her—who can know the real reason? I have already told you, things were different in those days. Epilepsy was a disease that aroused powerful fears, and those who witnessed an attack fled, as if from demons. In general, these things were family secrets, and professionals such as yourself were not everywhere. There is no cure for the disease, we were told, it is God's will and possibly hereditary. From that time on I took upon myself a number of restrictions, which puzzled or angered my friends. First, I could not allow Tsipora to play among children, lest the illness strike her in public. I would teach her the subjects I knew at home, and bring in home-teachers to teach the subjects I could not. I would shape my own life to hers, forge a new way of life where she would not need others, and most importantly, I would safeguard her by living as healthfully and purely as possible.

I was stunned by the strictness revealed in these decisions, like the verdict of a rabbi. I was also shocked to see how distorted the stories were that circulated about Dvora and her daughter. It was not at all Dvora at the center, but rather her daughter and her illness. The stories I had heard now seemed mean by comparison. And did Yosef go along with your decisions? I asked.

I was the mother and I took care of her, was alone in the house with her, in charge of her education. Yosef accepted my decisions without protest. Why should that surprise you?

You mentioned the interest people took in your unusual childrearing methods. Even I couldn't help hearing all sorts of strange versions of the story.

For example? she asked coolly.

Forgive me, I said, with mixed anxiety and relief. They say that Tsipora became ill much later, and that her epilepsy doesn't explain your decision not to send her to school and to keep her away from other children. Some people say that even if it were true that she had epilepsy, that was no excuse. Others have said that Tsipora was never ill at all, and Tsipora began having quasi-epileptic fits at puberty—no earlier—as a result of malnutrition, what you call the strict diet you took upon yourselves. And as for the diet, I said, hurrying to unburden myself, everyone thinks that the diet is about your condition, your indigestion—not some effort to improve Tsipora's condition.

And some no doubt told you, she added mockingly, that I just hallucinated all these illnesses; that there is nothing wrong with Tsipora but her strange mother, and that I, too, am healthy in body, if not in spirit, just pretending to be ill, or that I have a powerful imagination, eccentric writer that I am. But tell me: Why would I want to steal the joys of youth and friendship from my only daughter? Am I not a mother who rejoices when my child is happy?

I shrugged.

Perhaps I was such a talented teacher that I longed to continue my profession at home, she continued to mock. And when she got older, with her father so busy with his various pursuits, perhaps I needed her companionship, her services. Or I may be a tyrant, a mother who enslaves her daughter for cruel pleasure. As for the father, he did not intervene on his daughter's behalf, because it was more convenient for him if she stayed home with me, leaving him free to come and go as he pleased.

I would never think of you that way, I feebly protested.

Do not be so quick to defend us, Amia, she said bitterly. Who can say where the border between truth and fiction lies? In every story there is some grain of truth, certainly you must think that, whether it is overt or hidden from our conscious minds. The human soul is a mysterious thing, the greatest riddle there is.

We were silent, and the rain thundered against the windowpanes.

Tsipora will be drenched to the bone, Dvora said, a catch in her voice. I sinned against my little girl, she continued as if speaking to herself; but only because I wanted to shield her from dying or even worse, from the curse that hangs over her head and mine. We spent so many beautiful hours together at home, many years later, when we had returned to Palestine and Tsipora had grown. I made up many stories just for her—

things I never wrote down, fairytales and stories about the rabbis, embroidered with my own memories—and she would sit at the foot of the bed with the wide intelligent eyes, swallowing every word.

Tell me one if you remember, I begged.

I can remember telling Tsipora about the town from which I had come. She asked me many times in her childhood to repeat it, until she could finish the sentences for me. And so, it seems to me, the story went. Immediately Dvora's storytelling voice, the melodic one that I so loved to hear, broke through from the past: What was it like in the small town? Fields and forests and gentiles, many gentiles, and in the middle of it all a strip of land, white with snow in the winter and golden in the summer sun, and from it arose the fragrance of Torah. How can I portray such a fragrance? It is hard to say, but that was how it was, the rabbi of the town studied Torah, and the boys in the yeshiva studied Torah, and the old men in the synagogue studied Torah, and the little children in the cheders, well, they studied, too.

I could see the vision before my eyes: Dvora a young woman, her face smooth and full and her body strong but with the same fierce seriousness in her eyes, lying on the bed in a long dress with lace embroidering on its high collar, and on a stool at the foot of the bed a thin girl with the same black eyes and hair, her beautiful face turned to her mother. She toys with the fringes of the cover, stroking the velvet, and her lips move along with the words singing out in the room. I study too, the little girl would say when her mother arrived at that point of the familiar story, her voice barely audible. Tenderness and dedication suffused the picture before my eyes, Madonna and Child, and only the absence of a smile on the faces spoiled its perfection.

People had no gardens or fields, Dvora continued, they did not sow nor reap, but they had their holy books, and into these they delved. It said in their books that evil would come if they left the straight path; but it also said that if they searched for God with all their hearts, He would bring them back to their Land. And since the first thing had come true, there could be no doubt that so would the second. Although the land was far away, the heavens were close, and that was where they sent their prayers every day: they prayed for dew and rain when the Land was thirsty there, and on the Fifteenth of Shevat, while snow continued to fall, they celebrated by eating fruit, since that was the birthday of the trees over there. The town, after all, was only temporary. And even though they continued to build houses, marry off their children, buy and sell, they never ceased to long for the Land of Israel. If a house were painted, they left a black square in memory of the destruction of Her temple; and whenever anyone mentioned Jerusalem, they fervently added: "May she be rebuilt and reestablished."

Before my eyes the picture of mother and daughter had magically transformed into a different one: Yisrael with the lock of hair falling into his eyes beside the bed of our youngest son in his room, in our house in Jerusalem. Around his bed a pine railing, a colorful quilt folded over it. Photographs of all kinds of airplanes decorate the walls. The child's bright hair wet after his bath and the smell of soap rising from him, lying in his blue pajamas, waiting for his bedtime story and goodnight kiss afterward. Yisrael pulls a wooden chair from the desk and sits beside the bed, long fingers running through his hair, and he smiles calmly. "Tell me about your childhood," begs Eliav.

I didn't notice for a long time that Dvora had fallen quiet, her eyes gazing at me by the glow of the lamp. I don't know if my eyes filled with tears or if the loss was written all over my face.

What are you thinking? Dvora asked tenderly.

I came to myself. I don't know, I whispered, something strange happened, like a dream—but I didn't fall asleep.

And what did you see?

First I saw Tsipora, a little girl, listening to your story. Then the picture changed, and I saw my husband telling our son a bedtime story, as he did, in fact, every evening.

And what did he tell him? she asked with genuine interest.

It was so strange. Eliav was born when we were around forty, and his father was extremely close to him. When the boy was no more than two, I would hear Yisrael on winter nights after his bath, "Come hear a story from when I was a little boy." And little Eliav would always ask him, when he was older, in those very words, "Tell me, daddy, about when you were a little boy." And he preferred those stories over all the fairytales or stories in the books.

And what would his father tell him?

Stories about growing up poor in Tel Aviv in the thirties and forties, the oldest son of a family of workers, in an attic that was built onto the house of a rich old aunt. The games he invented with pots and a broom-stick; the neighborhood wars between the children of the Carmel Market and the Yemenite Settlement; about his mother, who was always angry and worried; his younger brother, who always tagged behind him; about the happy day he followed a group of Australian soldiers to the Tel Aviv beach and they gave him candies he had never tried before; about a dar-ing expedition to Lod with a pole and a box to pick *sabras*, the fruit that he sold to the rich kids on Hess Street.

I cried. I had been carrying this ache in my chest for a very long time. If only I could remember more of his stories. If only I had sat and lis-tened as hard as I could instead of snatching a phrase here and there while I washed the supper dishes. If only I had recorded their nightly conversations. Why had he chosen to tell that little boy so much? Did he know their time together would be so short? And what about me? Had I finally become a recorder of stories in order to find, at long last, his lost stories too?

The key scraping in the lock and the squeak of the opening door brought me back to Oliphant Street. Dvora lay perfectly still on the sofa, and Tsipora entered the foyer, her ill-fitting coat drenched and a headkerchief dripping around her face. She looked like an old woman, older than her mother. Don't worry, Mama, she said as soon as she en-tered, I wasn't outside in the worst of the rain, I waited inside a stairwell with three cats who were curled around each other, taking refuge there just as I had.

I dried my eyes and checked the tape recorder, which had stopped. How long had our silence continued? Had we fallen asleep? I must be getting home. I arose and worriedly looked out through the window at the glistening street.

Tsipora entered the living room after a few minutes in a warm robe, a pot of tea steamed in her hand. She sent a rare smile in my direction, as if grateful I had kept her mother company on such a dark night. Then she sat down and poured three cups of weak tea.

Amia told me today about the bedtime stories her children heard in their house, and I told her about the stories I told you when you were a child.

I knew them by heart, but I begged you to repeat them to me again and again anyway, Tsipora said wistfully. What sort of stories did you tell in your house? she asked me.

My husband also liked to tell the children stories about his childhood, I said, happy to have her join in, but I usually read to them from books I liked. They loved *Wild Children*, by Tikva Sarig from Beit Hashita, which is just an edited series of the memories of different children about growing up on Kibbutz Tel-Yosef.

We have good friends in Beit Hashita, Poznanski's children, right, Mama? Tsipora said. The children in Tikva Sarig's stories grew up in Tel-Yosef just about the same time I was growing up here in Tel Aviv, or maybe a little later. And immediately she added: Did you know that there's a settlement called Beit Yosef after Papa?

I nodded, while Dvora ruminated aloud, I always thought that children enjoyed real-life stories much more than those bizarre fairytales people invent for them.

She exchanged a glance with me in which we agreed to keep each other's secrets, and I took my leave from the two of them and went along my way.

fifteenth encounter

In the days following our last meeting, memories and fragments of my conversations with Dvora Baron flooded me. Distracted, I would hurry to finish work so I could go home and listen to the tapes; at night, Dvora and Tsipora floated through my dreams. My friends watched with bemusement, "Look at Amia, she's off in her own world again." Only my young son demanded the attention he deserved, and complained if he saw me glued to the tape recorder again, "Why are you writing about Dvora Baron? Who's interested in her anyway?" He liked it better when I was working with fighter pilots.

The night before I drove to Tel Aviv I dreamt about Dvora in her youth, a disturbing dream. I saw her in her long white dress walking down straight white streets that led to the sea, her feet not touching the ground. Young shoots beside the sidewalk bent their branches in salutation. A few steps behind her marches a little boy in short pants—little Rami, from one of her stories—or maybe Yisrael, following the Australian soldiers? I try to catch up with Dvora to tell her about three stories of hers I found, which no one else knew existed; but I can't reach her, and she turns a corner and dissolves into a curly little cloud.

What a transparent dream, I thought when I awoke, wrapping the heavy quilt around me. There was still a little time before I had to wake my son up for school. Dvora says to me, Don't think that you can catch me. And I say to her, How beautiful you are to me. Wait, I know things about you that even you don't know.

Today I shall tell you about my exile in Egypt, Dvora began, as I was setting up the tape recorder between us.

One day the news came that war had broken out. Turkey joined in, and a pall settled over Palestine. The Turkish herald paraded along the streets of the city announcing that there would be no surrender, that capitulation was no option, and that the consular powers of all other countries were hereby revoked. Anarchy was unleashed. The Turkish flag rose high on every flagpole, and foreign citizens became prey for any corrupt official wearing a tarboosh. Editorials praising the Sultan's generosity in the Zionist papers, including our own the *Young Worker*, were no longer any use. The war brought great poverty—even to us, who were not living in luxury in any case—and hunger visited our house. At the center of the city a gallows was erected, right in the marketplace, so all should see and tremble. That same day a quivering body was seen on the gallows, twitching until it subsided. At night, as the trees stood at silent attention and the laundry flickered between the roofs, the Turks wrapped the dangling body in a blindingly white sheet, and a black fear fell upon the city.

At first we were still trying to save the paper. We felt that it must continue to appear, for the sake of our readers. It was our duty to keep them informed, to keep their courage up, to advise them. The printer agreed to print for free and we saved on overseas postage, since Palestine was cut off in any case. But censorship became tighter every day and new decrees were issued each morning. Yosef acquired Ottoman citizenship, but precisely for that reason he became an easy target for every Turkish official and his whip. Because of some notice in the news he was arrested and dragged into the Turkish headquarters day after day. A miserable cycle of searches and evasions began to take over our home life, she said, sighing.

Suddenly she turned her head in my direction and asked worriedly, I already told you about that, no?

You mentioned some of it, I said soothingly, but it doesn't matter, go on.

My memory must not betray me before we are done, she said and turned to gaze at the ceiling with renewed concentration.

Once, toward evening, when Yosef was playing with Tsipora on our porch, a policeman came to arrest him, but since Yosef was crouching, he did not see him. A friend who happened to be walking by immediately realized what was happening and tricked the policeman into going off somewhere with him. But the same thing happened again, and finally, after they tore our house apart looking for him, Yosef was arrested and brought to Jaffa and from there, along with other activists they had caught, to Jerusalem. I knew then, she said in a whisper, that he would never return. We had already heard in Tel Aviv about the fate of those who had been rounded up in Damascus, and my heart prophesied evil, for myself and my daughter. But luckily, this time I was wrong. Dr. Ruppin and his emergency committee came through, the Consul Minister Morgenthau rushed to the rescue from Constantinople, and the group was saved.

But one Thursday at the beginning of winter, when Tsipora was nearly one year old, exile was decreed for all citizens of enemy countries, immediately and without delay. Yosef was nowhere to be found, but the husband of the next door neighbor arrived with the news, followed by a Turkish policeman with a whip in his hand. It was lunchtime. I stood with Tsipora in my arms, watching a scene I had difficulty believing, as the man with the whip followed the neighbor into his apartment. I saw my neighbor opening drawers, taking out a few valuable possessions, and I saw the expression on his wife's face. And then I shook myself and knew it was really happening.

My neighbor was a practical woman and immediately got to work: she extinguished the fire in the stove, flung open the doors of her closet, pulled out armfuls of linen and a few good clothes, and put them all in a wicker basket; she took a cloth sack and filled it with whatever she could find in the pantry and in the icebox; added her Sabbath candles, sweaters for herself and her daughter for the road, and she was ready.

In the meantime, Yosef had arrived home, he, too, with a Turkish policeman at his heels, and I understood that nothing would help, not his supplications, not his Turkish citizenship, not the intervention of prominent men on our behalf. We too were to be exiled.

What should I tell you? She gestured helplessly. How can I describe it? What does a tree feel when it is pulled from its soil, its tender roots wounded and torn? Something broke inside of me. Leaving my house in Lithuania had been excruciating, and only my love for the land had helped me find a home in its wilderness—and here I was uprooted and homeless again. Like our ancestors we were led down to Egypt, to a country not our own, a foreign language, alien customs. I went as if I were going to my death, toward disaster and hunger and annihilation, with no hope. "Soon we will return," Yosef consoled me as we hurriedly packed, but he was as desolate as I was and I did not wish to be comforted.

At the edge of Neveh Tsedek we met some other people we knew, exiles like us. They seemed dressed for a holiday, for some reason, their hands filled with bundles and traveling cases. Rumors passed that we were to be transported to Egypt, that an American ship—still neutral—was docked in the harbor, and now we were to assemble in the community house.

I will never forget that walk: I marched among the exiles like the Prophet Jeremiah. The neighborhood showed signs of abrupt departures and violent removals. People had been taken away from their lunches. Dishes were strewn on porches, coverless pillows draped gates, where they had been left to air that morning. A dog searched the crowd for its owner, whining softly.

Groups of young men who had been exiled looked as if they were marching, holding their heads up higher than they ever had. At the center of the neighborhood officials of the secret police pranced back and forth on their horses, and from every street a flood of exiles streamed forth, pushing each other along the sidewalks. Young students who had been born abroad were dragged from schoolrooms while their teachers tried to reassure them and shield them from the aggressors' whips. Two elderly sisters were taken out of their apartment. The older of the two lay on the sidewalk and announced that she had no intention of budging. "If they want they can take me in my coffin," she said, but as long as there was life in her bones, she herself would not go. I longed to stretch myself out on the sidewalk as she had, but I continued to walk with trembling legs, Tsipora in my arms.

Tell me, Amia, she turned to me with a terrible look in her eye, how much can a person survive such a march? How is it that my heart did not stop beating right then and there?

You must know that, I tried to calm her. We can take, apparently, much more than we think we can, although every great trauma certainly damages and changes us.

It was a tremendous rupture, she said. Certainly, anyone who finds themselves in a foreign land knows what it is to be no more than a rock or a piece of wood, an obstacle in everyone's path. And here I, who had just begun to strike roots in the soil of the homeland, was being driven off to a life of wandering. I, who would lose my balance just crossing the threshold of my home. Perhaps I heard an echo of my ancestors' terror at always packing up and leaving for a new place, which always brought with it—I knew—a new path, with many twists and turns.

She sank in her thoughts for a few moments before she continued: The community house was crowded with police and the exiles sat down on the sidewalks around it, each family with their bundles beside them. In the meantime, the order was announced from the steps of the building that no more people should be rounded up as the ship could not hold them. A shudder raced through the crowd, since many of the people there had been taken from the streets and were anxious to be reunited with their families. A woman stood up to beg that she be allowed to run back and fetch her little boy; one of the Turks came and pushed her with the butt of his rifle and she let out a shriek and stopped.

I didn't realize it was so terrible, I said, simultaneously ashamed of my ignorance and stifling my skepticism: Was it really? Was she exaggerating?

When evening fell, Dvora continued in a hard, emotionless voice; the order finally came for us to leave. The policemen went first, the families followed, and around us, surrounding us on all directions, walked the secret police. We walked five or six abreast, obediently and in order, without anyone crying or moaning, the grimace of self-restraint on every face, infants and packages in our arms.

The large American warship lay at anchor in the Jaffa harbor. It swayed a little offshore, she said as if seeing it before her eyes, the mouths of its enormous cannons pointing toward the city. I saw the admiral gazing at us in astonishment from his deck as we embarked. But he had agreed to take this motley crew of people, after all, who were being exiled for the crime of loving their homeland, all done according to international law. The Turkish officials worked with Oriental lassitude, taking their time going through packages and clothing, confiscating everything so that nothing should leave the country that was not supposed to. Finally, the commissar announced, waving his long whip in the air— the long, eternal whip I knew I could never escape—that we were leaving the land to which we would never return, and the ship raised anchor and was off.

Dvora was silent for a long while, and the room was utterly still. I stood and lit the lamp in the corner, straightened Dvora's blankets, and waited.

I do not remember how long the journey lasted, she contined. A deep darkness came over me. It seems I was led about by Yosef like a rag doll, until I found myself in our small apartment in Alexandria. A chapter of utter strangeness began; years of evil, disease, and poverty for my family.

But I've heard people say that Egypt wasn't as bad as the exiles thought it would be, I boldly argued. There was plenty of good, cheap food, the Egyptians were friendly, and besides, everyone knew it was temporary and soon they'd be back in Palestine.

Dvora responded angrily: Do not generalize from their experience to my own. There is the stalk of wheat that bends in the storm and the one that is torn apart by it. Some banded together in exile and others struck out on their own. We joined up with a few families, sharing a courtyard in Alexandria, an émigré tribe. Gradually, our neighbors began to admire the purity of our dealings, the way we kept the courtyard clean, and the sweetness of the songs of our homeland that drifted over the wall. My housemate, Nechama, was a true woman of valor, not only taking care of her own family but also taking in a few boarders and watching out for Tsipora and me. She was truly our guardian angel.

In Alexandria we lived by the seashore, as in Jaffa. The doors of the neighboring gentile courtyard were always open and the women would beat their tattered mattresses and stretch ropes on which to hang their faded laundry. The women talked to each other when they went for some air at the end of the day, just as they did beside the well in my town. In

poverty and distress all people are alike, I saw; and even if the neighborhood was a poor one, tendrils of bougainvillea climbed the white
walls of the houses and airy curtains fluttered softly in the windows. The
district was lush with greenery, and from the roof one could see the
sea and sailboats floating on it as if they were asleep.

The pillar of our courtyard was Nechama. She transformed her
gloomy flat into quite a pleasant place. She bought a few sticks of used
furniture in the Arab market, she sewed beds of cotton wadding, she
brought a kerosene stove into the kitchen, and soon the house was suffused with warmth. Since food was plentiful and cheap, as you said,
Nechama could cook up lavish meals as good as any she had eaten in her
Lithuanian town. Outside she hung a sign: "PRIVATE LUNCHES." By
the first week she had five regular customers and soon was bringing in
a decent income, leaving her husband free to study Torah or work for the
community, as he wished. Some tenants in the courtyard were actually
better off than they had been in Palestine, and soon they were going off
on tours of Cairo or the Pyramids at Giza.

But our situation could not have been more different, continued
Dvora. I arrived in Alexandria weak and ill, barely able to care for an
infant. At first I had dysentery—amoebic dysentery, the doctors in Palestine told me after we returned home years later. That is what caused
the digestive problems from which I still suffer, so I could not eat most
foods without aggravating my condition. I also had a bad cough; but what
kept me in bed was a broken heart. It hurt to look at our decrepit flat:
mold blossoming in the corners, cabinet doors hanging off their hinges,
the tattered sofa. I could not survive in such a charmless environment,
but I lacked Nechama's energy for improvements.

As soon as rumor got out that Aharonovich had arrived in Alexandria,
visitors—refugees from Jaffa and thereabouts—began to appear in the
courtyard. They came dressed to the nines, looking important enough
for our Greek landlord to strew fresh sand at the entrance and push aside
a few of the clotheslines in their honor. Women activists would arrive
to organize sewing circles to make shirts for the refugee children. For
our neighbors and visitors, Yosef was a walking newspaper, transmitting
to them detailed reports about what was happening in Palestine each

morning. He reported that the situation was serious and could get worse, but to me he sounded like a medical specialist, acknowledging the seriousness of the illness but knowing exactly what had to be done to avert the crisis.

You aren't one to put your faith in doctors, I thought, but I kept it to myself.

He and his friends were already busy doing what had to be done, she continued. Winter evenings they would gather at our house for meetings. Weaving together a speech from little scraps of paper, Yosef would relay news of the Diaspora to the people assembled. Despite the bad news, he gave his listeners courage. Sometimes they drew up lists of people who could help the refugees inside and outside the detention camps, and the next day he would go see what he could get from them. Sometimes bankers would come to our shabby apartment and he would set chairs around the room and at the table, and since there was no one to serve tea, put out some cold treats—almonds and honeycake—and open a few boxes of cigarettes.

And you? I asked, already knowing the answer from her gloomy gaze.

I became weaker and weaker in that strange land, until my strength was gone. I spent most of my time in bed, in a dark, still room off to the side. There were days when my temperature climbed until I was quite feverish, and one evening I remember seeing my father walk through the door with my traveling clothes in his hand, and then he sat by the side expectantly. I was filled with compassion for Tsipora, who would remain an orphan, and I told my father I was not yet ready to accompany him. When I awoke, I asked Yosef in my delirium whether he intended to leave me here, in a strange land, and he answered "No," with what sounded like a repressed sob. "You shall return when we return," he answered emphatically, as if he were swearing an oath.

I do not remember how long I was ill, or how many times. In the winter I would crawl into bed again, and when spring came I felt a little better. Nechama took it upon herself to provide our meals, preparing especially nutritious dishes to make me strong. She brought me hearty vegetable soup, fruit compote, and porridge with butter and egg yolks. Between meals she would come by with a glass of warm milk. Little

Tsipora would play quietly around my bed or would sit in Nechama's kitchen, silently watching everything that happened. Luckily, she was always such a good and quiet child.

I did eventually recover physically, but something inside had broken for good, Dvora said, and even on better days, I knew my dejection was only awaiting its moment. While I stopped writing and editing, Yosef was becoming increasingly caught up with his own hectic schedule. Aside from the community involvements that ate up his time, he had to earn some sort of living. What little work he found involved enormous efforts for meager wages. In desperation he considered taking his family off to America, but his letters never arrived, and no one could help with the arrangements. At first he gave private lessons, and then he taught in a Hebrew school for refugee children. Every day he taught for five hours, and since he was inexperienced, work left him physically and emotionally drained.

I remember how he arrived each afternoon from the city, wolfing down a vegetable cutlet from Nechama's kitchen and emptying his soup plate in a few swallows, and then he would take out a few notepads and lose himself in a cloud of cigarette smoke. Each circle of smoke that multiplied and thickened around him took him further away. He did not notice the baker arrive and put a loaf of bread on the couch or the vegetable seller weigh his vegetables on the threshold. Turning the pages, he would mutter some phrase from which I gathered that he was worried about people who needed a hot meal, or about children with no shoes. The absence of news from besieged Palestine was a source of continual distress. What could be done to help out there? he thought. Yosef would send off letters and telegrams to America and Russia, searching for ways to send money to Palestine, but wherever he turned he was met with apathy and disinterest. Finally, he would collect his notes, take a pack of cigarettes, and rush from the house. Again we were left alone, Tsipora and I, in our desolation.

Once in a great while, when he had completed some project, he would really come home. Then he would shout his greeting as soon as he bounded into the courtyard, gathering clothing from the line as he walked, looking around with wonderment as if he had just returned from a long journey. Then he would notice the empty cough medicine bottle and that the window in the bedroom was not closing properly, and immediately get to work fixing things. This time, the lamp in my room was also lit at nightfall, and he sat and told me what was happening in Palestine and in the world.

He had a day of rejoicing, too, when it seemed we might be allowed to publish the *Young Worker* in Egypt. He came to my room and excitedly told me how he had begun to attack the problem, requesting material from people, organizing volunteers, planning a benefit party to fund the enterprise. At the end of this rare domestic evening, Yosef lifted Tsipora and sang a quiet, melancholy tune until she fell asleep in his arms. These evenings of grace brought me some respite; but just as often there would be a knock on the door, and in would come the secretary of the community headquarters to announce that so-and-so had arrived from Cairo and a meeting was being called. Quickly, he would lay Tsipora down in her cradle, say goodbye to us, take his hat, and hurry after the messenger. He even forgot the outdoor key when he left, so I waited up for him, lying awake until late into the night.

How strange that is! I said, letting go with my thoughts. You were such an independent young girl; as a young woman you lived alone in a big foreign city, and then in Jaffa as well; and after your marriage it was so important for you to keep your freedom. Yet in Egypt you seem so dependent on the support of a husband. Exactly the trait you appreciated in him—that he would let you go your own way—was what ended up angering you so.

Dvora was silent, thinking over what I had said. Finally she responded: It is true. My life went off track starting from the exile. I became ill and never got over being cut off from the Land of Israel. Unlike Nechama, whose name means solace, I could not be consoled with the ease of everyday life. Perhaps if Yosef had been more supportive, as you say, even for just a short time, I could have been cured; but he, too, had stomach troubles, and I could sense how much he suffered from his poor health, the endless efforts on behalf of the community, his knowledge that he was not doing a better job caring for me and for our little daughter. I was a yoke around his neck, she said sadly. But at the same time I envied his active, full world, while I was stuck in bed.

You hinted a few times that the damage done in Egypt was irreversible, not only to your personality but also to your relationship with Yosef.

Dvora nodded her head. In Egypt we thought that when we returned home, everything would go back to normal; but it did not work out that way. The independence I had as a girl never came back; or rather, I was left with the independent spirit, which increased with the years, but lost my material and physical independence, my freedom to act. I never completely recovered my health, and it was difficult finding foods that would not hurt me. In time I could write again, even in Egypt, but it was a different kind of writing, more mature and utterly closed off from contemporary reality. The interest I took in my immediate surroundings dwindled and my focus on the distant past intensified. I had less energy, and could no longer write and edit at the same time.

And your relationship with Yosef?

It was burdened after that with mutual grief and guilt over our disillusionment and distance. Heaviness hung over the house, and within it there was little joy. Not surprisingly, Yosef was increasingly drawn to matters outside the home, covering a sad family situation with frantic activity. But he continued to take an interest in me and my creative work, managing the entire practical side of our lives, and he stood by my side whenever I needed him. Do not think this was nothing, she said. I have seen many worse marriages in my day.

And perhaps, she said in a brighter voice, I have painted this period in my life in too dismal colors. True, it was difficult at the outset, but things got better over time.

How long were you in Egypt?

Nearly four years. Under Nechama's dedicated care I stood on my feet again, and she was the one who told me that I had regained the radiance of youth. With the other women of the courtyard I went out each morning to the vegetable dealer's wagon, chose a loaf from the baker's basket, and brought the coal bucket up from the cellar. I painted the house and decorated a bit with some scraps of colorful fabric, and finally also returned to writing.

Tsipora, who was beside me through all this, was my soulmate from that time on. I began to tell her fairytales even before she could talk, and slowly I got her accustomed to the language of stories, and her young soul swallowed every drop. Often at dusk we would sit together, I in my bed and she in her cradle, and I would rock her with my hand and tell her whatever crossed my mind. Very soon the room would fill up with the sway of movements and images from distant days. I would tell her the stories clearly and in the greatest of detail in the darkness of the room, until I knew that she was seeing the images through my eyes. Her breath came quickly from excitement when I told her about Jerusalem in its days of glory and about the land, which contained everything: fields and orchards, fortified cities and great wealth.

So the little girl grew and grew more beautiful. The British army made advances until one autumn day in the fall of 1917, while we were sitting down to supper, the student who lived in our courtyard came in to say that news had arrived that the Land of Israel would be given to the Jewish people.

You mean the Balfour Declaration, I stuttered, and she nodded emotionally.

We dropped our silverware and laughed a great laugh from the depths of our being. For the first time since we had been driven into this city we felt ourselves worthy of walking erect, free of the burden of two thousand years of humiliation, inferiority, and timidity. A hunchback, if one were to take his hump off his back, must have this same feeling. Yosef's eyes radiated with the light of a prisoner under a life sentence whose hope had been extinguished, when he is suddenly brought out into the day. Not landless exiles—thrown from owner to owner like useless utensils—but citizens of their own country.

But our return took a long time indeed. While the activists in Alexandria set to organizing our transfer to Palestine, Yosef was trying to edit something else in Hebrew, after his failure with the *Young Worker*. After a long struggle with the censorship board, he succeeded in publishing a single short issue, *In a Foreign Country*. There was not much room in it for everything happening in the upper reaches of the world—the Balfour Declaration, the Russian Revolution, the Peace Conference—but it was a Hebrew periodical that warmed our hearts. Just then, Yosef became ill again, exhausted from the endless struggle and long wait to go home. Sometimes, late at night, he would whisper that he was afraid to see the devastation we would encounter upon our return, and perhaps it was better to tarry.

Then we were told that Palestine had been conquered by the British, and a first letter from Brenner arrived along with bulletins from the party, telling us to come home. News was beginning to spread about our friends who had survived and about the enormous hardships the Jewish community had experienced. The longer we waited for permits, the more we longed for the land. Boys from Palestine, in rags and shabby shoes, arrived in Egypt to look for relatives and fill their hungry bellies. They told us about the suffering in Palestine, the terror and brutality of the despots. With no protection from foreign consulates, the Jewish population was caught between the Turkish whip and the deep blue sea. The many dead were laid to rest in hasty funerals, without mourners, under the blazing sun or stormy rains. The imposed silence was terrible, for public mourning was forbidden. Hunger plagued the land, and on every road the secret police lay in wait and took from everything that came their way—crops and people. Terrible cries rose from the prison cells; but far away, the boys related, British gunfire already echoed, and people said it was the Messiah's trumpet and soon their troubles would end.

Then my neighbor Nechama began going around to the stores, buying things out of season to take back to Palestine. The balcony overflowed with sacks of rice and flour, and everything was made ready for the journey. At that time Brenner's suggestion to publish a collection of my stories reached me again. I asked him to wait until our return so I could contribute my opinions about the writing, which I had not taken with me to Egypt. How interminably stretched those days of anticipation!

Finally, the day of Exodus came: the day after Passover, 1919.

On the last day of Passover I said to Yosef that I wanted to go out with him for my first walk through the city. He had come to know every part of the large city, and despite his sickness, he brought me to places he knew I would enjoy. I saw meadows and roses and lovely palaces, houses of pink marble, with statues of alabaster children guarding their entrances, garden benches inlaid with shell and fountains, whose waters glittered like silver dust in the sunlight. In the great park by the fading light I was filled with awe at the rustle of the trees, the chirp of the speckle-feathered birds, and the rainbow of drops at the sprinklers on the grass. The celebratory mood of the day, our last day of exile, colored everything we saw with the tints of paradise.

And the next day we did indeed leave, with Nechama directing the operation. With a small pack the exiles went down to Egypt and they went up again with goods aplenty, furniture and kitchenware and clothing, and food as well, whatever we could preserve, from the abundance of Egypt. Nechama had bought linen and woolen suits and suede shoes for us too, because she did not enjoy anything if others were not enjoying as well.

We returned by train, by way of the army camps. How surprised we were when we stopped in the desert to see Jewish boys in uniform, who greeted us with cool drinks. It turned out that they were Lithuanian and Polish boys, who had ended up here by way of the United States, and who had been appointed to serve as border guards. And so we experienced the exodus again by passing through the desert.

At daybreak I announced to Tsipora, who had awoken in my arms, that we had arrived, we were here. For we could smell the familiar scent of the orchards in the distance, and everyone in the carriage rushed to the windows because you could see by now, you could see. Even Yosef, who had been sick during the journey, seemed to revive at the smell of the land wafting through the windows. The land appeared before us with her green blanket, leaping to meet us, trotting beside the windows, joyous and moist with dew and radiant in the rising sun.

Still caught up in her emotion, I remembered how my daughter and I had returned from a trip to Egypt after the peace treaty between Egypt and Israel. We came back by bus, and after crossing the border, as we drove through the south between the tilled fields on straight roads with modern cars—how clean and progressive our country looked to us! But I didn't want to diminish Dvora's moment of joy with my own story.

sixteenth encounter

A wintry sun was painting the short shadows of the bare trees against the sidewalk when I arrived at Oliphant Street around noon. Because of the blue skies and early hour, and because our previous meeting had ended on an encouraging note, I climbed the stairs of the old house more lightly than usual.

It's beautiful outside, I said to Dvora as I entered. Shall I draw the curtains and open the window so you can see for yourself?

I have no desire to do that, Dvora said softly but with her usual determination. The air outside is humid and polluted with automobile exhaust. Why open the window—to hear the buses roar by on the next street? At one time, when we first came to live here in the late 1930s, this was one of the only houses east of Yehuda Halevi Street. A large orange grove surrounded the house, and I could smell the sweet blossoms and hear the song of the birds from my bed. The roosters on nearby farms crowing at sunrise was music to my ears, unlike the screech of automobiles. But now that asphalt and smoke have conquered the city, I want nothing more to do with the tumult outside my windows.

Again I felt the heaviness of her presence close in on me. But the sky was still blue and the sun still shone, and trees still glistened with the recent rain, I said to myself, clinging to the pleasant feeling with which I had entered. It will not help her at all if I sink with her into gloom.

We got to when you returned to Palestine from Egypt, I began.

Yes, it was April 1919. The warm reception when we arrived gladdened my heart and contributed to Yosef's recovery. Greetings were published in the journal when we returned and a festive convocation was held in our honor at the *Young Worker* House in Jaffa; but for me it was just a fleeting illusion of well-being. Although our return did lift my spirits, there were not to be such good times, such high spirits, ever again in my future.

I did a swift mental calculation: Dvora Baron was thirty-two when she returned, a young woman who belonged to the elite of the tiny Jewish community in Palestine. What was the problem? And maybe things weren't really so bad, and it was instead her gloomy present that colored the memories of the aging and lonely Dvora Baron. Suddenly I thought of Sylvia Plath, and I asked myself at what age the young poet had committed suicide. I remembered something about young children, about the constraints of a husband and home in contrast with her desire for freedom and creativity. I must look up the story again. And thus I was caught up in my own thoughts, not listening to Dvora with my usual attention. Fortunately I was taping the conversation, I thought, and even said to myself, It's not an easy thing, Amia, to be drawn again and again into her sad and saddening world; so you run away, running for your life.

Somehow, this thought brought back my concentration.

New winds were blowing in Palestine then, Dvora was saying in a stronger voice. The world had changed, and we with it. The October Revolution, the end of the Great War and, especially, of Ottoman rule over Palestine, had profound effects on us all. The confirmation of the British Mandate over Palestine, the Balfour Declaration, the appointment of the first Jewish commissioner in Palestine—all of these things seemed to us like harbingers of messianic redemption. Only Yosef continued to write columns warning against exaggerated hopes, and issued the call for a revitalization of the settlement as an independent national entity. The third great wave of immigrants began to arrive by land and sea, and construction sites were everywhere, especially in Tel Aviv, which was growing by leaps and bounds before our very eyes. The writers who had scattered gathered again in Tel Aviv, and the journal was launched once more. But Aharonovich was no longer just the editor of the journal; his name had spread, and he had a hand in every aspect of the regeneration of the Jewish settlement. Great debates raged on our balcony on topics that had ceased to interest me: the establishment of a unified labor union, volunteering for the Jewish Brigade of the British Army, and so on. Yosef was involved in all these things; his poor health never stopped him from attending an event, and he even traveled abroad frequently on behalf of the party.

My father was like that, I said to Dvora. He, too, was an important leader in the settlement and often traveled around the country and abroad. My mother, with her three small daughters, was left to take care of those down-to-earth details of daily life that he was too grand to think about. Once he went off to Europe for three months and ended up staying for a whole year. When his old parents arrived from Russia, it was my mother who made sure that they had everything they needed in our cramped house.

And how did your mother accept her fate? Dvora asked curiously.

I sensed as a child that she was embittered, that she felt that a great wrong had been done her. Only later did I understand that it was Mama who had been the brilliant student, and that being female had robbed her of pursuing a career. And in fact, when we grew up and she went back to work, I could sense how much taller she walked. But when I grew up I could also understand the enormity of the task that my father had taken upon himself, the sacred work, really, of community organizing, and I knew that in a society there must be those who accept such responsibility.

As the pillar of smoke and of fire that goes before the camp, she assented. Tsipora also saw things that way, she said as if surprised by the thought. She knew how sad and lonely I was when her father was away, but she respected his work and held no grudges.

But you were the one who stayed home with Tsipora! I exclaimed.

Of course. She was always at my side, for I decided at that time to keep her from school and teach her myself, with the help of home-teachers, if necessary. But the girl was also her father's daughter, she said, and sank into her thoughts. He told her about his work on behalf of the community, and sometimes took her along on trips. Since we returned from Egypt, she said as if suddenly remembering, I have gone on only one excursion, on Passover. We arrived in Haifa, at the hotel. We had planned to visit the Jezreel Valley, but Aharonovich got into an argument with the hotel owner over some trifle and I lost the desire to continue.

Aharonovich and Tsipora hiked along Mount Carmel all day, and I was left alone at the hotel. I sat on the balcony, she said dreamily, I saw a few palm trees and the first grass of spring, so green and beautiful.

The description moved me, although I wasn't sure why. Was she giving me a glimpse of the early flickerings of her reclusiveness? Was she telling me something about her difficulties with Yosef? Was she hinting that she saw more in the grass from her seat on a balcony than a traveler who encountered all sorts of landscapes? But she had moved on.

I kept far away from public matters. Yosef went alone to the conferences and celebrations of the Jewish community, and I avoided accompanying him even to the most important events. At the same time, however, I returned to writing, editing, and translation, and participated in establishing various literary journals, like *Maabarot*, edited by my close friend Yakov Fichman. My home stood open for visitors once again, especially on Fridays and on the Sabbath.

There was something wistful or nostalgic about her story, and I felt a rush of sympathy for her.

Who were these visitors?

A mixed group, she answered. First and foremost, writers: Yakov Rabinovitsh, for whom I had such great admiration, Barash, Fichman, Shimoni, Temkin, and others. We spoke about literary matters and traded books in Russian, French, Hebrew—that was the beginning of the great push to translate world classics into Hebrew. Gifts of books always brought me joy and soon filled our bookshelves. Yosef also knew that a book was the greatest gift in my eyes. Beside the writers, who visited me nearly every Sabbath, were pioneers, the men and women workers visiting Tel Aviv from the cooperative villages and settlements; I loved to hear about their lives. These people knew me through Yosef, but some of them became my friends too, and often stayed over at our house. When they discovered my abstinence from meat, they brought me produce or dairy products from their farms.

Tsipora sat with us, she continued, and would show off her knowledge for those who had some Torah from the houses of their fathers. In her childhood we studied the weekly Torah portion, and our Sabbath guests would test her on what she had learned.

So those were active, sociable years, I said, but I hear you stressing that they were your activities, the guests were your guests, as if Yosef was being pushed further and further outside the circle.

It was not I but his work that kept him outside. I was very glad when he was home and joined in the conversation with our visitors. We loved to hear about the great big world around us from someone who was such an idealist. I remember his harsh words against military education to bloodshed and violence, his concern about narrow class consciousness and the weakening of Socialist fervor among the new wave of immigrants, the Third Aliya. But you are right to notice, she added, that the circles of our lives more often were separate than conjoined.

And why didn't you send Tsipora to school when she reached school age? I returned again to that delicate issue.

At first it was because I hated educational institutions, kindergartens and elementary schools, that run according to a set model. Vulnerable children are required to separate from their loving parents each morning anew, to act mature before they are ready. Later—as I told you—Tsipora was kept home because of her illness, she curtly answered.

So the illness was discovered then?

Around that time, she said evasively. I could not avoid thinking that perhaps it was the mother who wanted to be near her gifted child—with the father gone so often on trips—so she clung to her belief that no one could teach Tsipora better than she could.

Jaffa under the British Mandate was not a comfortable place to live. At the end of the summer, with the scorching heat, the hooves of the camel caravans pounded dully along the roads. Columns of dust rose around them, darkening the domes of the mosques and the palm trees behind them. There was only cactus to shade the traveler trudging toward the city gates. At the entrance to the city, between the walls, the picture softened somewhat. Houseplants grew in the shade, and at the fruit stand the watermelon was radiantly green even under its layer of dust. An Arab grocer plunged his knife deep into it, while juice vendors with polished trays stood at the crossroad, calling: "Lemonade or cherry juice."

More than once during the summer notices were posted on every street forbidding the eating of fruit or drinking unboiled water because of a cholera outbreak. The price of produce would drop drastically, and policemen in the marketplace would confiscate all forbidden products "by order of the law." Wounded tomatoes, wallowing in their juice, and dead fish with bloated bellies would roll in the sand. Garbage piled up everywhere.

Then we left our little house in Jaffa and moved to a spacious one in Tel Aviv, close to where Chayim Nachman Bialik later built his, she explained. That was when they started to build a new neighborhood with smooth sidewalks in the north. The smell of paint and wet gravel arose from the new lots, and the merry music of construction sounded. Within the hazy radiance of sky and sea glistened the skeletons of half-built houses, and it seemed that they were springing up as we watched. From a distance it looked like the camp of a conquering army, striding forward with the confidence of the triumphant, while the wasteland, with its ruined vineyards and jackal lairs, retreated in disarray. Bulldozers uprooted hills from their places. Refugee boys from various countries spread out with their tools, and before you knew it, a new street arose, with two rows of single-storied houses.

When the neighborhood was finished I would walk along its streets, enjoying the beautiful houses, the clean sidewalks, and the children chattering in Hebrew, playing happily outside without fear. The freshly plastered houses had a kind of satisfied smile they caught from their owners. Outside the houses white laundry swayed on a line, and a few miraculous blades of green broke through the desolate soil here and there. At night, when the houses were lit within, the windows gazed at passersby with beneficent eyes.

How different this was from Jaffa's alleys. Although they were separated by only a strip of sand, moving from Jaffa to the new neighborhood in Tel Aviv was like leaving a fortress—a Jewish fortress with a lock and gate—for a place that bordered on non-Jewish land, and where instead of the hum of Sabbath prayers only the hiss of the kerosene stove could be heard. But there was a Jewish dairyman there who delivered fresh milk each morning, and farmers brought their produce from the settlements to sell.

The house that had been built for us was entirely white. A row of pines shaded its courtyard, where we put up a swing for Tsipora. At the entrance to the courtyard, two half-gates opened to embrace visitors. When we first came, golden autumn leaves stood here and there in glistening mounds, exuding the scent of moist vegetation. We lined the books inside the glass bookshelves, set a table and chairs for our guests in the spacious dining room, and arranged new aluminum cookware in the kitchen. We had the great faith and little means of those who move from tents and huts to a real dwelling place, with their own four walls.

And in front of the houses—a golden square of sand. Beyond that, the sea sprawled askance, as if stretched to the corners of the sky. It was a view that aroused solemn thought, and the first time we left our courtyard of our house, we walked toward it in meditative silence. Here we hoped to see the ships come in, bringing immigrants from all the exiles of the world; for their right to do so had already been announced and duly signed by the powers that be.

In fact, boatloads of immigrants soon began to arrive at the shore at the end of the street. They usually arrived early in the morning, horns breaking into the sleeping city with glad tidings. And the immigrants—some were like survivors of a shipwreck, people with broken bodies and weakened spirits, still swaying, unused to solid ground beneath their feet; and some were boys, strong-bodied and powerful revolutionaries, muscles taut in their arms and sleeves rolled up, as if they were ready to start work immediately.

It seemed to me that it had been a while since I had heard Dvora speak in her storytelling mode, the one I liked so much, and I had assumed it was reserved for stories about her childhood. Her descriptions aroused distant, faded memories in me, too. Suddenly an ancient childhood chant rang out in me. When had I last heard it? When my father had sat with me at suppertime, trying to persuade me to swallow another spoonful of porridge? This is how it went: "Who comes there? Who comes there? A boat with a chimney and a captain's chair. What do you hold? And to where do you sail? I bring Jews young and old, to the Land of Israel." I was happy to remember it and considered telling Dvora, but no opening materialized.

Strong emotions seized us when we saw the newcomers. They dispersed in all directions to various settlements throughout the land; but for weddings or funerals, they gathered again according to their hometowns and spoke the old language amongst themselves. When they sweetly sang their father's melodies together or ate forgotten dishes, the wife trying to remember her mother's recipe, I saw that the embers had not been entirely extinguished.

And weren't there problems in those days absorbing new immigrants? I asked. Did all those immigrants find their place in this country?

Certainly not, she replied in her schoolteacherly tone. There were immigrants who, in their previous lives, had lived in lavishly furnished houses and owned summer cottages, girls who had worked as kitchen help, laborers who had worked under bosses in warehouses; here, there was the burning heat and a kerosene stove that smoked, the wealthy man who hires himself out as a simple construction worker, insects everywhere in his shack, and sand and sand. Some returned to the Diaspora and tried their luck in foreign countries. There were those who, embittered by fate, took their own lives. Some died of heartache, leaving a widow and small children, and these were our holy martyrs for the land. In eulogies we said that the Land of Israel had not accepted them with open arms, for she does not always respond graciously to those who seek her favor. The land was hard, quick to anger, having been left for dead for two thousand years. Even the pioneers and young workers, who seemed so accustomed to life in the country, often gave in to loneliness and homesickness for the house they had left behind, for absent parents. More than once I heard one of those young men pacing in his room and singing with enormous pain, and I understood that this tanned and muscular man was an orphan, with no mother and father, no brother and no relative in the wide world.

One day Nechama, my neighbor in Alexandria, arrived for a visit, she suddenly continued. She saw me as a rabbi's daughter, and came to tell me her dream as she would my father in the old country. In the dream it seemed she was supervising a few enormous vats, in which all sorts of good food from the land's bounty were being cooked for the newcomers. For the immigrants to Palestine were coming in droves from all sorts of countries, and they needed a hot meal when they arrived. They took out all the mattresses from her house and spread them on the grass so people could rest. And then, from the smell coming out of the vats she could tell that she needed to stir the food lest it burn, but she was too short, unfortunately, to reach. For the first time in her life she regretted that she had not grown, when she was growing, just a little bit taller. Still sad, she awoke and understood that the smell she had noticed in her sleep was the jelly roll, which it was time to remove from the oven.

That was how that good-hearted woman told it, Dvora said fondly, and I answered that she *was* big enough, at least as large as her deeds.

Among the immigrants were old acquaintances from my hometown. I heard that Gitl's old father had arrived, and eventually I learned that he had lost his wealth; without his business dealings he began to study midrash like his grandfather and in time, joined the Zionists. When news of the Balfour Declaration reached him, he thought that he might yet live to see Gitl, his only surviving daughter. Father and daughter came to visit and told me that some faithful young boys had taken care of the old man throughout the voyage, and escorted him right from the shore to his daughter's farm. I have never seen an old man happier than he.

One day Mina arrived, my childhood friend from the town. She arrived at my house without advance notice. We hugged wordlessly and sobbed, Dvora whispered, each crying to herself for those who were no more. I asked, my friend answered, and it seemed as if we were walking arm in arm through the town, street after street.

That was when Mina told me that the great synagogue in the town had burned to the ground—the synagogue in which my father had prayed when I was a child. It was not the gentiles who had set it ablaze but it had burned on its own, on a Saturday night, at midnight. They heard thunder, although there was not a cloud in the sky, and suddenly, tongues of fire burst through the walls of the synagogue and its windows looked as if they were running blood. Nothing was saved, for the flames had cut off all exit. The water that was carried from every well only fueled the blaze, like oil. Before all eyes the building was consumed, and by morning nothing was left, as if it had been ripped clean off its foundations. And many said, Mina continued with wide eyes, that it was to our credit, since synagogues in other towns were desecrated and looted, while ours was taken as a perfect sacrifice, rising in flames to the heavens.

By the end of the war, while we were still waiting for a permit to return from Egypt, Mina and her husband had already immigrated with the first of the postwar wave, and their house in the settlement awaited our visit. Before much time had passed I took Tsipora, a basket of salty crackers, shelled pistachios, and peanuts, which I knew they did not have in the village, and we traveled to see them in the communal farm. How happy I was to see my childhood friend healthy and sound in the house her husband had built. It was an isolated house, a garden on one side and a shed on its other side. A solitary pine stood at the center of the courtyard. A few doves perched on the roof of the shed, and from within it came the angry crow of a rooster. A single donkey was tied beside the bushes. Mina's husband had golden hands; he could have squeezed honey from a rock. Together we walked through the well-irrigated vegetable garden, radiating in the sunlight. A rubber hose with golden stripes coiled like a snake at our feet, here and there a puddle of water shivered, and around the puddles, birds chattered. The plants beside the house resembled green muslin. Those are tomatoes, Mina explained to Tsipora.

Mina's husband, who had been a lumber man in Lithuania, had an especially close connection with the earth, and it responded in kind. Strawberries and apples blossomed under his hands, and he fashioned vessels for the kitchen and courtyard from wood and stone. He, who was himself a recent immigrant, surrounded himself with young boys new to the country, sectioned off a corner behind the family house, and instructed them in farming with a shovel and hoe.

Toward evening my friend set the table and chairs under the pine tree in the courtyard, and brought Tsipora a plate of sour cream with fresh cheese and a bowl of porridge. For us she prepared potatoes roasted in their skins, pickled cucumbers, and coffee made with chicory, as Lithuanians like it. I remember that visit as clearly as if it were today.

Did you ever consider living on the land, in a kibbutz or communal farm? I asked.

Dvora looked at me as if I were a simple child. We have already spoken of that. It is true that I saw these people as the salt of the earth, she said, but how could I join them? They worked from morning until night, women alongside men, on the land, in the kitchen, with the livestock—and I was sickly and weak. Yosef, who had been an agricultural worker in his early days in the country, was also incapable of the hard labor expected of pioneers, and in any case his activities were considered a great contribution to the community. But I followed the settlement project and the progress of my pioneer friends from a distance, and my heart was always with them. And you, she challenged me, have you ever been a country girl?

No, I replied, although in the youth movement they talked about "self-realization"—which meant going to a kibbutz—but I understood very early, from a few short work-camps, that my place was not there, that I needed more privacy and freedom than a kibbutz would be prepared, in those days, to give its members. I reached the conclusion that I was, in the final analysis, a city mouse.

And I, as the asphalt grew wider and closed around me, as the orchards and vineyards and the song of sprinklers in the night retreated, felt more and more stifled and hated the urban monster more intensely.

As if to prove her words Dvora was suddenly seized by a fit of weary, deep coughing that reddened her face. I got up and helped her sit higher in the bed, and Tsipora entered, alarmed, holding a cup of water. Again she sent an angry glance in my direction, as if it were my fault her mother had become tired.

After Dvora had relaxed, she smiled at us. I frightened the two of you, she said, but I am still alive.

I don't think you've eaten a thing today, Tsipora pleaded.

It is better that way, her mother refused.

No, you must eat the porridge I cooked for you for lunch.

Tsipora brought a tray from the kitchen, and on it was a bowl of something white and thin. Dvora began to eat from it, bit by bit, like a bird.

What did you make for Mama? I asked Tsipora.

What she always eats, practically the only thing: Quaker Oats. She also eats one kind of potato, and that's all.

It is very nutritious, Dvora said, and does no harm. I can only digest the lightest of foods.

But one must eat a variety of food, the doctors told us, Tsipora explained, wearily. It isn't enough to eat cereal and milk and potatoes.

You eat, Dvora said to her. I am nearly seventy years old; we may conclude that my nutritional habits have succeeded.

She sat raised regally against the pillows, eating slowly. There wasn't the faintest tremor in her fine-boned hands.

Look, she said, people wash themselves, get dressed, and take care of other physical needs in private; but eating, which is essentially one of these needs, they are sure to do in public, making a great display of it.

My father used to say the same thing, I exclaimed.

Tsipora came back into the room with three cups of tea, and sat with us until the doorbell rang. A man with a Yemenite accent could be heard laughing and saying something to Tsipora. Dvora caught my questioning glance, That is Pinchas the water carrier, who brings us well water.

Excuse me? I asked in amazement.

Drinking water, pure water from the well. Water from the faucet does not touch our lips, since it is full of harmful chemicals. That is how the sages of Israel imagine they are purifying the water, she said scornfully.

So you mean you don't use water from the faucet, not even if it's boiled?

Exactly. Pinchas brings us a bucket of spring water every day and takes back yesterday's bucket. That is his work, and we pay him for it. He is an excellent man, she added, and where else could you find a Jewish water carrier who whispers chapters of Psalms as he works?

Where does he find well water in Tel Aviv? I considered asking, but I was too dumbstruck to speak, trying to catch a glimpse of the man as he left the house. During the day, I thought, is when you get to see the real workings of this house.

Tsipora, who had heard her mother's words, added, It isn't just his salary he gets from us. Mama takes care of him and his family however she can. When someone sends us food from the settlements, his children get some too, and she also gives them books and enough money to live on.

Stop! roared Dvora. I am not such a great saint. Pinchas has a very large family, all of them living in one poor room, and we have more than enough for our needs.

I looked around at what seemed an exceptionally modest apartment, with nothing superfluous, at the faded blankets covering Dvora, at Tsipora's shabby clothes. Is that what she called "more than enough for our needs"? But the two women seemed utterly satisfied with that appraisal of their situation. They make do with the barest minimum, even of food, of their own free will, like nuns. This is the widow of the founder and chief executive officer of one of Israel's largest banks, I thought in amazement; and immediately I responded that even when she talked about the time that Aharonovich was alive, it sounded like they were fairly poor. Was everyone like that then, or was there something different about this particular family? But then Dvora had very nearly boasted about their white house in Tel Aviv. So how could I clear up this confusion in my own mind? Ask her to tell me about their economic situation? I immediately dismissed that option.

Set up that machine of yours, please, Dvora said with a bitter smile, and let us continue.

Tsipora immediately arose and left the room, carrying the tray and dishes with her. Dvora sank back among the pillows, her black eyes fixed themselves on the ceiling.

The joy of returning home, going back to work, and reuniting with old friends and new immigrants was quickly extinguished by bad news. My brother, Benjamin, had finished his medical studies in Kazan, married, and I was confident that the day would soon come when he too would arrive among the new immigrants. The news of his death from typhoid fever struck me like a thunderbolt on a clear summer's day. That was a few months after we had returned. It was my nephew Barukh, the son of my eldest sister, who brought the bitter news to my house, she said in a hard voice.

I have already told you the few details we knew of his death, she said. And with unusual brevity she added, My hopes that he would cure Tsipora and me of our illnesses were shattered. He was the only one on whom I hung such hopes. Even today I mourn his death.

I sat, sharing her silence.

Before very long, riots broke out all over the land. Trumpeldor and his comrades fell at Tel-Chay, and anti-Zionist demonstrations heralded riots in Jerusalem. The gentile terrors had reached us in our homeland, too, and I heard the whistle of the approaching whip. The Arab I had thought was flesh of our flesh was rising up to kill us. After that I knew that Ishmael was not a true cousin. He had appeared humble and peaceable as long as he had been oppressed, as were we, by harsh masters. We had talked of how fine it would be to live together in brotherly harmony, working our land side by side; but now, with the changing times, the burden of the Turk lifted, he was revealed in his true colors: a wild beast of a man, as the angel had said to his mother, whose hand shall be against everyone. Sarah, with her mother's intuition, apparently saw even then that one fine day he would rise up against her son and demand a share of the inheritance God himself had given Isaac for eternity. That was why she said: "The son of this servant girl will not inherit along with my son."

It's amazing how you transform yourself into a rabbi's daughter in the flash of an eye, I said.

But Dvora ignored my comment completely and continued.

In the spring of 1921 the riots reached Jaffa. Brenner, who was living with the Yitzkar family in the Arab section of Jaffa, was murdered along with the Yitzkars and the young writer Tsvi Shatz, who had come to try to save them. Please understand, Amia, she said, looking into my eyes, Brenner was the cornerstone of the structure we had built, had begun to build, with such immense effort, and his cruel death symbolized the breakdown and bereavement of our efforts to take root in the land—the abysmal despair he wrote about so often. Like Aharonovich, Brenner had arrived in Palestine as a worker, but he could not handle the backbreaking work, not digging ditches, not stone-cutting, not in the fields or orchards. Finally, he decided to return to literary work. He was a frequent contributor to the *Young Worker,* and nothing happened in Palestine or abroad about which he did not express some sharp opinion in his writings or on the lecture circuit. The writers in Jaffa congregated around him, and for all his pessimism, he was always willing to put his shoulder to the wheel to help someone out. They say about Brenner, she added warmly, that he was an excellent teacher when he needed to find work at that during the war. When the Turks announced the expulsion decree, he and his students from the Herzliya Gymnasium were exiled to one of the villages and he continued teaching in the lap of nature. After the war he dedicated himself to writing and editing again, and was even about to publish a volume of my stories. Although I often disagreed with his opinions and did not see the Diaspora as harshly as he did, he was as dear to me in life as in his death.

So what is left in my life? she asked, with deep pain.

I understood that there was no possible response. I sat thinking about how she had described Brenner, who had been a friend, at such length, while she had talked about Benjamin so briefly this time. Perhaps one sorrow could not be separated from the other, I thought, and it was easier to mourn Brenner than her beloved brother. Yakov Rabinovitsh was also gone, having been run over by a car in 1948, and most of the other figures of that period had already passed away. One mourning encompasses all these, I thought to myself, but Brenner had described particularly well the despair of these old new-Jews, and maybe that was why Dvora Baron felt so close to him in her dejection.

It certainly was a difficult period, I finally said.

Yes, until it ended with our resignation from the editorial board.

And then you decided you wouldn't set foot outside anymore? I asked.

Not exactly, she said, but there was no resistance in her voice; I shall tell you about that some other time, she concluded.

seventeenth encounter

Beautiful and harsh was our regenerating land, Dvora began our next
meeting. Her eyes were set cavernously deep, and she greeted me somewhat indifferently, as if I were no more than an extension of the tape
recorder. Her pale skin was stretched taut across her high cheekbones and
her black hair lay wild against the pillow. Even before I had set up the
recorder, she was deep in her memories.

I particularly remember the heat waves, which began before Passover,
she said. In the park near our house the perfume of the citrus trees rose
like white incense, and purple buds multiplied on the margosa trees from
hour to hour. As the blossoming continued, fledglings began to appear,
splashing deep notes, filled with longing, into the air. In the vegetable
dealer's basket, on a bed of wonderfully green cabbage leaves, ripe strawberries burned deep red.

How beautifully you paint the picture, I cried, Even the smells.

I enjoyed describing landscapes in my stories, she replied, for me it
was embroidery, embroidery with words. That was what young Basya was
like in my town, my friend Mina's sister, and I learned it from her, she
said.

Basya's embroideries were the masterpieces of our town. She could
fold entire worlds into the corner of a canvas, no larger than a child's
palm. They said she worked "out of her head"; and it was true that she
never copied from books, embroidering things she had seen in her own
imagination, lit by her own light. Basya lived in the bakery, and women
came and went with their pots that had been simmering in the oven,
but something made them stay out of her way. When the girl worked,
no one made a peep, and they closed the door softly when they left.

When she finished a picture, her sister took out a new canvas for her, a smooth cloth that to me was like the primordial material of creation, before God had brought forth grasses and trees that radiated His brilliance. These embroideries brought eternal spring to the sooty rooms of the women of the town. They became a sort of spiritual treasure, a new interior measure of beauty. When people rushed to save their valued possessions from a fire, these canvases were always first among them.

I never heard anyone talk that way about embroidery, I mused, only paintings and sculptures, or important books.

And why not embroidery? Because it is woman's work? she asked, without waiting for a response.

In my childhood I was enchanted by Basya's artistry, she continued, and I saw how the local women loved her work. Today I recognize that the greatest kindness one can bestow on artists, who strew the sparks of their soul in every direction, is to gather these pieces together so they can be preserved.

That's what I hoped to do for you, I wanted to say, but the thought frightened me and I kept silent. Instead I heard myself saying, I wanted to talk to you about that, actually.

See how balance is restored in the universe, she said, ignoring me. Artists collect the sparks of being: they see, remember, imagine, and then weave a picture, a tale, a piece of embroidery. The imagination, like the sun, shines not only on the fortunate but also on the lowly and oppressed, somehow weaving together the ripped fabric of their lives. The prisoner imagines what it is to walk freely, and the exile returns to the native soil.

She is talking about herself now, I thought. Shut within these four walls, she imagines she can go where she pleases and spin stories from these experiences. No reason ever to leave.

As if reading my mind Dvora continued, It is just the same way with me, the last of the storytellers of the shtetl. They say that history destroyed that world, but I see myself as a kind of photographic negative, which remains after whatever was photographed has itself disappeared. Is it not my duty, then, to set my impressions on paper?

There are many artists whose names do not appear in encyclopedias, she said. I once knew a photographer, a young man, who had the gift of bringing out the good and beautiful in everyone—each spark of nobility or generosity or tenderness. Those he photographed experienced a deepened self-worth, and began to stand taller and respect themselves and others more. He exceeded even his own considerable powers when it came to photographing his crippled mother. He revealed everything that had been concealed, brought it to perfect clarity, and showed her herself in that way. All her humility, her pained love, her terrors, and her regrets, the stifled sob—all this he absorbed in the form of light rays and projected in every wrinkle of her prematurely aged face.

Basya's brother, her words sang, was also an artist and a poet, who loved nature and divided his time between the countryside and the world of his imagination—although nothing remained of his work after he died before his time. As he lay on his deathbed, Basya asked him softly, truly as if speaking to her soulmate: "What are you feeling?" "Nothing," he answered, "only lightness, I am so light I could take off and fly like a bird." The next morning he told his sister that they seemed to be cutting hay in the meadow. "I can tell by the fragrance," he said. He asked her to open the window, in which the meadow was reflected by the rising sun, and he stayed like that all day. He died with his eyes open, his wide eyes flickering in the brilliance of the sunset.

Years later, she continued, in a chain of associations that stunned me with their elegance, I heard Tsipora talking with her father one evening. She was seven years old then, I think, a gentle soul, and her grasp on the world seemed so fragile to me. The two of them sat in the courtyard at dusk, she on his lap, watching the sun set into the ocean, which spread beyond the sand to the furthest horizons. Together they watched the birds that dipped and soared above them. And then Tsipora asked her father: "Papa, why does a bird get bigger when it flies up in the sky? First, when you see it on the ground, it's so tiny, and then it gets higher—and it grows."

Tears began to stream down Dvora's cheeks, but she continued to speak in a firm, singing voice as if she did not notice. "The bird?" Yosef answered seriously. "The bird gets bigger because it goes higher. Everyone who leaves lowly, material things and goes higher—also gets bigger."

I will never know if Yosef knew that I had heard them, but I secretly believed that those words were directed at me, and I found comfort in that thought.

I put out my hand to caress her shoulder and felt her body respond. I gave her a tissue, but she held it, not drying the tears flowing freely down her face. Even now she could arouse a man's love, I suddenly understood, and drew back for a moment, shaken.

I envy birds, she smiled. If God had done well by me, he would have granted me wings.

It's no coincidence that they talk about flights of fancy.

Yes, I take off on flights of fancy without wings, or even legs, really, she said. Do you remember the story I told you about my sailing off down the river on an ice floe? It was a courageous attempt to pass from this ugly world to another, finer one. Certainly the vessel I chose for my journey was a strange one; but human beings have always used whatever was at hand. One sat on a kerchief spread on the water, and another flew off in a flaming chariot with steeds of fire. Even Jacob, on that wondrous night in Bethel, had some sort of ladder on which he would climb up to God.

And how did we arrive at this juncture? she asked, after a few moments of silence. I was thinking of telling you about our resignation from the editorial staff of the *Young Worker*, and here we are in the upper heavens.

I don't know, I answered, still reluctant to disturb her train of thought.

Dvora raised her shoulders in amazement and smiled. Seeing me glance at my watch, she said, in a businesslike tone: Let us continue.

In those first days after our return from Egypt I sensed a kind of renewal in my stories, as if in sympathy with the land being reborn. Those were good years for writing, and I knew for the first time that I had a real grasp on my literary work.

What do you mean? I asked. You'd been writing for twenty years by then.

True, I had been writing since I was a child; but there is no comparison between the scribblings of an inexperienced girl and the work of a mature person who has known suffering. The things I had written in my youth were worthless rags in my eyes. I had no desire to read them again, and would not agree to their republication. In contrast to what I wrote after my return from Egypt, since 1921, she hurried to add. I only sensed the change later, of course.

I do not have many stories, Amia, she said, turning to me; they came very slowly. A writer cannot always be burning, and one must write only when that fire burns within. Stories are forged in a deep furnace before they appear before the eyes of the world. In the long nights of wandering I polish one word after another, each period and comma, until the sentence sings clearly enough in my ears to put down on paper.

How do you write? I wanted to ask. At the desk, or did you write your stories lying down? I had not yet spoken my question aloud, but Dvora correctly interpreted my looking around the room, and said, No one has ever seen me writing. Creation requires absolute solitude.

Could you explain to me how your mature work is different from your earlier work? I asked. You know I am not a literary critic.

Neither am I, she chuckled. Do not ask the baker what makes his dough rise.

But anyway, I wheedled.

There were many Russian, French, and Scandinavian writers who influenced me, and from all these strands, and the people I met, and the events of my life, I wove my own plots, in my own style. In later stories this weave became simpler, less full of protest. The singularity of a character became more important than their class background. My early stories struck me as too vociferous, without any sense that things have their own reasons in this world, and that each calamity has its consolation alongside. My later stories suggest that even if one cannot know the reason for the evils of this world, she said with some hesitation, there is no greater wisdom than the acceptance of one's destiny.

Like you, I said.

Dvora continued, in her bookish manner: And so, my early stories are angry and try to change society, since in my youth I believed that was possible; but in the later ones I see the suffering that comes upon this earth as part of human existence, and I try to shed some warmth and light on the sufferings of my characters by the very fact that I describe them. And I later understood that one should not work one's material too much; explanation only further obscures things. One must learn to direct one's vision so things became visible in their own light. The intelligent reader can sense what is there in the darkened room, in the spaces around the page.

I wish I could learn your art, I thought.

I never achieved the result I wanted in my writing; but which artist is ever satisfied? she said. At first I was just an apprentice to the craft of writing. It took me many years to find my true voice, and since then I have stood my ground without further influence by others. And now, in the last few years I see greater clarity in the few stories I have published, which strive toward harmony rather than beauty. If they were paintings, they would be circles—not lines—she concluded, without further explanation.

But although my stories were critically acclaimed, she continued, for many years I was unable to publish a collection. The first attempt fell through before the Egyptian exile, and the second died with Brenner. Other attempts also failed. Bialik was about to publish my works with Dvir Press, and then changed his mind for some reason. Later good friends, among them Yakov Rabinovitsh, tried to publish a volume with Shtibl; but that did not work out either. You probably do not know that in those days Hebrew publishing houses were still based in the European capitals, in Warsaw and Berlin, and all manuscripts had to be sent there; only an occasional volume was published in Palestine. The publishing industry in Europe was struck with serious financial crises in the 1920s, and overseas negotiations were difficult. The project seemed hopeless.

Were you very upset about that? I remember how distressed I was when I couldn't publish my first stories, I said.

Really? she asked in surprise.

At one point, I was suddenly determined to be a writer. I had made up and written down stories as a little girl, as I told you, and my father would send them off to various contests, and I even won a few. In high school I wrote a story about Tsipora, the wife of Moses, based on commentaries and legends I had found, and I presented it as my final paper in Bible class. I laughed, and Dvora joined in.

I would have enjoyed reading that.

I succeeded in taking my teachers by surprise, so they were forced to grade this unusual paper, but eventually they understood that a lot of research had gone into that story. But when I started university I got completely involved in my studies, and over the years I stopped reading fiction and only read professional literature.

I went back to creative writing because of an impulse I understood only many years later. It was my sabbatical year. We lived in a cold part of the United States, shut inside for most of the winter, at home or in the office, while the whole world was hidden underneath a blanket of snow. I loved to look out at the white world, the mysterious world, with its tall black trees, entirely naked, sticking up like masts. But I hated to go out, true Israeli that I was, and in my free time I would sink into reading, dreaming, or writing letters by the picture window. That was where the idea for my first book was born, and there, in a burst of work unlike anything I had ever experienced, the writing was done in a space of a few months, until spring.

I remember one night I was writing about a young woman whose husband had fallen in battle—he had lost his way during a patrol and froze to death in the desert. It was night, my husband had gone off to bed hours before, and the children were asleep on the top floor. I sat at the old desk we had found at a junk shop and immersed myself in the description of her character, her mourning, and her recovery. Time stood still. Suddenly it seemed to me that the sun had already risen, and surprised, I got up with a jerk to open the door in order to see the dawn illuminating the snowy world outside our warm and sheltering house. In so doing, I spilled an inkstand that was on the table, which was still open from when I had refilled my fountain pen a little after midnight. A black stain spread on the golden carpet, which swallowed it like a thirsty giant.

That was when I realized how tired I was after the concentrated effort of writing and the sadness of separating from my character, who was no longer in my imagination but rather on the page before me. Looking at that terrible stain I started to sob like a little girl. Yisrael woke in the next room and came in sleepily in his flannel pajamas, squinting his eyes at the drama.

"What happened?" he asked. "You haven't slept at all? Where did the stain come from? Why are you crying?"

I hugged his warm body, letting myself feel his strength. I had a hard night, I finally said, but I wrote a good chapter, something real. It's a little like giving birth, I tried to explain, although he hadn't asked.

When he saw that I had calmed down, he went to the bathroom, brought a bucket of soapy water and a few cleaning supplies, and together we bent down to work on the stain.

I don't know why I told you about that, I stopped in embarrassment, it's just important in my life. Then I saw that Dvora's face had changed, the usual dejection transformed into something else.

Because you too embroider stories, she said. I was happy to listen to you; usually I am the storyteller.

That's as it should be, I replied. In any case, that was my first great writing moment. As for being published, no one rushed to accept that work. But I'm talking too much. Where were we? I asked in confusion. I think we've lost track of the time.

For a moment we were both silent. I had given up the attempt to reconstruct our work. Before my eyes, Basya and her poet brother hovered over a desk set in the drifting snow.

The track of time, you say, Dvora finally spoke. Time is not so straight and simple. Early and late roam freely within us, and knowledge takes her tools wherever she finds them. Today I think that time is not measured by hours and years but by the shape of the life it contains. An hour like the one you described is worth entire lifetimes.

That hour was a turning point. But we have talked about me enough today, I said, finally catching hold of the thread of our interwoven memories. You were describing your difficulties in getting published. Was that very hard for you?

I may have been angry, but I do not think I viewed it as a true failure as long as critics continued to praise the stories that appeared in newspapers and editors continued to ask for new ones. A writer cannot sound words unless they find an echo, and it is this echo that encourages the writer to continue. But when someone feels they are calling into a void, their energy flags. It was never like that with me and even now I have found a receptive listener, she said proudly as if I were not sitting there before her. Anyway, she remembered, in those days, worse things than not publishing a collection came along to occupy my mind.

I dedicated myself solely to writing, she continued, only after we resigned from the *Young Worker* in 1923, about three years after our return from Egypt. That episode was a landmark in Aharonovich's life and my own, each in our own way.

What happened?

There were many factors in what was a difficult decision, because our lives, and even Tsipora's life, were so closely entwined with the paper. Please understand, the birth of the journal week in, week out, was the central event in our lives. The journal reported on everything that happened in the Jewish world, in the settlement, in the party; it provided a forum for talented writers in Palestine and in the Diaspora. And we did most of the work with our own hands: we courted writers as if we were asking for a personal favor, we edited, prepared the galleys, and so on and so forth. Yosef himself would sometimes work late into the night at the printers, correcting the final proofs and waiting to see the front issue emerge, like a father awaiting the birth of his child. He would bring the journal home early the next morning still warm, and only then would he rest for a bit, before it started again. I too labored unceasingly over the journal, sometimes in desperation when a holiday was approaching and there was not enough material for a literary supplement. While Tsipora was still an infant crying endlessly, I would rock her cradle while working on proofs, editing, correcting and correcting, until the writer himself felt that that was exactly what he had meant to say. For over ten years that journal ruled our lives.

Even so, there were people who thought they could do a better job. They argued that Aharonovich should have an editorial committee rather than deciding everything on his own; that the journal was not receptive to the work of ordinary workers, but only published the elite; and that it did not provide the balanced coverage of everything that happened in

Palestine as it had at first. Some interpreted this to mean that the journal lacked its earlier intensity and originality, that it had grown distant from the world of labor it was supposed to serve and express. We considered these charges very seriously, but we rejected them, and were inclined to see them as an expression of a political struggle in which Yosef, in his integrity, had failed to hide his unpopular views. There was the controversy over the establishment of a federation of trade unions, which Aharonovich opposed, or the question of forming a Jewish Brigade in the British Army. In any case, we suffered tremendously from the barrage of criticism.

But it isn't unreasonable to suggest, I ventured, that the long-time editor of a journal should hand over responsibilities to someone with fresh, new ideas.

One might also weigh his experience and connections, you know. At the time we accepted the situation with mixed emotions. I was hurt by the ingratitude of the community, and saw the journal as a child we had nurtured and were now compelled to abandon; but I also longed to be free of our servitude. As editors we could barely scrape by. I knew Yosef would be offered another job: after all, he was an important man, and our situation would certainly not worsen. I hoped I could dedicate myself to writing and translating at home. In retrospect I will not budge from my belief that the journal deteriorated after we resigned—although some friends thought differently—and there is something to be said for changing guards. New forces were streaming into the land in those days, no less worthy than ours, in what was called the Third Wave of immigration, and there was some logic to clearing the way for them. But that was not how it happened: Yitzchak Lufban took the editorship upon himself, and my friend the poet David Shimonovitz became literary editor. The journal ran by the old formulae, and the people who ran it had immigrated when I did, with the Second Aliya.

Even after all this time, Dvora sounded as if the whole episode was still capable of wounding her.

When we announced our resignation from the paper, it sent shock waves through the public, and there were people who tried to persuade us to rethink our decision; but we were truly humiliated after a mocking article about our resignation appeared in the Purim edition. Tsipora was listed as one of the people who had resigned, and the house we had built in Tel Aviv was mentioned, as if we had hoarded a king's ransom through our work and were living in the lap of luxury while unemployed workers went hungry.

People involved in public affairs can never escape criticism, I said. My father, in his years as a public servant and organizer, was burnt enough times, and we, his family, shared the insult. As a little girl I would wonder whether he had done something to deserve the criticism, until I realized that the media worked that way and no one could make a clean escape.

Nevertheless, I was not prepared to be sullied by public matters again, she said forcefully. Scheming, ingratitude, and lies hurt me very much. A sin was committed against us, and the apology that came sixteen years later is evidence of that.

What do you mean? I asked.

A few days after Yosef's death, in 1937, an emotional letter arrived from the person who had written the satirical piece, begging my forgiveness. He admitted that he had intentionally hurt us and his conscience was bothering him now, although in later relations with Yosef he had continued to defend his actions. But what use is a letter like that, coming so belatedly? The wound could not be healed.

Still, she continued, it was an important crossroads. First of all, the paper that was the bridge connecting Yosef and me vanished beneath our feet. After that, a space opened up between us, each in our own world. It seems to me that happiness never again visited our dwelling. Yosef, who was called upon to manage the Workers Bank, drew into his shell, his principles hardening. He was faithful to his new work but the satisfaction and excitement he had known at the paper, for all the difficulties, were gone.

From a journal to a bank? I wondered aloud.

It was not as radical a transition as it might appear today. The Workers Bank was as important an organizing tool in those days as the journal. The same leaders filled the various positions, and they acquired them not because they were economists or businessmen but through their loyalty to the Zionist settlement and the party. The bank managers—there were two, Aharonovich and Brodny, who later became my closest friend—were first and foremost public servants. Although Aharonovich was not particularly experienced in finance, he had been involved in the workers' kitchen and helped establish a cooperative store in his early years in Palestine. Mathematical skills were less important than the ability to forge a relationship of trust with the public. After his death, many people told me that Aharonovich had succeeded admirably at this task. But perhaps, she added slowly, there is something in your reaction: perhaps this transition signaled Yosef's relegation to the margins of political life, because of his unpopular opinions. Who knows?

Slanderous tongues did not stop wagging after that, she said angrily. I heard people say that Aharonovich had left the public arena because of my sickness and Tsipora's, finding himself a comfortable position in a bank with a fat salary so he could devote himself to being our nurse-maid. He was dedicated to taking care of us, but there was no grosser lie than that. Despite his poor health, Aharonovich responded to every demand by the union or his party, working for many institutions and organizations, in finance, in culture and politics, speaking to youth groups and giving freely of his time. He was rarely at home. His salary was so small we could barely make ends meet. I am not complaining, she added, my needs have always been modest and that was how I raised Tsipora; but I hate lies. Once I was in Haifa on my way to the Jezreel Valley when I realized I did not have enough money to complete the trip and was forced to turn back.

Dvora spoke with a helpless rage. I could not remember her speaking of her husband with love, even in their first days together; but the affront she felt for the wrong that had been done him still smoldered.

And since then you have shut yourself in your house?

Dvora nodded, and sat in wounded silence.

eighteenth encounter

The last time we parted, moved by the stories we had shared, Dvora had promised that at our next meeting she would talk about her seclusion. My brain buzzed anxiously with possible explanations. I was going to hear Dvora's version about what strangers saw as the primary riddle of her life: why she had withdrawn into her house and the nature of her relationship with Tsipora.

In the months of our acquaintance I had gradually begun to see her image more clearly. This image, as any person's would be, was complex and self-contradictory; but it was also somehow coherent and human. Reclusiveness is not simply a neurosis, I knew, or a symptom of depression and retreat from the world. Great men and women had chosen to live that way, and that may have been what allowed them to be great. But this type of monastic existence was a riddle that held a powerful attraction for me and I felt as if I were standing before sacred ground, not daring to step inside the circle, as Dvora herself had quoted her dead mother: the place in which a person stands alone with the murmurs of their heart is holy, and no stranger must approach.

She began the conversation exactly where my own thoughts left off. Well then, we have come to the riddle, the essential question of my life according to public opinion, she said mockingly, Why I hide myself in my house. If I say it is because I have no interest in leaving the house— her voice rose and dipped in Talmudic singsong—no one would believe it. And if I say it is because I am ill, they would remain skeptical. Two strange women, Dvora and Tsipora, they think and shake their heads, I know. Fine, so that is the end of this discussion: I am an eccentric and bizarre woman.

You really are a unique person, I said, hoping she didn't really mean to end it there. And the long seclusion has certainly added to this aura. There are people who pass on the street and say: "The famous writer Dvora Baron lives on the third floor of this house. She hasn't crossed the threshold of her house for more than thirty years now, you know."

I have been unique from earliest childhood, she said with a rage I couldn't comprehend, for years before my seclusion, as you call it. I was unique within my family, my town, the city. What other little girl studied Talmud with her father, daring to make legal decisions when he was absent? What other young woman, having lost her faith, would go off to study gentile culture in a big city?

True, I admitted, and tried to steer us back to the topic; you were unique, and you knew it. But from that to your seclusion—

Do not worry, she said, like someone promising a candy to a child. I will explain the matter as best I can this evening. I dedicated myself to this question during the long years in which I did not leave my house, and talked about it with the closest of my visitors—a few of them were educated in psychology as well, she added with a smile—and I tried to arrive at a conclusion I could lay before you today. Never was anyone more prepared for the inquisitors, she said.

I leaned against the high back of my chair, listening.

The day on which I most felt the imperative of justifying myself was after Aharonovich's death, when I did not go to his funeral, she said in a restrained voice. Although his health was always impaired, he died very suddenly, sitting at my bedside. I, who was more gravely ill than he, survived; and he, the active, vigorous one, suddenly expired. That was in 1937, fourteen years after our resignation, she calculated, although it was clear to me that she was well prepared, as she said, for this conversation.

At the end of his life Aharonovich had involved himself more closely in literary matters again and had agreed to serve as president of the Hebrew Writers Union. He was also working on the business side of the literary journal *Libra*, in which he sometimes published a piece of his own. In the days before his death he came down with a bad cold, but he had already begun to rally. He was still at home and was reading Philo's

History, I recall. It was about a week before Passover. Suddenly, sitting on your very chair, he fell over. A heart attack. I had assumed I would go to the cemetery with the crowd that had gathered before our house on Maggid Street; but I descended three stairs—and turned back. I felt I was not going to be able to bear it, she said.

And I—the opposite, I said. When my husband died in his sleep, around a week before the Jewish New Year, also suddenly, I felt a powerful burst of energy, and even insisted that I be allowed to carry his body with the men.

She examined me and finally asked, How old were you then?

Forty-seven.

And I, she said, was forty-nine, nearly fifty, when he died. And she immediately continued, What an opportunity for the gossips! But I was more familiar with the phenomenon of reclusiveness than they, both from personal experience and from my reading and thinking about the issue.

Look, Amia, she said, as if she were finally getting to the heart of the matter. In actuality most poets, writers, composers, and philosophers— and to a lesser degree, painters and sculptors—spent much of their lives alone. You investigators of the soul say that man is a social animal who needs the company and affection of others from the cradle to the grave. You say that good relationships, especially love, are the sole or best source of happiness; but it is not that way, and even the Bible supports my position, she smiled, where it says: "And all you who seek the Lord shall go to the tabernacle which stands outside the camp," for no one can be alone with God—that is, be alone with the spirit of creation—unless they leave the clamor of community and find solitude. For someone of your generation, who will not count the Bible as an authority, one may find examples in the lives of great creative people, from Kant to Spinoza to Kafka. Many of them lived in voluntary isolation, had few close contacts with other people, and never had a family of their own.

What about Sartre and Simone de Beauvoir? Did she know about them? I snatched the thought, and then realized with a start, she is older than they. But she continued in a rush.

God did not distribute creative gifts among humans with the most lavish hand, she continued. Many envy the artist, and so artists are often reviled. But is it true that every artist is a little sick? Does freely chosen isolation bespeak misanthropy or failure in love? I see things differently. Not all great artists are emotionally disturbed, to use the language of your colleagues, just as not every person who is shut in their house is a miserable neurotic.

People differ. There are people, perhaps only a few, she said with pride, for whom freedom is a natural condition, who were born to freedom. Happiness and pleasure come to them through their work, whether they write, compose, or solve scientific problems. At times, happiness is nothing but the satisfaction of a good sentence on the page and the possibility that this sentence will somehow survive on the planet for a year or two after you have gone. The happiness of love, which all poets seek, what is that really?

After a moment of silence I realized that she was waiting for an answer. How can you answer a question like that? I thought, a little frightened. The feeling that I am not whole, I stammered, that I can fill in what is missing with a mate, who will become one with me—maybe only for a moment, during sex, maybe.

I feared her scorn, but she merely said, It was Plato who spoke about the myth of the primeval human, who was complete in itself, with four legs and four hands, male and female together. The gods punished this creature for its pride and split it in two, and since then each human being searches for its lost other half.

I nodded, touched at hearing Plato from her lips.

Let me say, she continued mockingly, that I never considered lust or sex any great honor to human beings, and certainly not a measure of health and happiness. Only a small-minded person would assume that happiness necessarily entails a successful sexual relationship. The wide road to happiness for the masses—just find the perfect mate. To my mind, Freud's theories have wrought great damage by equating man's desires with the animal within. Spirituality may bring an ecstatic sense of harmonic wholeness with the world—in my opinion, that is happiness—but one can achieve very little through satisfying physical needs.

Are you telling me, I asked boldly, that you never enjoyed sex?

In my generation people did not talk that way, she reproved me, but I will answer anyway. I have already forgotten whatever physical excitement I felt, naturally enough, in my youth. Today the entire subject seems absurd and overrated, aside from the commandment to be fruitful and multiply, which is the greatest commandment of all.

You also eat practically nothing and deny yourself sensual pleasures.

I enjoy music, a good book, a beautiful sight—but you say I am an ascetic. Perhaps I am; conquering one's impulses, the conquest of the flesh by the spirit, elevates humanity above the animal world, although many human beings live immeasurably worse than animals.

But there's something else about you, if you'll allow me to say it; you're not young, but I can still sense the provocative woman in you, the woman who attracts men.

Thank you very much, she said, with a deep, booming laugh. In my youth I stole men's hearts effortlessly. For years after that many of my visitors had a romantic interest in me. Among my closest friends the men far outnumbered the women, and when they surrounded my sofa in the darkened room, I often knew what was in their hearts. Later I understood that my behavior expressed intentions I never meant. I had no wish to accumulate admirers. True, at times I enjoyed the flirtatious talk and the caressing glances, but we never went beyond the imagination. I enjoyed talking about love, she said with a whimsicality that surprised me. When the mood took me, I loved to read love poetry, to hear gypsy romances. If my feet would have cooperated, I would have gone dancing from time to time, she said, waving her hand in a delicate rocking motion, and I didn't know if she was teasing me or expressing a hidden desire. But in reality I cut myself off from all physical pleasures without any great difficulty, she concluded.

Flirting—yes, and sex—no? I thought in confusion. Could this be the portrait she's painting now, when she's nearly seventy, and things looked different when she was younger? Or maybe the point was that she had to be in complete control of every situation? She spends her life on her sofa, the world revolves around her while she, the sun at the center of her universe, governs the path of the stars around her. But what is she really? A sick, malnourished, poor old woman, who hasn't left her bed for thirty years, I thought, my head spinning.

I just remembered that you translated *Madame Bovary*, which is all about sensual love.

True; but we were talking about seclusion.

I'm sorry I interrupted, I said, and waited for her to take the lead again.

The point is that what is called my seclusion is nothing like what we imagine by a withdrawal from society. After we left the *Young Worker*, I felt a great deal of rage at the community in Palestine and had no interest in socializing. Mourning Benjamin, worrying about Tsipora, left me uninterested in parties and celebrations. That was how a style of living gradually formed, in which I did not step foot outside my house, and inside I spent most of the time in my bed. But I did not withdraw from everyone; I did not seclude myself from human society. Tsipora was always with me. In her childhood I taught her for a few hours each day and directed her reading and schoolwork. As she grew, her life and my own life and work became bound together. As soon as Tsipora began to decide things for herself she became the buyer, cook, and nutritionist of the house, as she became editor, typist, and agent for my stories. When I felt bad and after my eyesight failed, I would dictate to her and rely onher proofreading. Thus she came into contact with the world in my stead, she said thoughtfully.

And Yosef, too, she continued, when he was alive, for more than ten years after our resignation, was obviously part of my world. Although he often traveled, he would talk about what was happening, and through him I lived in the outside world as much as I desired. Aside from them there were family friends, who faithfully visited from the city, kibbutz, or the communal farms, and just ordinary people who would come to the house in the course of their activities. Nearly every day between six o'clock and eight o'clock p.m. we had visitors in the house. But these became fewer and fewer in the course of time, she added in a different voice and stopped.

I hear that you turn away many people who would like to see you.

True, I have grown tired. There are people I would rather not see me in my present state, and others who would disturb my peace of mind. There are people I consider my friends, like Shoffman, whom I have never met face-to-face, and obviously many of my good friends are no longer among the living, she added. In the last few years I have sometimes felt lonely and abandoned. Yes, she said, even I, who chose this way of life for myself. There is nothing to be done then but to go to the window and look out at the bustling world or to ask my neighbor Leah to bring over Dan, her little son, she smiled sadly. Nothing banishes the darkness like the smile of a child.

But I am opposed to the notion, she repeated forcefully, of regarding a person who lives apart from the crowd of events and people as more unhappy than someone deeply engaged with it. Moreover, whoever wishes to do creative work cannot live in the heart of the crowd. A human being, I believe, has two impulses: to descend into oneself, communing with one's thoughts; and to break out of oneself to the outside world. I have always felt these two impulses simultaneously, and have known that dedicating myself to one path would entail giving up the second. In my youth and during my first years in Palestine I was more actively involved in the affairs of other people, and as I grew older I found myself more and more drawn into myself, shrinking from the tumult outside.

Do you know that Jung also talks about introversion and extroversion as two complementary aspects of the human psyche, I asked. He even says that in the second half of life there's often a transition from one to the other, usually from outside in and from body to the spirit. He explains somewhere else that human development is a journey from imbalance to balance, between the contradictory poles of the personality. For him that's what the circle, the mandala, symbolized.

Dvora looked at me without interest, although also without mockery, and said, I have not reached any balance, I have just chosen one pole over another.

But you said that you keep in touch with your friends and take an interest in what's happening around you.

So be it, she said, and again I felt that I had disturbed the flow of her thought. Maybe this meeting is especially difficult for her, I thought, which is why she's so sensitive about interruptions. So are you satisfied? she challenged me suddenly.

Satisfied with what?

Satisfied with the explanation for what people call my reclusiveness, she jeered.

I decided to take up her challenge and shook my head no.

I was gratified to see a pleased expression spread over Dvora's face. Neither am I, she smiled and then sighed, let us try again.

Most people are sociable throughout their lives, she said, but in my experience there are unusual or adverse conditions that may effect an individual's development. A trauma, for instance, can result in an inability to live with others. These people may became reclusive and develop the capacity for listening to the imagination and the fountain of creativity God gave them. Then writing, art, certainly science as well, may take the place of family or love. I believe that creativity is bought through suffering and self-denial, and that artistic inspiration will not easily visit a life of luxury and joy. But it is nonsense to say that one is a substitute for the other.

What's one and what's the other? I asked. This is how she studied Talmud with her father, I thought, and how she taught Tsipora.

Love and creativity, she answered patiently, the forces that are central to the human soul. One person desires love, connection with others, and the second, freedom and the courage to explore the depths of the spirit. Psychology, she said carefully as if she were trying not to hurt my feelings, deals only with love and sex and gives no honor, nor even place, to the freedom of the human spirit.

She seemed to expand and soar as she spoke, like the bird she had mentioned at the previous meeting. I do not wish to overestimate my worth, she said, but some people contribute to the spiritual wealth of the world—and not much to people around them. Apparently, I belong to this group. I have spent my life exploring myself and people I once knew, descending to the roots of this reality. These things are done in private, like prayer and meditation. The important moments in my life were those in which I arrived at a new understanding and expression of what I saw in my mind's eye. I do not understand how one can do such work with people around.

Ordinary people tend to their needs, she continued proudly. As long as the sun shines its light on them each day and they have their vegetable spread on rye, they think that fate is treating them kindly. What else do they need? Love, you will undoubtedly say, but I think they lack inspiration.

I do not mean to denigrate love, she said after a few moments, during which I had been lost in my thoughts. Sometimes I think that a human soul is nothing more than the sum of its loves: the people and places it has encountered. That is why, when someone loses the person dearest to them, they feel as if their life has been drained of its significance. We might conclude that one's own meaning is bound up in the beloved other, she said, lost in thought.

What are you thinking about? I asked, although I knew.

About my brother, Benjamin, she said without hesitation. When he died my life lost its luster. And my father. I loved those two more than anything, for only they knew how to illuminate the darkness of my life. For years not a night went by that I did not dream of my father, and, even after ten years, the news of my Benjamin's premature death retained its devastating power. Many times I would hear something, read something, encounter some difficulty, and immediately think, What would Benjamin say about that? What would he do in my place?

When I had the breakdown that was caused by my mourning, she continued, I found that solitude held more consolation for me than the company of other people. Everyone knows that mourning customs differ among different peoples. Jews mourn by removing themselves from the ordinary habits of daily life, although there is no suggestion that complete isolation is recommended. For me isolation was necessary and urgent, even during the mourning period for my father, and later for Yosef, and especially for Benjamin. I did not have the opportunity to sit for the ritual seven days of mourning or to light memorial candles, and there was no grave to fling myself on, she said in a stricken voice. And then the stories reached me about the destruction of our town, and finally the destruction of all the Jews of Europe.

In their attempts to persuade me to leave my house, her words were distant, some of my friends said that I had transformed mourning into a way of life. Perhaps they were correct; but they did not know how much I mourned. There was some respite in silence, in peace, in internal reflection. As if there were some journey that I must travel now that I have been left alone, until I arrived at the solution to the loss, to how I could find my place here in the absence of those I loved.

It is like prayer, she said as if speaking to herself, not to God, which is the business of the collective; but rather, a way of bringing one face-to-face with oneself, with the wise woman inside, to use your words.

I was glad she remembered.

If prayer has any purpose, she said, I no longer believe that it is because it elicits the help of God in heaven but rather that it brings internal harmony, the desire of a grieving heart. Silence also helps pain, she added, the silence in which one listens with no need to find answers, the peace in which to dream. The silence of one who lies in bed, she continued as if she were still dreaming, without making the slightest effort to move a muscle, liberating one's thoughts and emotions to wander in inner space, to encounter new and better images of world. These are the teachings of the Christian monks, and we Jews have something to learn from them.

I tried to summarize my thoughts while her silence lengthened. So after a loss people draw peace from isolation and silence, because a new inner world is created in this peace, like a new life story arising in the imagination from the ashes of the old one?

Something like that. You remember, she said with an effort, that you once asked me why I told stories about Chana, the little girl who was like me, the daughter of a small-town rabbi, except that she lost her father when she was very young, at ten or eleven years of age—as opposed to what happened in my own life. Creation is outside time, and even in our own lives time may break loose and twist sideways or backward. I wished to put orphanhood at the center of my stories, at their beginning, with all other losses radiating from it or under its shadow. Do you understand?

But it is not so simple as all that, she continued with a sigh. Loss alone does not transform a person into a writer.

You need talent for that; but certainly you've heard, I said, that a therapist sometimes suggests that their client express some distress creatively—by keeping a journal or writing letters, drawing or sculpting, whatever suits them.

Therapist-client, she said; those words are not in my vocabulary. If someone is an artist, loss will increase their need to create. And then, if they overcome their sorrow and complete some creation, it will become a healing power, coming in place of what was lost. When one changes the world in the imagination, she continued hesitantly, something may be felt to change in the external world too. Creative work can overcome our insignificance in the face of destiny, perhaps even raise the dead. This is what is meant by *Tikkun Olam*, the mending of the world. Do you understand?

I nodded, although I was not sure I was following her completely.

The important thing is that all this occurs within oneself, and for that one needs isolation.

So there are a few factors in recovery, I boldly attempted to rephrase her words. The creative expression of pain is first, and that draws others into the sorrow, faceless, nameless others—an anonymous audience. Along with this goes the sense of reviving what has been lost, and then, if one's creation merits attention, that too can help alleviate the pain. All this reminds me of a story I once heard about Felix Mendelssohn, the composer.

Dvora turned her gaze to me expectantly, while I tried to draw forth the story from the recesses of my memory. In fact it's somewhat like your story, I said, grateful at the miraculous workings of memory, which had provided the details just when I needed them. They say that Mendelssohn had a sister who was slightly older than he was, also a musician, and he was bound to her heart and soul. Although he was married, everyone knew that it was his sister who came first. She died one fine day at the age of forty, apparently from a brain hemorrhage. Mendelssohn fainted when he was told, and he never recovered from the blow. Shortly after his sister's death he traveled to Switzerland, and there he composed a powerfully emotional quartet, a kind of memorial to his sister, which is considered unequalled in all of chamber music. There were those who said that this was a turning point in his work, but he did not live long enough to develop the new insights since he died a few months after his sister, in similar circumstances.

And I have sometimes thought, Dvora said, that the stomach ailment that has plagued me for decades now is nothing more than the echo of the typhoid from which Benjamin died; even if they are only imaginary pains, the suffering of the mind can be greater than that of the body.

And a moment later she continued: That is a beautiful story about Mendelssohn. It helps one understand how artists seize their pain. Perhaps they are frightened to recover from such mourning, since healing holds the danger that their creativity may run dry. But there is also the notion of cosmic repair—the recognition of an order that grants meaning to loss. The goal of isolation is knowledge, the knowledge that life and death are only two aspects of the same order, just as winter and summer, destruction and rebirth are waves, advancing and retreating from the shore.

So in your long isolation, you have come to terms with destiny? I asked.

At times, she sighed. But I have my weaknesses. Sometimes I plunge into self-pity, railing against the cruelty of fate, longing for a world where the good does not always drag the bad behind it. And you, have you achieved some acceptance of your husband's death?

I don't know, I evaded her question. That's not the kind of question I'm used to dealing with, I added; and she tactfully dropped the subject.

She too had grown tired, apparently, and her eyes were practically shut. Come tomorrow morning, she continued, as if she were in charge of my time, and we will continue.

For a moment I considered protesting that I had other plans and that

I needed some space between one plunge and the next; but something in her fragile figure beneath the blanket made me promise to come the next morning.

I phoned home from my friend's house in North Tel Aviv, explained my absence, and asked them to cancel tomorrow morning's appointments. This was the climax of our story and it was impossible to stop now, although Dvora had been too weak to continue that evening, I explained to my daughter, apologizing for the difficulties I was causing because of the demands of my work.

nineteenth encounter

It rained furiously all that night in Tel Aviv. I tossed and turned restlessly on the hard sofa in my friend's living room, and woke in the morning feeling troubled and heavy.

I did not sleep a wink last night, Dvora greeted me when I arrived at her house an hour later. I do not generally see people at this hour, when I am not myself.

But she was already on the sofa, hair combed and gathered at the neck, long dress covering her body. The curtains prevented the gray morning from brightening the room, and the corner lamp burned instead. Nothing changes here, I thought in amazement.

I also barely slept, I answered.

Dvora smiled affectionately. Troubles? she asked.

My brain is teeming, I answered. Things do change somewhat, I thought. Here we are, communicating in telegraphic morning style, which we'd never done before.

We were quiet, allowing our energy to recharge. Tsipora entered, dressed as usual in her brown sweater, with the white socks peeking out over the tops of her boots. Do these two ever change clothes? I wondered.

Tsiporaleh, prepare a strong cup of coffee for our guest.

Gratefully I asked, And you?

I had two cups of tea and a piece of toast before you arrived, she answered.

We sat in silence. The steaming coffee was served, with a slice of toast and jam. Warm smiles passed among us, enveloping Tsipora as she came in. The merry sound of children on their way to the school at the end of the street could be heard through the closed window, punctuated by the rhythm of a ball bouncing against the sidewalk. Where is Eliav now? I worried. Had he managed to get ready for school without me and did he remember his sandwich, the key—

Quiet, quiet, I calmed myself by taking measured breaths, sipping the hot coffee. Some modesty, please, the familiar internal dialogue continued, you can't be everywhere at once, and the world will keep spinning even without your constant supervision.

I thought about Kafka last night, Dvora said in her lovely voice, and immediately all reality outside the room vanished.

And I thought about you.

What were you thinking?

No, tell me about Kafka first.

And then you will tell? she asked like a little girl.

I promised.

Kafka's letters to the women in his life always attracted me as much as his stories, she began. He was unable to live with a woman, and directed all his love from afar. In one letter to his beloved he wrote something like this: "You once said that you would like to sit at my side while I wrote. If you were to do that, I could not write at all." And then he continues in these words, which are etched in my memory: "A person can never be alone enough when he writes, there can never be enough stillness when he writes, and the night—can never be black enough."

When I read his letters, I understood that he had been frightened of love all his life, love that would be realized in a shared life. He felt it as a threat to his sole possession: the slender thread that connected the parts colliding and struggling within him. Without writing it was clear to him that nothing could protect him from madness, from the abyss. And so, the person Kafka needed most was also the one who most frightened him.

And why were you thinking about him last night?

Let us not rush to easy comparisons, she said, and in any case he was an infinitely greater writer than I. But there you have a sick and isolated man, and a great artist at the same time. And you, it is your turn. What were your thoughts last night?

I was thinking that maybe mourning in your life was an incentive for isolation and creativity, even though it's clear that you've always been both sensitive and talented, and didn't suffer great or overwhelming losses early in life, as some other artists we know. But where did you find the ability to be alone for so many years? I couldn't bear it, even for a week or two. Maybe that's why the whole thing is so fascinating to me.

Have you ever tried it? she asked.

No, I always had children, a husband, work. Once I traveled to Greece for two weeks, but even there I was with a group of women. Maybe in the future, when no one depends on me any longer, I'll go off to an ashram in India or get myself a single room in the Eitanim Psychiatric Hospital in the mountains of Jerusalem, where a few of my friends work.

She didn't seem to get my joke about a mental hospital as refuge. If so, then how do you know you could not bear it? she asked.

I just thought about the times when my house is full of guests, I said to her, without knowing whether my association was at all relevant, even if I love them all, even when my older children come home for a visit.

And what about that? she asked, when I stopped.

I get this feeling of relief when they all go back to their own lives. I dump the butts out of the ashtray, air out the blankets, scrub the bathroom. Slowly, after their footsteps and smells have disappeared along with the notes of the music they play, the house, my private world, comes back into its own, like a circle closing on itself again. Only my little son doesn't bother me. Even when he brings his friends to the house or roughhouses with his dog, he doesn't break my imaginary circle. Someone can touch the circle—but never enter. They can come in sometimes, very rarely, I corrected myself—but only at my invitation. And if someone breaks through—it hurts, it bothers me, it demands to be repaired.

You see? You also have the tendency to close in on yourself. And I too enjoy the company of children. Sometimes the neighbor's or housekeeper's children would come to me even in my gloomiest day, and then light would penetrate the darkness. Sometimes I felt I was frightening them—a black woman on a sofa—but I always found some way of entertaining them.

And Tsipora? I asked.

Tsipora, she considered, no, I have never felt her disturb that circle about which you spoke, the holy of holies that must not be touched. Perhaps because she remained a child, she said slowly, perhaps that is why I never allowed her to become an adult.

When I did not respond she said as if to herself, I turned her into my shadow; but what sort of life could she expect in her condition?

I don't know, I said, but it's obvious that the two of you love each other very much.

Dvora turned her face toward me and smiled gratefully, although clearly she did not see the matter as closed with that.

So we have agreed that I did not entirely withdraw from human society, she said, but only exercised the right to choose with whom and when I would socialize. And once a person starts down such a path, it may not occur to them that they could end up chained to their house for over thirty years.

Just a minute, I continued. You asked me to tell you what I was thinking last night. Two ideas crossed my mind, and I wanted to hear what you think of them.

Dvora listened seriously, without the scorn I usually perceived on her face when I slid into psychology.

The first idea was that only some people have the talent for being alone, which is crucial for the development of creativity. And people with healthy experiences in their childhood, who trust their parents and family, may have an easier time being alone and can develop the desire for it. The determining factor in this regard is if an infant or young child experiences the conditions in which to "be alone in the presence of the mother." That is the only way a person learns to listen to their inner world.

Dvora nodded her head vigorously. Thus far psychology passes the test, she announced. Indeed I had the advantage of such conditions in my childhood. You remember, I told you how my childhood bed stood across a thin wooden partition from my parents, and their presence was very palpable. While I was still an infant I would play in the kitchen while my mother and older sister did housework, or I would hide in a corner of the community house while my father dealt with community affairs. And at night I often overheard my parents' conversations. They were always close by me.

It's the same in therapy, I explained. Often the therapist says very little while the client proceeds with the journey into oneself, as if alone but with the support of a sympathetic presence in the room.

And perhaps that is why I was able to bring up the story of my life before you, she said as if struck by a new discovery.

Although I'm not your therapist any more than you're mine, I protested. Even so, the idea pleases me—being alone in the presence of someone who feels for you, as we do for each other. It reminds me of winter nights in Jerusalem, when I would fall asleep tucked into my warm bed while my husband was still sitting in the study. In the stillness of the house I would hear the night noises, hints of his proximity: soothing classical music, rustling pages, a spoon clinking in a mug of tea, a mild cough, the rattle of a typewriter. It was especially pleasant on those nights he was most distant, most absorbed in his own world. When I thought about it, it seemed to me that I was remembering nights from my early childhood, when I lay in my crib and heard my father, returning a book to the shelf, or my mother, finishing up the dishes in the kitchen. They were not involved with me, but their presence infused me with a sense of security.

Dvora smiled tenderly. These days it is Tsipora who is always present at my side, moving around the house with her light step and making me feel safe. There is no voice more soothing, more soporific, than the rattle of her typewriter in the next room.

Now listen to the second of my night thoughts, I continued. Take a slightly older child—let us say five years old—who begins to encounter the demands of its parents and environment, for instance, upon entering school. Such children may feel that many expectations have been placed on them to behave properly, so they can be their parents' good little boy or girl. Families can be very demanding; children who are interested in keeping their parent's love may try very hard to behave accordingly. In this way, a gap gradually builds between the true "I" of the child, which remains inside, and the public "I," the false one, who is worthy of praise.

Depression is the result, I concluded, with utter bluntness.

That is the word you have been avoiding these many months, have you not? she asked in a whisper. As a doctor refuses to present a sick person with the name of their malignant disease.

Not true, I insisted. Why would that word be forbidden? How is depression so different from sorrow? Some degree of despair and depression exists in everyone's life, and each of us responds to life's blows in our own way. It is true that depression could explain the unwillingness to get out of bed, the lack of appetite, and the various physical ailments; but I do not see you as a depressive, since I always found your words alert and fluent and I sensed that you also took an interest in me. Believe me, I am not trying to put you in any medical category.

And you would not succeed if you were to try, she said. I have experienced deep despair, but without losing interest in life. On the contrary; I would consider someone sick if they did not feel despair in the face of what I have undergone in my life.

True, I said, hurrying to leave the danger zone before Dvora banished me from her magic realm. But the same split also leads to a desire to be alone, I continued, in order to find expression of the true self. And perhaps this hidden self is better expressed through creative work than through contact with people. Such a person might be drawn to describing relationships in literary form, which would constitute an involvement with human beings without necessitating any direct contact. I thought, I concluded hesitantly, that you might find some of these ideas useful.

Let me think about them.

We sat in silence for a few moments, alone, I couldn't help thinking, in the presence of another.

This split, Dvora said from within a supreme effort at focusing, has its roots in the fact that I was born a daughter and not a son. My parents expected another boy, like Benjamin, and although they loved me and gave me everything they could I always felt wounded and ashamed of being a girl. This was brought home to me, in fact, each day Benjamin went off to learn in the study hall and I was left alone; when the boys played wildly on the slope above the synagogue, and for us, the girls, there were rag dolls. I wanted to be with the boys in their games, in the synagogue, and the study hall, she said with fury, and instead they wanted to turn me into a little fool, who would stand in front of the kitchen stove and rock the cradle when the baby cried, and nothing more. Fortunately, my parents soon understood that I was no less intelligent than Benjamin, and my desire to learn was as powerful as his. The harder the books my father brought me, the more I surprised him with my progress, and eventually I was granted a partial exemption from helping my mother and sisters with the housework, and became a study hall girl, called upon to perform what I had learned before the guests: some strange hybrid creature. But I always sensed that I have been granted an education by charity, not by right. I was never one of the boys, but was always looking at them from behind the partition of the women's section. Sometimes I did not know if I were a girl or a boy and what it was I should be striving for, she said bitterly. I did not know a single woman on whom I could model my own character. The closest I could come was a female Benjamin.

So, I continued, maybe you felt in some way that only when you were alone could you be yourself, without the need to justify yourself or answer to anyone's requirements.

Perhaps, she said. Being the wife of an activist in Palestine was even further from my nature than being the rabbi's daughter in a small town, she added with a smile. I would escape to our house from the tumult of the editorial office, from the workers' arguments, far from anyone's eyes, in order to be alone. And today my inner self finds no place in the noisy Israeli city. The inner I has no part in all this, she said, searching for the proper words. At first it was free will, and in the course of the years, force of habit. I only see a narrow strip through my window, through those who continue to visit; and that is me, the reflection of that small world, and alongside it the old world of memories. Small and large simultaneously, she corrected herself, since it is possible to see the whole universe in a drop of water.

One morning when the tide was low, I suddenly remembered, I went down to Jaffa beach with a friend and we sat on a rock, it was like a long, low cliff stretching parallel to the shoreline, and stared at a small hole, really just a crack in the rock. We could see the water inside it rolling in miniature waves, a crab scuttling after its prey, and tiny fish flitting from one end to another. I stuck a finger into the little pool, and the motion of the water changed, circles after circles forming around my finger. The mighty ocean with all its power, its creatures, in the cleft of this rock.

That is I, Dvora Baron, she echoed my words, this house, closed off from the outside world, the sofa in the darkened living room, my old dresses, the books on the shelves, the words on the page—those are me; and outside—the noise, the progress, the light, the great strangeness, I could not be like that.

As we sat in silence, a bird chirped outside the window, a desperate, shrill whistle, like a mother warning her nestlings of some danger.

I can still see that same dear friend before my eyes, I said, trying again to break into the thread of her thoughts. I don't know what makes me think of him, but I feel as if he were sitting here with the two of us. He lives alone. At about forty, he began to feel very sad and restless, after a long period of working closely with other people. He wasn't running away from any particular trouble, except for the obvious difficulties he had in finding time for himself, to read a book or listen to the music he loved so much. And while we all resign ourselves to such situations, my friend understood that he would have to leave the rat race behind before it was too late. He strapped a knapsack on his back, said goodbye to everyone, and went off for a few months to be alone in the wilderness. What was he looking for? Some peace and quiet, he said, nothing more. I just want to experience this completely, being alone, he said, to experience solitude and quiet for long enough to know what they taste like.

Like Elijah the Prophet, she said, so softly I could barely hear her.

For a few months he lived alone at a wildlife observation station. In one of his letters he wrote to me:

Today I went for my daily walk at dusk. As usual I listened to the stillness. The day was nearly over, and night was about to be born in great tranquility. Here I have felt the tremendous natural forces that work in silence. In the night sky I saw the movements of the cosmos. In this cosmic harmony my private despair shrank to a tiny grain and finally disappeared. Death seems close, so close I can touch it, and if it were to beckon, I would sink into its arms without a struggle, knowing that when the sun rose I would be born again as a snake, a butterfly, a star—what did it matter?

When he finally returned from the desert at the end of the winter, he was someone else. I settled into my own self, he explained, and it revived me.

You love him, she said simply.

We were silent again. The winter sun emerged from behind a cloud, and made its way through the drawn curtain, touching the room with a warm gold. The rain had stopped.

One must choose quiet and tranquility, and not have loneliness forced upon you, Dvora continued, drawing together the vanished threads again. In my seclusion and sickness I unintentionally found myself free from the daily worries about food, clothing, or money. As I learned to make do with little food and drink and distanced myself from people who disturbed my peace, I sometimes felt that I had passed from the physical to a spiritual plane, until I could carry on a conversation with the cosmos, with life and death, in my room, even if I were utterly alone.

You see, she continued to explain, my illness and revulsion with public life forced me to shut my doors against the multitudes. I did not know where it would lead, but once it had been accomplished, my solitude brought illumination, something similar to what happens to a nun when once she enters the abbey.

Like your friend in the desert, I loved tranquility and clung to it as best I could. In the long days, when not a living soul came to visit, I sometimes descended—or perhaps ascended—to hidden worlds. Sometimes, in the lengthening stillness, a person uncovers the perfect order that reigns in the universe and sees their own place within it. Now that I have grown old, I often miss people. But who has no regrets? she added, and at least I had my moments of illumination in which these stories were born.

I made a mental note to listen to the tapes at home and think again about what she had said. And then she surprised me, as usual, with an unexpected transition:

But those moments never lasted long. I often say that life is like a *krupnik*, she laughed aloud, a Lithuanian stew of potatoes, groats, fat, water, salt, and more. A *krupnik* comes in a single dish and it is impossible to eat each ingredient separately. Thus, alongside the life of the spirit, daily worries managed to drag even me into their orbit. The neighbor from the floor above, Leah, came in to show me how her little son had begun to crawl, and together we worked up some gossip about the landlady, who was stingy with the heat. The doctor Manya Merari came to visit, and ranted at me for lying in bed. The time for porridge arrived, Fichman and Barash were at the door wanting to come in, while Tsipora was entering the living room with the tray. You call that seclusion? I was moved by her hearty laugh in the face of the unexpectedness of life.

But I still don't really fully understand your lifestyle, I said, living here in an apartment, distancing yourself from people and writing about them in stories.

I love people, she said whimsically, from afar and in small doses, like Kant, for example. Do you know about him? she asked.

Of course, but I know very little about his way of life, except for the fact that he never left the city he was born in.

Correct. He lived in Königsberg, the same city in which Benjamin studied medicine, and at the same university, only more than a hundred and fifty years earlier. He was a gentleman-bachelor, you might say, she said in an uncharacteristically light tone, as apparently are many of the professors at the great European universities.

I listened, transfixed.

He never had a sexual relationship with a woman, she continued, and told his friends that there was nothing worse in the world than the enslavement of one person to the will of another. In his philosophy he also championed complete independence, never concerned with what others thought about the problems on which he was working. He did not isolate himself from contact with others, he had friends, women and men, conversational partners whom he loved to lecture about his ideas; but he always lived alone, and no one became his intimate. They say that he did not see his sisters, who lived in the same city, for twenty-five years. But see here, she smiled, this eminent man who strove for a life free of all limitations, was very meticulous, to the smallest detail, about everything that touched his life. He would awaken each morning at exactly the same hour, eat his meals and go for his daily constitutional with such meticulousness that his neighbors could set their watches by his comings and goings. And more, he guarded his health religiously, had a horror of filth and contagion, kept his house at a fixed temperature, and abstained completely from coffee and tobacco. He lived in this way to the age of eighty and died in the best of health at a ripe old age, she laughed.

And why are you silent? she challenged me. It is clear that your brain is responding to the invited comparison. Are you thinking about Dvora Baron's hubris in supporting herself against such a large tree?

You got me, I laughed.

Reclusiveness has been occupying my mind for decades, and all my friends have brought me stories and books about great thinkers who displayed similar proclivities. I could tell you about Marcel Proust, about Beethoven, about Goya—each has some strange connection with my own story.

I would be happy to hear, I said. I remembered one of our early conversations, when she listed for me, like a living encyclopedia, all the dishes of her town and how they were prepared. I won't try to interpret your stories and I won't make any comparisons, I promised; I wouldn't dare.

I felt the satisfaction in her look, the sense of superiority at the very kernel of her being, beneath all the bodily infirmities. That was how a very special girl grew up in her father's house, I said to myself, a lofty tree of the female sex.

Here you have an eminent writer, composer, and artist. Each of them created from within physical weakness, apparently, but that only begins to explain the matter. Marcel Proust, very nearly my contemporary, was always in poor health and died in 1922. He remained in his apartment from the age of thirty-four, when his mother and father died. Alone in his room, he devoted himself solely to perfecting his masterpiece, *Remembrance of Things Past*—a treasure that exceeds all others in world literature.

They say that when Beethoven became deaf at the beginning of the nineteenth century, she continued, he suffered the agonies of hell. And indeed, how great must have been the pain of a man such as he, when he could no longer hear the melody of the flute, the song of the shepherds. He said to his brother that it was only his art that kept him from taking his own life. Because of his disability, he distanced himself from society and grew suspicious in dealing with people, but scholars say that with his deafness his artistry increased. Beethoven could try out new musical forms in his silent world, free of the distraction of noises from the surrounding world. His internal ear was not at all damaged. He worked, like Basya the embroiderer, from his head alone.

So too with the artist Goya, who lived around the same time as Beethoven. After he fell ill at the age of fifty and also went deaf, he stopped painting noblemen and their wives and chose to paint whatever he found in his imagination. He no longer attempted to win favor with his art. The paintings he did after that are full of imagination and invention, describing the depths of human anguish, the nightmares that tormented his sleep, the compassion for those who suffered, and his disgust with tyranny. He painted those harsh, wonderful paintings on the walls of his house, and he lived out the rest of his days surrounded only by them.

Slowly I saw them arrive and gather round, sitting with their backs to the white walls in their mantles and flowing locks—Kafka, Kant, Proust, Beethoven, Goya, each in his place, erect on his chair, mute witnesses to our conversation. There isn't a single woman among them, the thought flitted by, but I let it go, trying instead to hold on to the moment for a little longer.

I want to go home, I said suddenly, surprising myself. This was the first time, I thought, that I had ended our meeting. I hope you aren't angry, I hurriedly added. It's just that I want to get back to Jerusalem before my son gets home from school so I can be there to greet him.

So why are you crying? she asked—she, whose vision was so poor. Did I not tell you that ebb tide and high tide always follow upon each other's heels?

I don't know. I was thinking about solitude, the despair and suffering that lie in wait for my children, when I won't even be there to lift their spirits.

Think also about the happiness, she said softly, about beauty, about the joy of understanding.

I nodded my head and thought: I want to feel my son in my arms. Just that, and nothing more.

I left the house with hurried steps, as if escaping from some trap that had nearly swallowed me whole.

twentieth encounter

And how will you describe me in your book, now that I have bared my soul to you? she asked provocatively at the start of our next meeting, which took place once again in the afternoon. Will I be a good or bad woman in your book?

I'm quite a long way from a book yet.

You are avoiding my question, she stood her ground.

I don't think that you'll be either good or bad in my book, I said, after thinking for a minute or two.

How's that?

You know very well, I answered. Last night I saw an amazingly powerful film by a Polish director who was trying, I think, to create a series of films about the Ten Commandments. The one I saw last night was called *Thou Shalt Not Kill*. It was terrifying. The murder was presented very realistically, you could hear the victim pleading and his gurgling death throes, and then, at the end, they showed the young murderer being hanged. But what was so amazing was that none of the characters were either entirely good or completely evil. The murderer was a bloodthirsty villain, but he had a sister and mother he truly loved, and there was no way to reconcile his sadistic enjoyment in killing the taxi driver with his consideration for his mother and longing for his dead sister. When he talked with his defense attorney, whose first client he was, they were just like any two people talking. The victim, the taxi driver who had been viciously murdered, was no great saint; he enjoyed harassing his passengers. The prosecutor, the judge, the wardens, the hangman— they were all human, people I might share a table with at a café. After the film ended, late at night, I stood and thought about how the director had presented the many faces of each of his characters, confusing the audience with what it means to be human.

And that is what your readers will be left with if they try to understand me? she asked.

They may be confused, but I hope the picture they get won't be a superficial one, and that they'll feel you as a human being. Let me get a wheelchair, I changed the subject, and take you to the movies. How long has it been since you've seen a play or concert? Tsipora can come too, I urged.

I am sick and cannot go out, she said, like someone repeating a password, and I knew that I was getting nowhere.

So what should we talk about now? I asked.

We have already explored the primary events of my life, she answered; from here on, the bridge of time crumbles and we are in uncharted territory.

Do you want me to ask questions?

She was silent for so long that I thought she had fallen asleep. That was how my life continued: long, gloomy, and monotonous, she suddenly spoke.

Impossible, I said, we have to find a way to bring your next thirty years to life. Even without milestones, we'll find a way, I repeated.

Look, she said in a slightly stronger voice. Most lives have milestones: parents grow older and die, children are born, grow up, choose a profession, marry, grandchildren are born, one finds a new job, travels off somewhere and returns, falls ill and recovers. And with me? Time stood still. Tsipora is with me as in her childhood, my parents disappeared into the darkness of the Diaspora, and I persist: writing a little, reading a lot, looking out the window. Only one event crossed the wasteland of my life since my seclusion, which was Yosef's death; and we have already discussed that.

Do you want us to end your story here? I asked.

She shook her head no. I have become accustomed to your presence, she said.

And I have become accustomed to yours, I answered, touched. Let's continue, then. I will ask you questions and you try to remember. It's perfectly clear to me that there are many more stories in your sack. And in the meantime, if you will permit me, I'll make us some tea to have, with the delicious cookies I bought on the way here, all natural ingredients, and I'll think about where to lead us.

I walked lightly into the small kitchen and set the kettle to boil on the old stove, looking around again at the poverty that pervaded the house, which had not been painted for years, and at the dishes that were mottled with age. The porter's water bucket stood covered on the cracked marble countertop. Containers of Quaker Oats lined the cupboard shelves, potatoes rested on newspaper, and in the refrigerator—a bottle of milk and frightening emptiness. Apparently, it's been a while since anyone from the kibbutz has visited, I thought. There isn't enough here to feed two grown women.

My hands trembled as I poured the boiling water from the old aluminum kettle to a china pitcher they used to prepare tea. And what if I couldn't manage to draw Dvora out any longer? Had I reached the end of the road? Was this like the Thousand and One Nights? I wondered. Don't die, Dvora, for lack of stories.

I served the tea, raised Dvora up on her pillows, and sat across from her.

In therapy, I said, when the client is unable to think of anything to say, we sit quietly, and there's nothing wrong with that. The impasse, I call these points in the course of therapy. Don't worry, I say to whoever has reached it, stay with the silence until something occurs to you.

An impasse is essentially an opportunity. If we don't run from it into chatter or small talk, something worthwhile will emerge. Sometimes I even help by making the situation concrete: I ask the client to imagine standing before a high wall that blocks their way, as if it were actually in front of them, and then continue their imaginary trip however they want. What would they do? Take a rest in the shade of the wall and wait? Turn and go back the way they came? Find some way to break through? Destroy it in their rage? There are many possibilities before us.

Dvora sipped the tea, sucking a cube of sugar between her teeth, and then lay back again.

Perhaps we should begin with history, she suggested. Over the years,

I followed what was happening, and there were friends of mine who were amazed at how much I knew about various events. But was that so surprising? The paper came to the house every day, and I listened to the radio when I wished, from time to time. I have known how to draw my own conclusions since I was a little girl. I spent many days beside my windowsill, looking out at people and seeing how they were doing. But it was mostly the friends that continued to visit me who told me what was happening in Tel Aviv, in Israel, in the world.

From the window of my house I looked out at the neighborhood. I could see people joking and talking, and sometimes celebrating together, weaving their lives into a single tapestry. In the evenings each family withdrew into their lit rooms, and only I was left. I loved to hear the ringing cries of the children and the gratified laughter of their parents; but sometimes my solitude deeply embittered me. All that was left me was to turn to God, she said ironically, but I had, after all, abandoned him, and thus forfeited my right of complaint.

Many sights crossed my vision on the other side of the window: the families of the other tenants in the courtyard, their Yemenite help, their pets—I knew them all. Once the couple in the apartment across the way got into an argument, and the husband cruelly flung his wife's lap dog into the street. While she was still in the gutter, along came the cart of Moussa the dogcatcher down the street, and the little dog was swept along with the other pitiful creatures, who, being homeless, were viewed as a public nuisance. I watched helplessly, she said, imagining the woman running over to the cart on the next street, hearing her dog bark, and rescuing her from Moussa and certain death. Another time I heard on the radio about Rami, the boy who wandered away from his parents, and I spun out the descriptions of the emotional reunion. Sometimes I sweetened reality by the power of imagination, as a dream may be sweetened. Do you remember? she asked.

I nodded, and Dvora continued.

But there are stories that no one can sweeten. A few years after Yosef's death, the Second World War broke out. Again the way was blocked to my hometown, where I had at least the graves of my loved ones. And I, who had always sensed the abyss awaiting us and the catastrophe lurking at the door, could see the terror in all its horrifying dimensions. My heart told me that a heavy cloud had descended upon what remained of the town, and my life became loathsome to me. I breathed a little freer when the battles approached us here, when I saw the fear in every eye, the blackouts at night and the penetrating wails of the siren, foretelling doom. When the sirens blasted the streets emptied below, the courtyard writhed with movement, and the neighbors scurried in panic. From my window I could see the people who lived in the shacks around coming to hide in the basement of our building, and only I was left in my apartment, looking out the window at the street, my body alive with anticipating one of the shells the enemy was raining upon us.

Once bombs fell in the neighborhood, and from my window I saw trees with their tops shorn off, uprooted columns and the smoking skeletons of houses, and heard from afar the forlorn shrieks of the wounded. Sometimes it seemed to me that these people were my own flesh and blood, living in the shadow of an identical terror, shoulders bowed against the next blow.

Eventually, a secure shelter was erected in the neighborhood courtyard, and a nightly blackout decreed. In the moments of respite between the all-clear and the next air-raid alarm the courtyard would fill up with the peals of people clinging to life's joys; but with the next raid darkness spread over the city like a black tent, fear leaking through it like raindrops from a storm cloud. The sea moaned in the west, and a baby's wail sounded in the distance. During the bombings I alone remained, frozen at the windowsill. Tongues of fire flickered like lightning in a cloud, and the residents of the neighborhood crawled like shadows down the streets on their way to the public shelter. There, in the belly of the sealed-off building, strangers sat beside each other holding babies in their arms, draped with kerchiefs.

I listened to her lyrical words with mixed emotions, glad that she had been caught up again in the stream of her stories, yet saddened by their content. I was struck again by the precision of her descriptions, although it seemed to me that different wars were weaving themselves together in her memory into a single tapestry. Tel Aviv had only been bombed twice in the Second World War. Was she thinking of the War of Independence? Today, her stories seemed like pieces of shrapnel, fragments of old memory without any sense of context or chronology. Dvora continued, oblivious of my skepticism.

On the first floor lived a young family. The husband worked as a guard in one of the villages, and the wife was home with her infant. One night the father was killed while on duty, and the frail woman could not cope with the catastrophe. The neighbor women raised the child until an aunt came and took him to her village.

After that we no longer heard a word from occupied Europe. We lived as if a wall had been erected before us that obscured everything that happened behind it; when the wall was finally breached and the first reports came, they burst through in a hemorrhage. Whoever has undergone surgery must know the feeling of waking from under the cloud of ether to learn that some crucial part of the body had been removed, and from now on it would be necessary to carry on with the shell that remained.

Dvora was silent for a long time, her face twisted with pain.

Who can describe the enormity of the disaster? she answered. Some of my stories that were written after we learned of the Holocaust hint at it, and others describe the catastrophe as if it had taken place much earlier, during the pogroms at the turn of the century. A person who has lost all friends and family, a bereaved mother, an orphaned child—one can speak of these; but I could never paint the entire canvas. I only dealt directly with the Holocaust in a single story, she said.

I remember; it's called "As It Is."

That was one of the last stories I published, and some wanted to see it as my swan song.

Tell me, I begged.

It is based on an incident that happened to me. One day after the war Tsipora told me that a woman, clad entirely in gray, sat on a bench before our house and looked at her every time she came or went. She sat on the bench each day with folded hands, like someone who has finished their business in this world and has nothing more to do. Once, when Tsipora passed near her, she stood up, clapped her hands and cried out in a sobbing voice three times, "Woe is me!" The passersby stopped in their tracks, and some of them turned and called out with her.

I gazed at her through the window for many days. When the winter arrived, Tsipora approached the woman and asked her if she had eaten and why she was sitting there. The woman said, "I heard that there is someone who lives on this street whose father was the rabbi of our town, and whose mother was a great saint."

Are you looking for Dvora Baron? Tsipora asked.

She said she was, and that she was Basya, who had helped my mother with the housework after her husband was murdered in the pogroms. "I have something to say to Dvora," she said to Tsipora, and Tsipora brought her up immediately. You remember, Amia, she turned her head to me, she was the woman I told you about, whose heart prophesied evil all the days of her life, and who worried about her children to an extraordinary degree. I had already heard that her six children were shot before her eyes in front of their house.

Basya did not want to drink anything in our house, she continued, she just put her hands, blue with cold, on the heating pipe for a moment, came into the room, and stood before me, where I lay on the sofa. I recognized her, and she, apparently, recognized me—but she did not say a word about my illness or remark on how changed I must have seemed. Forty years had gone by since I had seen her last.

She spoke her piece hurriedly, as in the days when she was in a rush to get to work. She said that since the "children" were gone, it was proper that they be written in a book, so that those who were here and their offspring who would follow should know that once there were people like them.

It has already been done, I said, they have already been written.

"All of them?" She was suspicious.

All six, I said, and I listed them in order of age.

"And did you say that Chaya was the best?" she asked.

The best, the most wonderful of all, I swore.

"Ah!" she exclaimed, like someone who had finally achieved what she had been long striving for, and she turned to go with a firmer step.

Nevertheless, Dvora continued, after that I could hear sobbing in the still of the night—what the prophet describes as the bitter, forlorn cry of a mother mourning her children.

In the silence that followed the rhythmic sound of Dvora's breathing could be heard.

You know, I began, you have sometimes told me that your life has been a difficult one, and your stories attest to that. But certainly there were good times too, even after you secluded yourself, no? Why is it that the bad is so firmly fixed in our memory? Do you know?

I am not sure that it is that way with everyone. Do you see your life that way? she wondered.

Sometimes, I searched for a way to explain. A few months ago there was a party to celebrate my having completed a job, after I had worked at it for four years. My co-workers succeeded in making me feel wonderfully loved and appreciated until I was practically drunk with it. That night, as I was falling asleep, I thought that I should try to save the memory of that perfect day, so I could have it like some magic pill on the bad days that would certainly come. It seems to me that good things are quickly forgotten.

It is hard for me to remember a good day, Dvora said, after my childhood. The most I could tell you about are days free of pain, pleasant visits from friends, the laughter of a child next to me, or the warm sun coming into the room, motes of dust dancing in the rays.

Tell me about your friends.

That is somewhat hard for me, she said after some thought. I am not much of a gossip, and my friends were well-known people. Some of them are still alive, and others have passed away, but their families and friends safeguard their memories. But perhaps like Basya's children, it is better that they live in a book and be known for their good deeds. And immediately she continued, Eizik, that is, my good friend Yitzchak Brodny, was my right hand in everything I did, and his visits gave me greater joy than anything. He was as bursting with stories as a pomegranate and his jokes kept me in stitches and made me forget my troubles. The women who read to me would ask: "Have you heard any new ones from Brodny?" And I would repeat them, and they would enjoy them too.

Who was he? I asked. His name sounds familiar.

He was a soul brother to Yosef, and the two of them ran the Workers Bank together until Yosef died. Although they belonged to different parties, there was true friendship between those two. Yosef, who was not a man who wore his heart on his sleeve, seemed to open up for him. After his death Tsipora and I were left without any support in this world, until Brodny took it upon himself to visit us and take care of everything we needed in the house, as if it were his own. The Workers Bank decided to provide for our needs, pay our medical expenses, and even more: Brodny himself, along with some other clerks at the bank, made sure that doctors came to us on house calls. He sent good women who tended the house, took care of Tsipora's hospitalization whenever that was needed, made sure we had the special food we ate—for we would never allow most foods on our table. There was nothing Tsipora or I required that he did not make the most diligent efforts to procure. Sometimes I was afraid to mention that I wanted something, because it would immediately be magically produced, and I, who was clearly of no use to anyone, had no wish to be a bother to a person who shouldered the responsibility of an entire community.

I looked around at the modest apartment, the faded blankets. I remembered the sparse kitchen, the old clothes of the two women. Surely bank managers lived in vastly better conditions. How could she possibly feel that she lived in the lap of luxury?

This time I knew she would see me examining the room and read my thoughts.

My needs are few, she said curtly, nothing is lacking here.

I sensed her wounded dignity and the sincerity of her contentment with little. Although I had never thought of myself as a materialist, her asceticism was foreign to me. Again I thought of a nun conquering fleshly desires, a strange but appropriate figure by which to understand this proud rabbi's daughter, on whom poverty had not left its gritty mark. I remembered Tsipora's remarks about her mother sharing what little came her way with those who seemed to need it. I had never heard Dvora speak of that herself.

Only once, she said, remembering, did I truly feel that I was poor. But it was because I was enraged, she smiled.

What was that about? I asked.

It happened about two years ago, she said scornfully. Two tax collectors arrived at our door like a pair of executioners, and at their demand, I got out of bed and led them around the rooms to show them my riches. This bookshelf and that threadbare rug were sentenced to be confiscated. It is a miracle that my heart did not give out right then and there.

A loud, deep laugh rolled from her lips. Today it seems funny, but then it shook me to the bone; and when I heard that Brodny was abroad on business, I put out the alarm to Avraham Braudes, the secretary of the writers' union, to come rescue me. How infuriated I was! My royalties from the books were meager, and my pension from the Workers Bank all went for rent and to pay a cleaning woman. No one could understand how we managed on that, while I was homebound, for more than twenty years! And suddenly I was a fat catch for the income tax people. What did they want from me?

Today I can laugh about it, she said, but then I cried, and I do not often shed tears.

How did it all turn out?

Braudes went up to Jerusalem, had a talk with Speaker of the Parliament Yosef Shprinzak and Shkolnik, that is, Levi Eshkol, who would later be Prime Minister, and that was that. At least the gossip columnists never got hold of the story. Whatever Braudes did apparently worked, because the assessors never came back again to torment me.

In most cases it was Brodny who took care and still takes care of things, she continued, and he also sends his emissaries, kind souls, to help us out. One of these was Dr. Manya Merari, a young doctor who lived with us for a short while; and the second, Rivka Preuss, one of the clerks at the bank, continues to watch out for us until this day.

When did the doctor live in your house? I asked.

Just after Yosef's death. I have told you how ill I was, and the bitterness of my soul made it difficult to find the strength to recover from the blow. Apparently I aroused the concern of Brodny, and he found a young doctor who would live in our house and monitor my health. Manya had just finished her degree and there was no work in those days for young doctors. Her pioneer husband was wandering around Palestine, working in road construction and agricultural jobs, so Manya agreed to come live with us and hold the fort. At night she slept in our house, and during the day she worked for a few hours at the Hadassah Hospital nearby. When her husband came for a rest from his labors, he would share her room. Manya was a dear woman. Under her care I was filled with hope that my situation would improve, but it did not work out that way.

How was that? I asked.

She took charge of my meals and made sure that I ate more than I was accustomed to, and a greater variety. Each day she or her husband, Eliyahu, would go to one of the cow sheds in Sharona and bring back fresh milk, which bolstered my health. After a few months, when my strength had returned, Manya demanded that I get out of bed and walk around the house, and I obeyed. She treated me with respect, unlike many of her colleagues. Although she was younger than I by many years, I became her friend and relied on her wisdom. She never pried into my affairs and asked no questions that did not have some bearing on our relationship. Thus she succeeded in bringing back the blood to my veins, at least for a while. It was still possible then, she said wistfully.

I do not remember if it was a year or longer that Manya lived in this apartment. After she began working at the Beilinson Hospital and stopped living with us, she continued to visit a few times a week, until she found a position on a kibbutz and our ways parted. She was pregnant with her first child and it was difficult for her to come. I remember one visit. Manya was a happy young mother by then with an adored six-month-old son in her arms. I was the one who gave him his name—Ariel—but then she disappeared from my life. Another doctor, also a very nice woman, Dr. Einhorn, took care of Tsipora and me, and I went back to my bed and my old habits.

And since then no other helpers have lived here?

For short periods only, she said, trying to remember. I seemed to have recovered from the crisis, and Tsipora had also become stronger after the mourning period and gone back to taking care of household matters. Sometimes there was a woman to help Tsipora with the housework, and sometimes a housekeeper lived here, or even a couple—husband and wife. After that, when times were hard, we rented out the third room, she said, and had our share of troubles with the tenants; but I do not wish to speak about that, she forcefully concluded.

Tell me more about your friends, then, I asked.

Aside from Brodny, she continued, characteristically methodical, I had my writer friends, a core of people who visited regularly and brought the smell of the great world into our house. Like King Saul, I was sometimes visited by an evil spirit or weighed down by the sickness, and then I refused to see them; but that did not stop them from coming again. Eventually I learned that we illuminate the people who come into our world with our own light, and the qualities we see in them are nothing but our own reflections. If we can no longer see someone's charm, as had happened with a few of my friends, our own souls have become damaged. To what can we compare this matter, she chanted in Talmudic cadences. To the sun, who once looked over at the moon, whose light was diminishing, and the sun watched and wondered. But something like that could happen only if the sun itself had lost some of its light.

That's a nice parable, I said.

Of all my visitors I loved Yakov Rabinovitsh best, she said. He was older than I, but he immigrated to Palestine the same year I did, after two previous trips. I knew him since 1913. We were few in those days, and Rabinovitsh already knew the meaning of solitude then. Once he wrote to me: Dvora, do not be alone; start a family.

For some time Rabinovitsh was among the regular contributors to the *Young Worker*, and that was how our friendship was cemented. He was a unique person, she continued, a true friend to many of the writers in Palestine of all ages. He was a free bird in his spirit and in his thoughts.

He was a writer? I asked.

Yes, of course. A writer, an editor, and a translator, with an original perspective on everything, she said, the itinerant conscience of the settlement. He was a speaker, wandering from one place to another throughout the land. I know for a fact that Rabinovitsh knew the name of every child born in the settlements, and could even recite the names of the cows in the dairy sheds. He had nothing to call his own. Not a house and not a family, no possessions and no position. He lived until the end of his days in a rented room and managed on what little he received for his articles and books; but he never owed anyone a dime, and was beholden to no institution or party.

Is he no longer alive? I asked.

In 1948 he was run over by an automobile and died of his injuries, she answered curtly, and tears moistened her eyes.

And who were your other friends among the writers?

Leave me be, she said wearily; if I forget to mention one of them, I will be ungrateful to my benefactors. Yakov Fichman, David Shimoni, and Zrubavel were at my side for many years, in true friendship, and Menachem Poznanski and Avraham Braudes and Asher Barash never despaired of lifting my spirits. Even now you may find them in my house on a Friday or Saturday evening, although they are not the men they once were and their visits are infrequent.

And women friends?

Fewer, but there were some, she answered thoughtfully. In recent years I have befriended a few women, but in my youth in Palestine I had just one special friend: Rachel Katzenelson, whose husband later became the third president of Israel, Zalmen Shazar. She was extraordinarily talented, she wrote beautifully and longed with all her heart for creative work, but life did not permit it.

Why not? I asked.

How can I explain those days to you? she said. The life of the mind was suspect then. Intellectual and literary work were considered a force that kept people from productive labor, from a direct encounter with the world and with other people. We all lived in the shadow of this intellectual suppression, and those who did not shut themselves off from the spirit of the times could not justify for themselves the mental engagement required by creative work. A woman and mother found it even more difficult to dedicate herself to intellectual work than a man. At the very top of the social ladder stood the pioneer, and those of us who lived in the city and worked at jobs that did not dirty our fingernails felt the need to excuse ourselves for not standing behind a plow—even if we were tubercular or had malaria. No virtue could compete with the labor of bricklaying or pouring concrete, on a road or in a field. Only the guard, who defended the land of the pioneer, approached him in value, she added. I was often amazed at the value system by which we lived. If a person was kindhearted, they would coolly remark, "So-and-so is a good man," in the same tone one might use to discuss a woman, "So-and-so has nice eyes"; while for a pioneer who had come to rebuild the homeland and haul heavy stones, they would enthusiastically sing his praises. They did not understand that being a decent person was infinitely more difficult that carrying stones up a slope. To be a good person is an unceasing uphill battle.

And Rachel Katzenelson? I asked.

She was very sensitive to criticism, and even more so to apathy or scorn. If she could not participate in the physical labor and earn the halo of the pioneer, she would at least dedicate her energies to the public weal. And so she submerged her soul in the details of publishing the journal *The Working Woman* and organizing the women in the labor union, she said sorrowfully. She once wrote an intelligent article about me as well, if I may say so myself. I liked what Rachel said about the place of the Land of Israel in my writings; she understood that I had not fled to the Diaspora, but that for me the Diaspora was the landscape of my childhood, my first homeland. Writers may sometimes need other eyes to see their own reflections, as I need yours.

Dvora sank into thought, and finally continued: Rachel only rarely expressed her creative spark, and she shared the pain of conquering the heart, as was required in those days, only in her private diaries. Only a few of her friends understood the enormity of the sacrifice she had made.

But you were neither a pioneer nor a community activist, I said.

Which was why it seemed that I had chosen an easy way out, she said with a touch of bitterness, but I could not have been, with my poor health. We have already spoken of that, she said wearily.

But maybe it was exactly the opposite, I suddenly thought. Maybe you got sick precisely so you wouldn't be forced to conquer your heart?

And I said aloud, Who else visits?

A few relatives. Some of my eldest sister's children—especially Eliyahu, who has forged a close bond with Tsipora. I often felt irritated with my relatives when they visited, and they sensed it and came less frequently. My friends from the kibbutz and the collective farms also visit from time to time. They come with the pick of their produce in their bags, bringing the freshness of the field and the joy of people who live by the sweat of their brow. My friends from Deganya took it upon themselves to supply us with potatoes and dairy products, especially during the years of austerity right after the establishment of the State of Israel, and without their help we would have suffered the disgraces of hunger. But our friendship does not depend on that. I always loved to hear the stories of the pioneers, and although my place was not among those who settled the land, my heart was always with them.

I was quiet, thinking about the generation who had founded our society and were now gone, about the high price paid by those who were too frail to do physical labor in those hard conditions, and about the other kind of strength it took to say, "I am different, and that is my destiny."

But the joys of living and the events of the great world came to me not only through these visitors, Dvora continued; on the days I felt well, when I looked out at the street or courtyard, I participated from afar in people's lives. I shared the sorrows of the little children, walking to school, rucksack on their backs, holding their father's strong hand lest he abandon them. How those children tried to match their small steps to his great stride, as he hurried to turn them over to their fates and get to work on time. I saw how people no longer had to make do with very little, earning a living by the sweat of their brow as my generation had. I could see the lives of the families in the courtyard: the Yemenite housekeeper who came each morning to clean, flinging open the windows and hanging the rugs over the sill; husband off to the office, leather briefcase in his hand; the missus in her high-heeled shoes going to meet her lady friends in a café; the young household help, trading stories when they were left alone in the house.

Again I see a war, she said after a few moments, as if she were turning the pages of some internal photo album or maybe reminding me that despite her isolation she still took it upon herself to know what was happening.

That was the War of Independence, she said, not so very long ago. The whole country was one army. In the courtyard opposite our apartment lived a family, a widowed mother, a few of whose children had been drafted. We watched from the window, Tsipora and I, to see how they were getting on. The soldier daughter, Zehava, stood tall and splendid in her uniform. Her brother, who studied at the teachers' seminary, was drafted as well and saw active combat. And then, during the period of the most serious shellings, Zehava decided to make it official—marry her boyfriend—and asked for a day's leave for the wedding. Her brother was amazed: "Now, with the country in flames, when no one had a cent in their pocket?" But she, Zehava, stood her ground. When her mother asked me to have a word with the young girl, Zehava told me that her friend, who was such a sweet young man, just a regular soldier, had joined a demolition unit and stared death in the face every day. Only now, with his life in danger, had it become clear to her that she would not live, could not live, without him. She felt as if she had been sentenced to death, but the decree had been temporarily postponed so she could still breathe and see the trees and sky, she said, and that was why she must marry him immediately, come what may.

The courtyard was in a constant state of emergency in those days. Between the all-clear and air raid signals, the women snatched the laundry down and ran to get their kerosene rations. The children hoarded bullet shells and shrapnel from the Stens or the automatics, or played blackout with shrill cries: "Turn out the lights!" Sometimes in the middle of it all an airplane would swoop as if it were falling out of the sky, frightening the birds on the rooftops. The children would cry "It's ours"; but then the siren would wail and the courtyard would empty in a matter of seconds. From the entrance to the shelter the landlord's son would announce: "Twin-engine bombers." At that second the thunder would roar, the air would fill with the shriek of explosions and drumrolls and trumpets, and immediately after that the sound of a fire engine and the familiar noise of the firemen.

I, who was bedridden, did not go down to the shelter with the other neighbors. I trusted my soul to God, lying in bed like a bound ram, watching the glint of the sacrificial knife at my throat. Tsipora, who refused to leave me alone, sat at my side. And who was as ready to return their lives to the Creator the moment He claimed them as we? she smiled.

If one day there was a lull, we all relaxed, and the young people came to visit me. They talked about how now that we had a land to call our own, it was no longer a matter of murderers and victims, but rather a battle between two camps. And I, for my part, would say, A gentile is still a gentile, even here. They would protest, "Look, we answer them blow for blow."

And at the very height of it all, the wedding was held, Dvora said in her storyteller voice, and I listened eagerly.

The mother took some sugar and oil from her small stock, sifted flour by the door of the shed, and picked out raisins. The ceremony was to be held in the community house, and the mother baked a cake. The family crowded into the tiny kitchen and prepared canapes for the reception. The soldier son arrived from his base with a present for his sister—a hen he had discovered in a grove near the base. How happy the mother was, for she could cook up a consommé for the wedding meal. But the son could not bring himself to slaughter the starved and abandoned hen.

The day the ceremony was supposed to take place bombs rained steadily. In a street further north a woman was struck while beating her bedding on the balcony, and here, in the very next street, a high-rise apartment building was hit just as the tenants were about to descend into the shelter. Groans and cries broke from within the smoking walls, licked by flames, until it seemed that the building itself was screaming. People went about the rescue work with set faces. From my window I heard acquaintances meeting on the street, calling out supportive words to bolster each other's morale: "Things will be fine."

In our courtyard, just as they were about to bring the hen to the butcher to be slaughtered, they found a white egg underneath her. What a treasure, at a time like that. So that poor hen's life was saved not from compassion but by her own merit. I myself saw the son, a proud soldier of Israel who had fought gallantly on the battlefield, hide his face in a khakhi handkerchief and sob with gratitude. Perhaps through the merit of that rescue, she concluded, we were all saved from the bombs, and Zehava married her true love and lived happily ever after.

Dvora smiled at me as if to say: You see, I found another story for you.

Look at that, I said, with satisfaction. When a woman talks about the War of Independence, she mentions the bombs and the fear; but she also discusses chicken soup and baking a cake, and saving a hen's life.

And perhaps all that is nothing but a parable and its moral, she smiled her wise smile.

And what is the moral? I asked. Dvora shrugged and smiled triumphantly.

The moral? That the time has come for you to drive home and cook your children some soup, she said.

How long our visits have become recently! I said to myself, looking at the clock in the car as I edged out into the dark street. Dvora's stories keep us both from noticing the time.

twenty-first encounter

Tell me about the award, Dvora excitedly began our conversation the following week.

You remembered? I asked.

Of course, she said, what did you think? Do tell, Tsipora wants to hear too.

I thought you were completely absorbed in your own affairs, I said to myself; and if Tsipora really did care, she could have come to the ceremony. After all, it took place here in Tel Aviv, not far from the library she goes to.

But why am I keeping score with these two? I stopped myself. It was wonderful, really moving, I said, one of those days we talked about that you want as a keepsake against the bad times. The museum hall was full of flowers and packed with people, Haganah and Palmach fighters, veterans of the struggle against the British and the War of Independence. I love every one of them. Beside me sat my three children in their holiday best. My father and two sisters came, and the people I had written about came up on stage in turn and said marvelous things about my book. What more could a person ask for?

I share your joy, she said, smiling tenderly, and Tsipora nodded in agreement.

Is it impertinent of me to preen like this in front of them? I asked myself. How long had it been since Dvora had experienced this kind of gratification? But their faces showed nothing but happiness for me.

You see, I said to Dvora after Tsipora had left us alone, once you asked me if you were suffering from depression, and I answered that I disliked psychiatric diagnoses; anyway, I didn't see you fitting into any artificial category. This evening, I really saw your capacity to share in my happiness. That's the best proof that the word "depression" doesn't explain who you are or how you live.

Good, said Dvora, I am glad to hear that.

Here you are, Dvora continued, a beautiful young woman, accepting an award for your book—not your appearance or sex. That is as it should be. I, too, was happy to receive the Bialik Prize from the Tel Aviv municipality, doubly so: because I was the first woman to win such an award in our country, and because I received the award from a woman, the Honorable Shoshana Persitz, the first woman to head the Department of Education and Culture in this city. But all my life I felt ambivalent about the fact that God had made me a woman. However much I liked my appearance in my youth, enjoyed the sense that men were noticing and admiring me as a woman, it enraged me if they saw my work as women's writing, if they took me seriously only because I was then the sole woman writer among all those men. Even as a child I was revolted by the injustice women suffered, and I often wrote about it.

I hoped we would dedicate a conversation to that, actually, I said.

We are of one mind, she answered approvingly, and we can do that today—although the matter confuses me. My thinking about women cannot be separated from my thoughts on marriage and love, and along with that, the whole matter of the translation of *Madame Bovary.* How are we going to find our way through this maze?

Slowly but surely, I answered. We'll enter the jungle and find a trail as we always do. And we were worried that there were no more stories, I added.

Well, it seems there are. The world of women is something that has been much on my mind from first maturity until now. I protested most vociferously in my youth; during my adolescence, as you would say. In my stories I cried out along with the wounded woman, without understanding anything or considering the other participants in the human tragedy. As a girl who would never be the town rabbi, and probably neither a doctor nor a pioneer, the rage grew within me, and every day brought new justification for it. It seemed to me that the women of my town were beaten and oppressed by cruel husbands, who lusted after their

bodies and mistreated their children. That was the whole picture, she said
scornfully, the unripe vision of my youth. The fact that I did not find
true love among the men I met after leaving home, found no one who
could understand my divided world, stoked my rage.

Your divided world? I asked.

Certainly, she responded impatiently, on the one hand, I was a young
woman who longed for a mate who would fulfill her desires and also
protect her, and on the other hand, a student, a writer just starting out,
with a fiercely independent soul. No one understood as I wished them
to, she said bitterly, and I poured out stories about the women I remembered from the town well, the market square, the women's section of the
synagogue. Stories from my own experience. That would be the first, earliest chapter of the *Chronicles of Women According to Dvora Baron*—if
I had written such a thing, she smiled.

Later I immigrated to Palestine, married, gave birth, established
myself, and it seemed to me that I had been wrong in my first writings, and that it was possible for a woman to find her way among the
thorns. Perhaps Palestine would heal the wound of women's oppression,
I thought, along with my women friends on the collective settlements;
that was a good period between Yosef and me, a period of shared activity.
How distant it now seems! she sighed. Was that really me?

And so we arrive at the third chapter, she continued. A woman is dis-
illusioned, discovers she has been deceived, and ancient grievances are
rekindled. I could link this to my growing estrangement from Aharonovich, an activist in the great world, while I was forced into seclusion
with a sick young daughter and no help from anyone.

So you hated Yosef's activism, I said, watching her pursed lips, her
blazing eyes.

An activist is never home, she repeated emphatically. At mealtimes he
was lost in his own thoughts. The family Sabbath was not his Sabbath,
and family holidays were not his holidays. While the shoemaker who
lived next door celebrated Sabbath with song and cheer among his children, I sat alone with Tsipora in the desolate house, leafing through some
book. If Tsipora fell ill on some stormy winter night, it was I who had
to ask the neighbor woman to sit with her while I ran through the

puddles to get the doctor. True, Aharonovich was not off getting drunk in a brothel, he was sitting through endless political meetings with his comrades, trying with limited resources to build a new society; but if that was his life, I wondered, why did he need a house and family? Why did he not live in a garrett like a bachelor and eat his meals in a restaurant?

I sat silently, stunned by the force of her anger against a man who had been dead for decades. Dvora breathed deeply, gradually calming herself, and continued in a more even voice. So the days of rage began again, and the protest surged so powerfully that I had to leave one of my best stories unpublished lest it bear witness to my rage. Instead, I put my energy into translating *Madame Bovary*. Even in Palestine, I could see well enough that the problems of women had not found their resolution.

And what did you do about it? the question was on the tip of my tongue. Just literary protests? Translate someone else's masterpiece about the diseased relations of men and women?

But while I was trying to formulate the question, she turned to me and asked, provocatively: Are you enjoying this? And before I could respond, she continued, Never accept a simple formula, as the rest of your colleagues do—even if it is tempting. A person of my age knows that there are two sides to every coin. Is Emma Bovary a good woman or a bad one? Certainly she was not a wise woman, she concluded. True, women suffer, but men are not exempt from pain. I have thought about the fate of Emma's poor husband, of her daughter. And who is to blame, after all? Apparently it was ordained from above, long ago, and there must be some meaning in it. Who are we to protest?

Tell me about the women, I asked. I promise I won't look for neat interpretations.

There are so many stories, she answered. I can see the women as if dancing in a circle, young women and old women, beautiful and withered ones, with bent backs or tall of stature, passing before my eyes in a chain. If they could lend one another a hand, fate would be kinder to them. Dvora let her head sink back on the pillow and gazed at the ceiling as she spoke, and I knew that soon I would hear her storytelling voice, singing from deep within her.

Fradl was my favorite, she began, but we will return to her later. First, there are images of the women I knew in my youth. Here is the servant girl I saw beside the river, thinking of putting an end to her life. What a bitter life she led! Her father was dying, and in her mother's house there was no wood for heating; and she was growing old before her time with backbreaking toil. That was how I saw her as she considered throwing herself into the river, until a passerby, a young man with a black mustache, happened by the bridge, and cruel hope arose again. Then there was the old widow, forsaken and lonely. At night she plucked feathers in her son's house and during the day she rocked her grandson's cradle and mended sacks. On the Sabbath she would sit at the corner of the table, trembling with fear of her daughter-in-law. But how bitter it was when she was taken as a maid in an invalid's house and there—God help us— there was not even someone to make the blessing over wine for her. A third woman's boorish husband abused her whenever he came home. The poor woman would set the table with a cloth and the tastiest dishes for him and he, crass man, would shout: "Don't you know how to make anything else? Again you put the cigarette box on the small table? Lummox, whore, you don't work and you don't earn!" he would shout and beat her, beat her. The fourth—she plucked feathers and sorted beans to feed her hungry children—felt a sharp pain in her stomach, but ignored it because her frail husband was always lying in bed. "It's nothing to worry about, and anyway, how can I think of my own little aches while he is practically a corpse?" she said at the well, and the next day she died an agonizing death. And the fifth, a hunchbacked, consumptive little girl, who lived with her widowed mother and baby brother in a cellar. She would restrain her cough whenever Berele's mother came to visit— Berele was the baby her mother wet-nursed—until the poor tubercular girl could no longer control her cough, and because of that her mother lost her livelihood. And who bore the brunt of her rage if not her invalid daughter?

These are horror stories! I exclaimed, at a loss for words.

What can I say? she said bitterly. Why could the old woman not say the blessing herself? Why could the young woman not return her husband's blows? Why was there so little pleasure in the lives of these women? In my youth I found no refuge from pictures like these.

Always and everywhere I saw their suffering. Those who were not touched by poverty or illness or fear of being put out in the street suffered at the hands of their husbands. That was how marriage looked to me: sometimes a girl was married against her will to a man she did not desire; nevertheless, each day, when she brought in some dish from the kitchen, she would lift up her eyes to him, like someone clambering up from darkness into light, with some anticipation of a friendly face. But the man turned his gaze out the window, which was scrubbed clean, of course, toward the meadow. And this estrangement, this ignoring of her and her existence, grew between them, until she felt a closer bond with the cow, who turned to her with affection, than with her husband.

Under the best of circumstances the woman kept to the homestead for five or ten years, putting in shifts at her husband's service. She washed, knitted, and patched, devotedly straightened the crooked and smoothed the rough. She gathered wood for heat at construction sites, collected scraps from the edges of gardens as compost for the two vegetable beds in her courtyard, grew beans and turnips, and then thought up vegetable soups and compotes to make from them. She created ex nihilo. And when the man came home, he sat at the set table, sliced the bread with strong hands, and gulped the soup she served; and through the rising steam he shot her a glance, in which a spark of contentment or gratitude flickered, and that was her reward.

Then one day it happened and the whole thing went belly up: the quarrel broke out—at first restrained, for shame in front of the neighbors, and then shouting and roaring he showed her his fists. The children took shelter like chicks in a thunderstorm, and the father, in a mad rage, knowing he could hurt her that way, lashed out at them too, beating them mercilessly, until one of the neighbors took pity and brought them into their house. "What cure was there for a house with no love?" the neighbors said. It is a malignant disease, and those whom it strikes will never recover, she finished harshly.

I saw those women come into the community house with downcast eyes to get their divorce, because they wanted it or against their will, hopeless and ashamed in their distress, ready to relinquish their pride or their bodies for the sake of the children. How it moved me to see the barren women, who after ten years were given a divorce and cast aside like a rag no one wanted. Some could support themselves by some sort of trade with the help of the neighbors, but others fell into abject poverty, and on Sabbaths would stand alone at the entrance to the women's section, like beggars. But the husband—he married another in the wink of an eye—and then made her miserable, too.

The rich women were no better off than their poor sisters, she continued fluently. My mother had a friend, a real saint, whose husband was a rich and evil man. She walked through the rooms of her house with quivering footsteps, on her face an expression of permanent fear—a face that served as a target. Her husband did not beat her, but he flung at her the slings and arrows of his ridicule, playing the game with the greatest satisfaction. He would grasp her chin with a manicured hand and ask: "From whom had she inherited her grace, from her stub-nosed mother?" And because at that moment she believed she was not beautiful, she really became ugly. He brought her ready-made dresses and patent leather shoes with high heels and narrow toes from the capital and she would be squeezed into them as if they were stocks. Despite her torments, she grew fatter and fatter, until the dresses no longer fit. She filled out, Reyze the cook said, because she swallowed humiliation and scorn, like a sponge that absorbs liquid. Only the servants saw her silent tears. Upon his return from a long journey her husband brought something new to tighten around her body—a corset. She looked at it with lost eyes, Reyze said, who was called upon to tighten the laces, but she did his will even in that.

Here, in Palestine, the whole farce was repeated once more. I used to watch the couple across the way from my kitchen window. It was impossible to miss his lovely habits, how he boiled when a woman friend came to visit his wife or when she took a few moments to care for her houseplants. Once he threw his supper into her face, poor woman, the cutlets and plate together. In the morning, when he had left the house, the woman covered her face with her kerchief, sobbing soundlessly. Outside, at the vegetable cart or talking with the neighbors in the courtyard, she put on a happy face. At home, she hurried to fry or cut something, wiping a tear or two with a corner of her apron as she moved about the kitchen. At night, from time to time, the sound of shattering emerged from behind the closed shutters. Once, in the morning, a crushed plant, surrounded with shards of clay and clumps of moist soil, lay in the courtyard, and beside it the dog whined pitifully.

The goal was a peaceful house and children who were cared for, Dvora said in a hard voice, and for that a woman was prepared to pay any price; if she got a bit of affection from time to time, the sun had shined on her and erased all her troubles. And sex, which of course no one talked about in my youth, was no source of pleasure for a woman either. That was the way of the world, I understood soon enough: A woman was supposed to fulfill her obligation to her husband by giving him her body as well, if only in order to continue the family and the nation. It was a commandment, and she must fulfill it with purity, she said scornfully. Thus the modest daughters of Israel, who hide their light from public view, would walk through the alleys on their way to the ritual bath before the eyes of the curious. Everyone knew them by name and knew where they were going and why, a kerchief pulled low over their faces and eyes cast down. For behind them, had they not left a house in disorder, a goat waiting to be milked, hungry children crying for their supper, and an unperturbed husband, who turned to her only to satisfy his needs? They were moody men who did not pamper their households or speak soft words to them, and against him the heart swelled with rage. It was not their desire for a little lovemaking that propelled them, but only their master's command and the holy duty, inheritance of their mothers, the commandment of life itself. These were the women who raised clear-eyed sons, weaned them and fed them on suffering. The sons were washed not with water but in their mother's tears, she said as if declaiming a vision, and they were sated, in the absence of bread, on the sorrow of her love, which they absorbed like nectar of the gods.

All these are such powerless women, I commented, but certainly you knew other sorts, didn't you?

Certainly, Dvora said, but there is no escape from the simple fact: In the circle of women who dance before my eyes that is the common image. I knew few women who took destiny into their own hands, or who lived in love and friendship with their mates, as my parents did.

Most of all I admired the women who forged their own destinies, she continued. Fradl, whom I knew in my youth, was that way, and in my eyes she became a symbol for the heroism of a woman who finally becomes her own master. I have written her story and you certainly know it, she said, but when she saw my look, she continued and told it:

Fradl had lost both parents, but she had her own nice house up the alley. She was a tall, attractive woman, who married an educated boy—her aunt arranged the match—who had some sort of business that took him away from home most of the day. He was not a bad person, she said, he freely volunteered to teach poor children arithmetic. Nevertheless, in their spacious rooms, among their fine furniture, a frozen stillness reigned. Dressed in the finest city clothes, she walked through her rooms mute with grief. A pale light came in through the curtains, the silvery leaves of her plants spread a whitish splendor, and between the walls of the house there was a deep chill. Only the blackened, impoverished alley could warm Fradl's heart with the life it radiated.

When her husband arrived home, the two of them ate from glazed china that tinkled delicately, but the silence between them was unbroken and the husband would read a newspaper or one of his books during the meal. When supper was over, the woman would slip away to her embroidery or to sit on the bench by the house.

How well you describe the alienation that can overtake a marriage! I said.

And you are curious to know whether I experienced it myself, she continued to hear the words I hadn't spoken. Certainly, I, too, knew desolate days with Yosef, especially after we had returned from Egypt. He was not a bad man, but he spent most of the day outside the house and it was hard for me, she said mildly. But there the similarity between Fradl and me ends, she said; you could say, at least, that she was a stronger woman than I, she concluded without explaining.

Please, I begged, go on with Fradl's story.

"It is a matter of the heart," the women by the well said, "and the best thing is for them to part." You must know that there is only one way to fill the emptiness in the life of a couple, although there is no guarantee that it will succeed: the birth of a child. But Fradl's only son had died before he was a month old, and again she was left with her husband without a bridge that could connect them. Sickness, too, can sometimes draw a couple closer, Dvora added. When her husband fell ill, Fradl cared for him devotedly. She swept and scrubbed his room herself and raised or lowered the curtain as he asked, walked around in cloth slippers so she would not make a noise, looking in them as if she were floating in the air. When his strength began to return, she took a chair out to the garden where the vines shed some shade, and brought out a small ottoman so the man could eat his meals out there.

But instead of returning her kindness, he just recovered and left the house. He worked at his business day in, day out, and came to the community house for conversation, or went down to the junkyard and played chess for hours with his friend who had just come back from the Talmudic seminary, she said with sorrow. When he came home in the small hours of the night, words and sobs could be heard from within.

After a while Fradl lost her beauty, and her attempts at adorning herself with bright dresses did not win back her husband's heart. One night we found her in the courtyard, lying on the ground in a twisted heap, like a piece of laundry that had fallen from the line. How this fine woman degraded herself for that man! It was hard for me to watch her ingratiating manner with him. In my eyes she became something negligible and unreal, and I had no more pity for her in my heart, only scorn.

Finally, the man left home and took a position far from town. He left his wife to live a "paper marriage"—like many women in town whose husbands had gone abroad to various countries—waiting for his letters in which he deceived her with easy promises and affectionate words. When he finally came for a visit, she ran to the ritual bath before everyone's eyes to purify herself for him, while he was gathering his belongings and turning back the way he had come.

It was then that a miracle happened and life rushed back into her as if she had been given a gift, Dvora said in a voice thick with emotion.

All that night Fradl paced back and forth in her room, sighing little truncated sighs with pursed lips, like someone trying to swallow their pain; but the morning found her sitting at the set table, eating her fill of what had been prepared the night before for the guest. When her aunt saw her bright face and the clarity of her thoughts, she understood that something had changed within her in the course of the night—what her modern daughters called a turning point, but which in her opinion was nothing but the bit of common sense that God had planted in her heart. Fradl dressed herself in a simple shift she still had from her girlhood days—unlike her usual finery—shut herself in a room with her aunt for many hours, and finally the two of them emerged and cheerfully announced that it was time to go and arrange for the divorce.

I saw Fradl's face when she came to my father's chamber, her blue eyes radiating again, like the eyes of her father the day he went to take his revenge on the gentile rioters up the hill. How beautiful she was as she accepted the divorce in the community house before the eyes of all the assembled, dressed as simply as in her youth, standing erect once more. My mother and her friends said that she looked more beautiful than on her wedding day.

A year had not passed before she married a different man, and a beautiful son was born. So they lived happily ever after, she smiled knowingly, until this very day.

Wonderful, I said. Did you know that Jung calls such stories "transformation stories," about the rebirth of the hero? In fact, what you described is a return to the very same sort of traditional structure, although with a more suitable mate.

True, Dvora answered with pleasure, but think about it: How could she do better in a small town? What sort of life could a solitary woman make for herself? Could she leave for the big city and study, as I did? Look, she continued, the big achievement of Fradl's life was the divorce itself, the fact that it was she who demanded it from her husband. For a man who hated his wife could give her a divorce and get rid of her according to Jewish law, but there was no such law for a woman: If she despised her husband, there was nothing to do but tie a rope around her neck and hang herself from the crossbeam, or throw herself into the well.

I knew women like that who sought their own deaths, she said, while Fradl, after she took her life in her own hands, married again.

So as your story about Fradl shows, I argued, you accept marriage as a potentially worthwhile choice in a woman's life.

And was I myself not married? she said, as if posing a riddle.

Nevertheless, I knew unmarried women with strong personalities who created a place for themselves in the community, she said, her face expressing wonder. Chaya-Fruma, from my town, was like that. She was an abandoned child, a crippled street girl with no parents. She supported herself by doing laundry in people's houses until she was married off to an old widower, who owned some cucumber fields and arrived from the village on the day of the wedding in a cart laden with produce. He too was always occupied with business, and with no sign of his affection his wife felt as if she were suspended over the void with nothing to grasp. Only the ill-tempered cow he bought her warmed Chaya-Fruma's desolate heart, and when she licked her hand with her sandpaper tongue, the woman's heart was filled with sparkles of light.

And then, she continued to weave her story, her husband suddenly fell ill and died. Chaya-Fruma withdrew from the quibbling of the children over the inheritance and asked only for the cow, and it was given to her. One rainy day she walked back to town with her cow and at the end of the bridge street she found a shack in which she set up house. She set up one room to live in and used the other half as a cow shed. She went back to work as a housekeeper and laundress, putting the cow in the care of the shepherd. In the evening, when they returned home, she set some fragrant fodder before her cow and sat on the stool beside her with the milk bucket in hand. This was the hour of communion for the two of them, Dvora said dreamily, their time together, which had the sweetness of mutual influence and the stillness in which those who are mute can hear the heart's call.

How beautiful, I said, people say that the greatest share of talk was given to women; but here the woman, like the cow, is utterly silent. They converse through the heart, I wondered aloud. You probably don't know about the psychologists, especially women, who talk about a special feminine voice, a language without words.

What of it? Chaya-Fruma's life tells more about women than a thousand expert witnesses. I can remember the line that would stretch each evening before the shack: the residents of the village coming with jugs to buy the fresh milk, all of them praising the cow for her good looks and sweet disposition.

So Chaya-Fruma became her own boss in the course of the years. She sold the calves—not to be slaughtered but for farmers to raise—and with the money she bought equipment to make dairy products, butter and cheese. She built a baker's oven in the yard outside the shack and baked rye bread and buckwheat cakes to sell. As she gained confidence, she began to invite a man of Torah, a blind old recluse, to her Sabbath table, and he in his blindness conquered the path through the depths of the woman's heart. Under his influence she began attending synagogue services, giving charity to the poor and needy there. She bought a candelabrum for the women's section so that the women who prayed there would have some light for themselves, instead of the dim reflection from the men's section. Anyone who saw her descending to the gulch to perform her acts of charity, wrapped in an expensive shawl, with just the slightest trace of her former limp, would have to wonder: Could that be Chaya-Fruma?

How beautiful! I said again. Now there is a triple union: the woman, the cow, and the blind Torah scholar. And here too, as in the story about Fradl, you noticed how a person's body and gait changes with their recovery from trauma and their increasing inner peace.

There is no better medicine than a healthy spirit, she responded.

And for you? I ventured.

Dvora smiled forgivingly. You never give your investigating mind a rest, Amia. For me it was just the same: my sorrow weakened my body. Or do you not believe that?

Another thing I said, taking advantage of this opportunity. Chaya-Fruma, like Fradl, finds her salvation only through the aid of another man—even though she does not marry him.

A woman could not survive alone in the shtetl, she insisted. Today things are different, and there is no doubt that a woman can now achieve a high spiritual level and a strong social position on her own. You yourself are proof of that, she said, and I did not know if she was making fun of me or not.

I'm no example, I argued. I had a spouse for many years, and it was while he was still alive—actually at his side—that I achieved my independence.

Fine, she said, but in the shtetl it would have been much harder, and a woman without a husband or sons was a useless vessel. Look, she continued, how could a woman live alone when even friendships between women were lacking? Women saw each other in snatches, by the vegetable dealer's cart or at the well, in the women's section at prayers. Their way of life isolated them, one woman to a household, and it kept them from finding solidarity with each other's pain. Do you remember my story about my mother and her friend the shoemaker's daughter and their secret encounters at night? Perhaps I only imagined all that; but I did not often see my mother chatting with her friends, the way women of your generation do when they meet in a café or even in a park, while they are out strolling with their children.

I couldn't survive without my women friends, I said.

Tell me, she said.

I don't know how to talk about it, I hesitated. Maybe that's the woman's missing voice that we talked about. There is a sympathy that forms in a glance, a caressing smile. We talk about the children, about our men, and we're actually talking about ourselves, like in my friend Anat's poem, which I read to you a while ago.

Yes, I remember, she said.

One of my friends is really just a neighbor, and I go down to her apartment for a cup of coffee nearly every day when I get home from work. We summarize our days in a nearly telegraphic style. She often cries—she's tenderhearted and has a hard life. Between the two of us I'm considered the strong one, but our coffee drinking is one of the sources of my strength, if you can understand that. The very fact that we sit together in a small kitchen is all I need to go on with my day. I generally visit another friend on Friday afternoons, during the loneliest hours of the week, when everyone is with their family—while I'm often alone. She cooks for her family in her spacious kitchen, and I absorb the fragrance of onion along with the smell of baking chocolate. It doesn't matter what we talk about, it always feels something like a mutual caress and that's what is important.

You, too, are a lonely woman, Amia, she said with amazement. Only loneliness lets us glimpse such depths.

No, no, I protested, I've given you the wrong impression. I'm usually inundated with people and events, more than I care to be.

Dvora looked at me doubtfully and said, I should read to you Rilke's letters about loneliness, although a man's loneliness is nothing like a woman's.

It's late, I said, suddenly feeling drained. I should be getting home.

Drive carefully, Tsipora called as I left, my bag heavy in my hand.

twenty-second encounter

The two days after our meeting were stormy, rainy, freezing winter days in Jerusalem. A hailstorm chased me home in the evening, and I pulled down the shutters, lit an olive wood fire in the fireplace, and sat on the carpet in the firelight to watch my son perform his card tricks. The next morning, the eve of the Purim holiday, we awoke into a world that was totally still and white. The snow that had fallen throughout the night had stopped all traffic, and the Valley of the Cross sprawled magically wide outside the window. "The world is wearing a white Purim costume!" the neighbor's little daughter called to me from the balcony; but this is nothing like the snows of Lithuania, where Dvora Baron was born, I explained to my son, who wanted to go down at once and build a snowman in the courtyard. The snow there stayed frozen for months, and horse-drawn wagons drove straight down the frozen river, I explained, as he hurriedly buckled his boots, ignoring my story completely.

The weather threw my schedule into disorder, and I couldn't make it to Tel Aviv as I had planned. With no possiblity of our meeting in the next few days, I felt a powerful urge to research some matters Dvora had spoken about. I snatched every free moment to browse the shelves of the Hebrew University library, and came home with my arms full of books. If she is a riddle, I'm finally going to solve it, I told myself.

During my spare time I read, and checked, and compared, and thought. I immediately dismissed most of the material as useless, and finally was left with just a few articles and books that seemed to shed light on a few unresolved matters: human development in midlife, the reclusive tendency, people who had withdrawn for extended periods, women artists, women who were bedridden for years for no apparent reason, and so on.

After the storm had passed, I wrote a letter to Dvora Baron to say that I expected to visit her the following week and that I would bring a few books that might have some bearing on her story. Would she discuss them with me? I asked. That way, I thought, she would be prepared for a certain deviation from our usual course.

When I arrived loaded down with my "material" I found Dvora smiling in bed.

I love books, she said like an eager little girl, and I am curious to see you in the role of professor.

Do not mock me, I slid into her old-fashioned language. These are just books I came across in the library, and I hope you will not see this as serious academic research.

Rest assured, Dvora said, a pleasantly expectant expression on her face.

Just a short introduction, I began, after I set up the tape recorder. Please don't be hurt by any personal comparison that may seem to arise. Let's say that I'm bringing you associations that haven't been worked through, thoughts that branch off into many directions, and you respond just as you please.

Including absolute rejection? she asked with unexpected mischievousness.

Of course.

How shall we start?

Maybe we should start with some history: this book summarizes one hundred and fifty years of expert advice, from doctors, mainly, to American women, especially during the nineteenth century. The writers emphasize how birth went from being the domain of women, who helped each other give birth naturally, to being a medical, male profession. At that point science began to deal with the mentally and physically passive woman, pushing aside the healing, compassionate woman, whose experiences enabled her to alleviate her sister's distress—this had disastrous consequences for women in our own day. Through this transition, I said, watching Dvora's curious face, women became eternal patients who were dependent on the advice of men. In other words, medicine preserved a social hierarchy: men ruled and women submitted; and even when a woman gives birth, the pinnacle of her life when she experiences her powers to the fullest—something no man can take from her—she does so at the mercy of a doctor, the male expert, who decides which of his artificial methods to use.

There are women doctors too, and I was fortunate to know some of the kindest among them, Dvora said, in a mild voice that did not challenge my words.

True, but they are few, and that is a belated development.

And so? she pressed me to continue.

The next point is that medicine, or physiology, constructed a theory in the nineteenth century about women being weak and delicate due to their sensitive reproductive systems. By her very nature, the doctors said, a woman was sickly and required the protection of men. One week a month, during her menstrual period, she was ill and should be confined to bed, and so too during pregnancy and lactation; and at other times, a woman's body was so fragile that anything out of the ordinary, from a heat wave to an argument with the servant girl, could send her back to bed.

How ridiculous! she responded, apparently seeing no reflection of her own situation in my words. Women are much stronger than men. Everyone knows that, and even in my childhood I noticed as much.

Working-class women may be strong, I answered in the spirit of the book I was reading, and in fact, those women worked at home and outside, gave birth, raised children in very difficult circumstances; but women from the higher classes, whose lives were somewhat better, were considered by science to be frail and vulnerable.

Is that possible? she grumbled. Is there any difference between their bodies?

Listen, I said. It's not hard to undermine these archaic viewpoints, and of course I don't buy them; but there's still something interesting there.

I will tell you the difference: With servants in the house and the children sent off to school, the woman has nothing to do, so she becomes ill with boredom; poor women could not afford that luxury.

Fine, I responded, upset that she was piercing my arguments with her wit before I could lay them out.

Listen, I begged again, you're right, but what's interesting is that there are many cases that justified these theories—as if women *were* more fragile in those days.

I, too, am a child of the nineteenth century, she cut me off.

Why was she making it so hard for me today? She listened to my personal stories attentively enough. Was she impatient with this vague theorizing? Or did she find it threatening?

A mysterious epidemic plagued upper-class women until the end of the previous century, I continued, bolstering the hypotheses of the medical profession. There are hundreds of case studies of women who took to bed and never recovered. They suffered from chronic migraines by the thousands, from weakness, from muscular aches and pains, from dizziness, nausea, chronic coughs, digestive problems, and menstrual irregularities. All these were accompanied, of course, by depression and melancholy. At conferences, the doctors agreed that the evidence showed that women were simply unhealthy creatures. One eminent gynecologist described the syndrome as "neurasthenia," I read in a free translation from the English book I had opened, peeking from time to time at Dvora's face:

> The woman complains of weakness and grows steadily paler. She loses weight, eats little, and when she does eat, she cannot properly digest her food. She is constantly exhausted, and everything drains her energy: sewing, writing, reading, and, of course, walking. She prefers to recline on a sofa, an armchair, or her bed. She reports that every activity costs her a tremendous effort, and that her body aches. She suffers from insomnia and requires large doses of tranquilizers. Periodically she has sudden emotional outbursts.

It seemed to me that a slight flush had risen in Dvora Baron's cheeks. She pursed her lips, but did not speak. I continued, "It was not a mortal illness, and no one ever died of it; but on the other hand, it was an illness for which no cure could be found. Many of its victims—women who complained that they suffered from weak 'nerves' and mysterious women's ailments—outlived their doctors."

So none of them recovered? Dvora asked softly.

There are very few known instances of recovery. One of those, a writer who lived during the last century, was Charlotte Perkins Gilman, who regained her health after leaving her husband and young daughter and started to write. She became very active in the struggle for equal rights for women, and among other things, wrote about her illness and the recommendation of the attending doctors—that she refrain from all physical or mental activity.

The doctors, along with the women's husbands, blamed the women for pretending to be ill, of course, she said with a knowing smile.

Not necessarily. For the doctors, this was an inexhaustible source of income, and for the husband, maybe he was proud of his fragile, pale wife, lying in bed all day dressed in a lacy nightgown, an eternal virgin-bride, don't you think? It was such a romantic image, a regular theme in popular literature. The artists also often painted ascetic beauties, reclining against the pillows, eyes clinging to the husband or doctor making a bedside visit.

And the husband fulfilled his needs elsewhere, she said quietly.

Almost certainly; but both the medical textbooks and the women's diaries describe the real agony these women suffered. Alice James, for example, the sister of two famous men, one a writer and the other a philosopher, described in her journal how desperate she felt about her weakness and inability to participate in the life cycle. She described the day she was informed that she had breast cancer—after twenty years of being bedridden with neurasthenia—as a happy day, because she had received tidings of death, the redeemer.

Dvora listened closely.

Contemporary feminist writers argue, I continued hesitantly, that the illness struck primarily—but not solely—married women, or unmarried women who had to run their fathers' or brothers' households.

Thus escaping the dreariness that is the housewife's lot, she said, when there was almost no other way of life open to women.

The illness, I added, freed married women from sex and continual pregnancy. It's no wonder that doctors viewed the root of the illness as a disturbance of the uterus, or of a woman's sexual organs. Suffering is the natural state of womanhood, the experts said, and that, apparently, is God's will. If a woman wished to alter her fate, she faced a united front of scientists and doctors. It was dangerous for a woman, the doctors warned, to strain her mental capacities. Education invited disaster, they wrote. If a woman burdened her mind with geometry or Greek, sterility or madness would result. Her body would cease to produce milk and her breasts would wither and fall off.

Dvora grimaced, and I saw again that none of this seemed to her to have the slightest bearing on her own situation. Soon she would ask me, I thought, panicked, why I had brought this stuff. But she rescued me by commenting, I was studious from earliest childhood.

So were a few of the great women of the nineteenth century, I said, although the day they matured and became women their studies stopped.

But Dvora continued with her comparison: I was never well off and never sought a life of leisure. Despite my illness, a day rarely passed without my picking up a pen. The stories I composed at home were the best I ever wrote.

I know, I hurried to answer.

The comparison is nevertheless interesting, she smiled; are we not coming to Freud and hysteria, which was also considered a disease with roots in a woman's womb?

Certainly, I said, but the classic hysteria of the last century came in sudden attacks, as opposed to the chronic disability of the neurasthenic state. Hysteria was also an illness that did not endanger the lives of its victims, but it was not fully curable. However a woman may have benefited from her hysterical attacks, and their convenient timing, it was useless to accuse her of pretense. Hysterical women enraged their doctors with the persistence of their illness, which could not be reasonably explained, and many doctors treated them with true sadism.

Until Freud arrived, Dvora Baron said.

At least he was an enlightened doctor, who argued that even if hysteria was imaginary, women who suffered from it were in fact seriously mentally ill and required treatment. Even faking an illness was a disease, perhaps a more serious one than hysteria or neurasthenia, and anyway, since Freud, psychiatrists and psychologists deal with the phenomenon, not the gynecologists of the previous century.

Does that matter? Her laughter was bitter but revealed a wise resignation. How often have doctors, psychologists, even just ordinary people argued, directly or indirectly, that I am pretending to be ill; and that if I wished, I could stand on my feet and dance in the streets. I feel no gratitude for what Freud said.

As you wish, I answered, and closed the book.

Finished? she asked, disappointed.

With this.

I thought you would talk about those women who spent years in bed.

Someone in particular? I asked, sensing she had some specific story in mind.

Florence Nightingale in particular, she said lightly.

You tell me; I have talked enough, and we still have many books here.

I do not know much about her, Dvora said. She was, as you know, a nurse, who insisted on her right to work at her chosen profession—despite the opposition of her upper-class British parents. They say that she heard God calling her to this vocation, and she could not reject the call. In the middle of the nineteenth century she was finally appointed to direct a shelter for sick women and she worked wonders there. During the Crimean War she led a group of women recruits to Constantinople to care for the wounded, and there, too, she worked miracles. Even during her life legends arose around her; "the Lady with the Lamp" she was called. Many owed her their lives. Florence Nightingale lived to the age of ninety, and died sometime at the beginning of this century, before the First World War.

In 1910, I said, but she paid no attention.

But not many people know, she added dreamily, that after she came back from Constantinople, at the age of thirty-six, this distinguished woman did not set foot outside her house.

Why not? It was my turn to ask, although I had two biographies of Nightingale before me.

Dvora gestured in an expression of helplessness and smiled mysteriously. Some said she was ill, she said, a mischievous twinkle in her eye.

But you don't believe that, I guessed.

Who am I to know about the life of an English noblewoman? Perhaps she was truly ill, or perhaps she suffered from that strange epidemic you described today. A disease of the body or the mind, a protest against woman's place in society, both of these—who knows?

But it's clear that Nightingale wasn't one of those women of leisure who declared a sit-down strike against their spouses, I said.

True. Nevertheless, her seclusion was nearly complete, and many of her friends were turned away at the door. But she continued her activities from home: She often wrote about health issues; exerted her influence on the British government in the area of public health, especially for the poor; worked for the opening of nursing schools; and was finally awarded one of the highest British knighthoods, the first woman in British history to achieve that status, I think.

Interesting, I said. I've been reading about her too this past week; there's a photograph of her in this book on the Victorian Age.

And you sat there as if you knew nothing about her.

I wanted to hear about her from you.

Dvora wagged a finger at me, but her warm smile belied the rebuke.

You scholar, you! she said affectionately.

The scholarship on Florence Nightingale doesn't match the legend too well. It presents her as a difficult, manipulative, and power-hungry woman who stopped at nothing—including exploiting her sickness and her saintly image in England after the Crimean War—in pursuit of her plans.

Which were virtuous, she said.

True; anyway, do you want me to read some of the analyses of her personality I have here? I asked.

Dvora nodded. I opened two books I had brought with me at the places I had marked. One biographer, an Englishman, is especially hostile. He says that Nightingale's true life started exactly when most of the public thought it was over. She returned from the Crimean War with her health ruined. The enormous strain of the previous two years had permanently damaged her heart and nervous system. Acute fainting attacks kept her bedridden. The doctors agreed that she was mortally ill, and decreed absolute rest. But she was a stubborn woman, I smiled and read, and rejected the decree, and from her sickbed she wound all of England around her little finger. The biographer says that the entire country was caught in her spell. How unfeminine of her!

Who wrote that? she asked with flashing eyes.

Lytton Strachey, I said, and showed her his photo—an English gentleman in tweed, with a short beard and gold-rimmed glasses. He died in 1932, and they say that he was a master at biography.

Dvora made a dismissive gesture and asked: The second book?

It was written by a woman, Nancy Boyd-Sokoloff, also British, and according to the title it's about three Victorian women who changed the world. The three of them—Josephine Butler, Octavia Hill, and Nightingale—worked at reforming the educational system, social work, and public health. They strode confidently into the public sphere, the writer says in her introduction, because each of them had a clear goal and a consciousness of her own talents. But Nightingale is the one who most interests us.

Because she was the recluse, Dvora completed my thought.

Yes, and that's why I wanted to read you the research—but only if you promise me you won't be hurt. The best biographers, the writer argues, tried to be broadminded about Nightingale's strange illness. But whatever the nature of this illness, clearly Nightingale took the fullest advantage of it: first, because she was ill she could order people about. People came to her, while she never went anywhere, and they came only at her invitation, never more than one at a time, and she received them only if she felt well enough at the moment. Thus she secured for herself complete control over every encounter. By the way, she was also known for the sharp things she said about people behind their backs, I said. I glanced nervously at Dvora's face without detecting anything—or was that a faint smile she quickly swallowed?

Nightingale's sickness, I continued, gave her the perfect excuse for not seeing those who disturbed her work, as she put it—which meant primarily the members of her own family. Her poor health was a stick to goad others: If she, a sick and frail woman, could do so much from her bed, how could they, healthy men with eminent positions, shirk her requests? Thus, by activating feelings of guilt and pride, she demanded a persistence and diligence that did not fall short of her own. No one dared to argue with her. Who could risk the possibility that his opposition would lead to the death of this saintly woman?

It worked, Dvora said with a chuckle, because she was involved in social reform, in politics. But if she had just been a writer, like me, what purpose could her illness have served?

Listen, I said, ignoring the personal note and leafing through the book in my hand, her sickness bought her the advantage of being able to deal with only one thing at any given time. It freed her from social and family obligations so her energy could focus, like a spotlight, on whatever goal she chose at the time: reorganizing the army's medical services, or hospital architecture, or establishing nursing schools. With the help of a small circle of friends she had recruited, she gathered enormous amounts of statistical data to bolster her positions. She was well off, but nevertheless sometimes needed the help of her family, her parents, uncles, sister, and brother-in-law. Being ill gave her the audacity to demand and accept their services without having to resort to hysterical attacks, as she had done in her youth. On the other hand, she did not hesitate to deter their visits on the grounds of her poor health. That was how, I said slowly and emphatically, she achieved a measure of independence by means of her illness.

So women have shrewd ways, she commented.

As I had promised, I made no explicit comparisons, merely saying that the writer summarizes the case quite sympathetically. Clearly Nightingale's illness, with which she lived for fifty years after it had been diagnosed, was pathetic. She payed an enormous price for meager profit. Who knows what her fate would have been had her doctors prescribed, instead of rest, daily work at the office or in Parliament? What if life had taught her to accept disappointment and compromise, to work toward a goal alongside men and women she saw as equals? Because she decreed seclusion for herself, I loosely translated for Dvora Baron, she fell prey to a world of tortured delusions, where old disappointments, ancient feuds, the demands of the self could find no corrective in reality. Only age and the grace of senility rescued her from this internal storm, finally bringing her, at the very end, to take the step over her threshold. Perhaps then she attained the distance and wisdom of Buddha, gazing serenely at the raging world?

I carefully closed the book, trying not to disturb the peaceful look on Dvora's face.

Are you tired? I finally asked. Should I make us something to drink?

As I helped raise her on the pillows, she stretched out a hand and stroked my hair, as if a lock were out of place.

Sometimes I think you understand me better than I understand myself, she said.

Then she turned toward the pile of books at my feet and merrily asked: And what else have you brought me?

A story that takes us back five hundred years; about a nun, I said, glad for her opening. It's this old book here; I found it with the theology books.

Asceticism is not a particularly Jewish trait, she said to me.

This story takes place in England as well; a student of mine chanced upon it. Would you like to hear?

Dvora nodded, although I sensed her reservations. This daughter of a rabbi, whose mastery of literature was no less solid than of the midrashic commentaries, still preferred not to hear about non-Jews. Christians and Muslims made her recoil, bringing to mind the pogroms of her childhood.

The heroine is an English noblewoman who lived in the fourteenth century and came to be known as Saint Juliana of Norwich. When she was thirty she fell mortally ill and the priest had already performed final unction, when she suddenly revived.

Born again, whispered Dvora, hanging on every word.

After her miraculous recovery she retreated from the world and gave up her family and possessions, isolating herself in a cell built into a wall of her hometown church. She lived there in solitude, supported by donations from the community, and except for a maid, who attended her and shared her silence, she saw no one apart from the worshipers when she participated in mass from afar—and then only through the grilled window of her cell. Among the medieval "ascetic saints," Juliana is considered the most important.

During her seclusion, I continued, looking at my notes, she had sixteen visions. She wrote them down in a book as they were revealed to her. These visions are called, in Christian literature, *The Revelation of God's Love,* and their language is archaic and difficult. Because of this, Juliana is also said to be the first woman writer in England, and maybe in Europe; but Juliana also won her place in history by her study of the feminine principle in theology. She was apparently the first to suggest characterizing God and Jesus as mother and woman. God was maternal, that is to say, Goddess, I stammered, and Jesus is also feminine in her writings. In her visions only Satan was an unattractive young man.

Dvora laughed shortly and asked, So during her seclusion she wrote?

A kind of automatic writing of her visions, and she also worked at self-mortification and prayer, as was the custom of holy hermits before her—most, if not all, of whom were male. The church had quite firm rules about everything connected with the daily life of a recluse: how to confess and repent one's previous sins; how to carry on a spiritual life, avoiding distractions and temptations and dedicating one's life to serving God. The secluded nun lived in silence, in poverty, with no luxuries at all. I know very little about the subject, I groped for words, but it seems to me that in Christianity a person who is taken up with the body, with this world, cannot attain the holiness in which God is revealed, as with Juliana.

It was not easy living that way, I said. Juliana spoke about her life only once, writing, "This place is a prison; this life my atonement. God's love is the only resting place." In the church's eyes as well this way of life was considered a kind of death, a dying to the world. For that reason, when a person's request for seclusion was accepted, a prayer ceremony very like a burial service was held. But the purpose was, of course, to arrive at a purification of the flesh and the soul's union with God.

These notions are foreign to Judaism, she repeated.

But what do you think of it? I asked.

Purifying the body or conquering the soul has no spiritual value in my life, she said, after prolonged thought. Who is strong? He who conquers his impulses, we say; but in my life, with this body, I had no other choice.

That is to say?

If I could bear the air, the water, the food that most people enjoy, I would gladly have done so. I am no nun like your Juliana, she smiled forgivingly. Do not set me among the saints.

While we were speaking, she had put on her thick-lensed glasses and begun to leaf through the Bible. Read aloud, she ordered, pointing with a long finger.

My hand trembled for some reason as Dvora handed me her Bible, pages softened with age.

> And Ahab told Jezebel all that Elijah had done, and how he had slain all the prophets with the sword. Then Jezebel sent a messenger unto Elijah, saying: "So let the gods do, and more also, if I make not your life as the life of one of them by tomorrow about this time." And when he saw that, he arose, and went for his life, and came to Beer-Sheba, which belongs to Judah, and left his servant there. But he himself went a day's journey into the wilderness, and came and sat down under a broom-tree; and he requested for himself that he might die; and said: It is enough; now, O Lord, take away my life; for I am not better than my fathers. And he lay down and slept under a broom-tree; and, behold, an angel touched him, and said unto him: "Arise and eat." And he looked, and, behold, there was at his head a cake baked on the hot stones, and a cruse of water. And he did eat and drink, and laid him down again. And the angel of the Lord came again the second time, and touched him, and said: "Arise and eat; because the journey is too great for you." And he arose, and did eat and drink, and went in the strength of that meal forty days and forty nights unto the mountain of God Horeb (1 Kings 19:1–8).

I took a deep breath and looked over at Dvora. Her lips moved and she continued in her sonorous voice where I had left off, word for word according to the text before me:

> And he came there to a cave, and lodged there; and, behold, the word of the Lord came to him, and He said to him: "What are you doing here, Elijah?" And he said: "I have been very jealous for the Lord, the God of hosts; for

the children of Israel have forsaken your covenant, thrown down your al-
tars, and slain your prophets with the sword; and I, even I only, am left; and
they seek my life, to take it away." And He said: "Go forth, and stand on
the mountain before the Lord." And, behold, the Lord passed by, and a great
and strong wind rent the mountains, and broke in pieces the rocks before
the Lord; but the Lord was not in the wind; and after the wind an earthquake; but the Lord was not in the earthquake; and after the earthquake a
fire; but the Lord was not in the fire; and after the fire a still small voice
(1 Kings 19:9–13).

Dvora fell silent. I asked if she wanted me to continue, but she shook
her head and stretched out her hand for the Bible.

And so? I asked.

You must see: forty days is the maximum period of seclusion for Jews,
and at the end of that time, a few extraordinary individuals, Moses and
Elijah, are worthy of seeing the godhead revealed as a still small voice.
And immediately after the isolation God commands the prophet to return to reality and perform a great revolution for His sake—not from
his bedroom, God forbid—crowning a new king in Syria, a new king in
Israel, and choosing a successor for himself, and only then would he be
allowed to die as he wished.

But Elijah's seclusion in the desert was a flight from terror.

And also his disgust with this evil world, which he loathed unto
death, she said, a deep empathy in her voice. Some of us find refuge in
the desert, like the friend you spoke about; and others, in a monastery
or their house. It is one and the same. What they share is an unwillingness to live in a world of machines or worse, among people, with their
scheming, evil hearts, she said.

I hadn't thought about Elijah the prophet, I said, because I read about
women all week; but you share something with the women we mentioned—Juliana and Florence Nightingale.

What is it that could connect such distant worlds?

To explain that I need another book, I said, drawing it from the pile
like a rabbit from my hat. This is about women artists. But it's late already, I said, suddenly becoming aware of the silence on the street and

the mounting chill in the room. You must need a rest and you haven't eaten anything this evening.

No, said Dvora. I am not hungry, nor tired. Let me just get up for a moment.

Tsipora appeared as if someone had waved a magic wand, supporting her mother. How could they coordinate so well? I wondered. I caught a mild dispute from the corridor: Dvora needed to eat something, and she refused. I got up and drew aside the curtain, revealing a cloud-heavy sky, street lights throwing rays on old piles of leaves, and an old couple, walking home hand-in-hand. I need to go, I thought.

But Dvora returned with an alert expression, eager to continue. She spoke shortly to Tsipora, Bring in the heater from the kitchen, Tsiporaleh; they have turned off the heat, but they cannot force us to go to sleep yet, can they?

And to me she said, I suffer from insomnia, so why rush? Can you stay?

Yes, I answered, my son is spending the night with a friend, so he won't miss me.

Dvora responded gaily, as if we were having a pajama party, I thought, lifting a book from the top of the pile. From the bedroom came the soothing clacking of a typewriter, monotonous and fluent.

This is such a fine book I wish I could read you the whole thing, I began. It was written by Caroline Heilbron, a literature professor in the United States, who also publishes detective novels under a pseudonym. She argues that a male artist's life progresses according to a recognizable plot of quest and discovery, while things are different for women. The lives of women artists are full of despair; they struggle with powerful anxieties, since there is no familiar plot by which to structure their lives. Do you understand? I asked.

Dvora nodded intently.

Here, this is what she writes about Virginia Woolf: She had enough despair to sap the strength of women artists for generations to come.

I have always sensed, she said, that you could not understand the depth of my despair.

I sat in silent agreement.

Listen, I said into the stillness, the writer argues that for a woman artist, one who strives to make her life her art—as a man might—something must occur, even if she invents it, unconsciously, of course, to make her life swerve from the ordinary feminine course, the traditional one, to another plot completely, a special, eccentric story.

From being a wife and mother, Dvora said slowly, to something unfamiliar and unique.

That's it! I exclaimed. A man has a period of apprenticeship that leads him, directly or indirectly, toward his goal; while in the life of a woman there's some kind of crisis, and only then can she devote herself to her craft. Sometimes it's a great sin, which takes her to the margins of ordinary society and frees her from their demands, and sometimes it's a retreat from the world.

Or an illness, she said.

But there is some pattern to the timing of these crises, I continued. They usually happened in the middle of women artists' lives. If it occured earlier, she would lack the strength to develop as an artist against the opposition of society; but when the crisis occurs in the prime of life, if the woman has some luck and was blessed with talent and an education, she might succeed at becoming an artist.

Thus, the lives of women artists often have two chapters, two different halves.

In the silence of the room, to the clacking of the typewriter, I could feel my words, my own life, being absorbed into Dvora's world.

My own life also has two very different chapters, Dvora finally said. In one I was active and sociable, and in the other I am isolated in this house. I wrote stories I do not like, the "rags," until I discovered the refined, correct way to write. I was an irritable and bitter young woman and now I have come to terms with the destiny of human beings on this planet.

You were independent and you gave up your independence, I tried to complete the picture.

I do not know, she said wearily, have I relinquished the independence of my youth? Did I become dependent on my husband, my daughter? Or have I achieved another kind of independence, like Florence Nightingale, at the cost of my two legs?

I once read another article about women, that in their prime their feminine tendencies are transformed into more masculine ones.

Stop! she laughed her rolling laugh. There is a limit to how much psychology I will swallow, even from you.

It's good to laugh, I answered.

This was a good conversation, she responded.

I began to gather my belongings, which were strewn across the room.

Do not go yet, she said softly.

I stopped on a dime and turned to her. Sleep here, Amia, she said. Tomorrow we will wake you at dawn and you can drive to Jerusalem.

I agreed, feeling the closeness that had grown between us. Tsipora was called to the room, and with a pleasant smile, she repeated her mother's invitation and went to make up a bed for me.

But before she left Dvora stopped her. Find the Rilke on the bookshelf, Tsiporaleh, please, and bring it here.

She isn't getting tired, I thought, so who am I to say anything? The book was produced—in German, I saw. Dvora put on her glasses and asked me to sit on the couch. She took a magnifying glass from the corner table and set it on the page. Then she pulled the lamp closer, until a circle of light spilled onto the page. Now we can see something, she said, with energy that was growing with each passing hour.

If you are wondering how we reached this point, I cannot help you. Let us say only that after you have kindly related to me such beautiful and intelligent things, I wish to return the favor. Rilke is one of my favorite poets, a great man. I shall read to you from his letters to a young poet, her smile revealing her thoughts: she, the older writer, was speaking to me, who was younger. He was only twenty-seven when he wrote them, but he was wise beyond his years, she laughed.

I sat comfortably in the armchair, my books in a pile at my feet, and listened.

He lived a dissatisfied life, the poet Rilke, wandering from city to city in Europe with one woman or another, and often alone. He sought his destiny in wretched hotels in Paris, in artists' communities in Germany, on the banks of Italian lakes; always in motion, always searching for himself, she said dreamily.

The absolute opposite of you, I said.

In this wandering, she said ignoring my comment, he was able to create for others an illusion of serenity, as if he knew his proper place in the universe. And that is how I understand his ten letters, which I sometimes turn to for inspiration and consolation.

To whom did he write the letters? I asked.

To a younger poet, an anonymous admirer, who had spent his youth in the same military academy in which Rilke had studied. He studied there, but he hated the place and suffered. The young poet, Mr. Kappus was his name, was unknown, while Rilke had already published thirteen books by that time.

Dvora began to leaf through the book, passing the magnifying glass over the pages, smiling and murmuring to herself.

What should I read to you? It is all so beautiful, so wise. Here, in the first letter, in which Rilke comments on the boy's poetry, which was apparently immature work: "I cannot discuss your verses; for any attempt at criticism would be foreign to me. Nothing touches a work of art so little as words of criticism," she translated aloud. "Things aren't all so tangible and sayable as people would usually have us believe; most experiences are unsayable, they happen in a space that no word has ever entered."

She continued to turn the pages, translating passages in her deep, confident voice, unhesitatingly finding the Hebrew words.

"You ask whether your verses are any good. You have asked this of others before. I beg you to stop doing that sort of thing. No one can advise or help you—no one. There is only one thing you should do. Go into yourself. Find out the reason that commands you to write; see whether it has spread its roots into the very depths of your heart. Ask yourself in the most silent hour of your night: *must* I write? Would I die if I were forbidden to write?" The descent into solitude he calls this journey, Dvora said, and how true that is. If the answer is affirmative, she continued slowly, "Then try," writes Rilke, "as if no one had ever tried before, to say what you see and feel and love and lose. Describe all these with heartfelt, silent, humble sincerity, and when you express yourself, use the things around you, the images from your dreams, and the objects that you remember." Or, she leafed, "All I can advise you is to keep growing, silently and earnestly, through your whole development; you couldn't disturb it any more violently than by looking outside and waiting for outside answers to questions that only your innermost feelings, in your quietest hour, can perhaps answer." And more, "Turn your gaze inward, to pictures of the distant, rich past; your personality will grow stronger, your solitude will expand and become a place where you can live in the twilight, where the noise of other people passes by, far in the distance." Finally, Rilke says, "For the creator must be a world for himself and must find everything in himself and in Nature, to whom his whole life is devoted."

Did you know that this letter was sent from Paris in 1903, she turned to me, during the period in which Rilke experienced the infernal suffering of a foreigner, stripped of his language in a hostile city? Knowing that enriches his words for me a thousandfold.

And all that was in the first letter? I asked.

Yes. The second one was written from Italy, near Pisa. Rilke directs the young man to read Scandinavian literature and look at Rodin's sculptures. In the rest of their correspondence Rilke discusses these artists as a source of inspiration and says, "Works of art are of an infinite solitude, and an artist must wait with deep humility and patience, beyond the reach of one's own understanding, for the hour when a new clarity is born."

And so he continues with his advice for young people who have lost the way, she sighed, leafing through the book. I caught glimpses of pencil marks in the margins: "Have patience with everything unresolved in your heart, and try to love *the questions themselves* as if they were locked rooms or books written in a very foreign language." And here, "Be happy about your growth, in which, of course, you can't take anyone with, and be gentle with those you leave behind."

How beautiful, I said, when Dvora had gently closed the book, and taken off her glasses.

How true, said Dvora. True for me, I wondered, or true for you? Which of us has been left behind?

From somewhere the ringing of an ancient clock could be heard. I counted eleven or twelve peals. This magical evening had come to an end.

twenty-third encounter

I thought about friendship between women, as you asked me to do, Dvora said the next time I came. In her black dress, wrapped in a gray sweater, she seemed paler and more drawn than usual. After opening the conversation and announcing the topic, she lay gazing upward and said nothing further.

Winter is almost over, I commented, trying to bring some lightness into the room.

I still feel cold, she responded, and the landlady is stingy with the heat.

I covered her with the extra blanket that had fallen to the foot of the sofa, and sat on the chair beside her. So tell me, what were you thinking about women's friendships? I asked.

I thought that you are my best friend, despite the age difference, she said, a smile spreading from ear to ear. You have become a very important person in my world, Amia. You have the ability to listen, a rare quality.

It's been years since I got such a wonderful compliment.

It was a great pleasure for me when you stayed the night at my house. You remember how I said that you were lonely; there is nothing wrong with that. But it is easier for a man, apparently, to live in true solitude; we women weave threads between ourselves and those around us.

That's exactly how it is with my friends and me, spreading a fine, strong network, I said, a spider's web, which actually is very sturdy.

Am I in the network too? she teased.

There was an elderly woman from my town who would come here during the evenings, she said. She sat for a while with her embroidery.

She could sit so that, speaking to her, I felt as if I were speaking to myself, and when the woman answered, it seemed to me that I was hearing my own voice. She did not read or study Torah, but none of my male friends were as close to me as she.

Friendship between women, she continued after a pause, often departs from the usual lines of class and education, as if womanhood itself provided a basis for companionship. That was how it was with my elderly friend, and even now, with a few ordinary uneducated women who visit from time to time.

I waited for her to talk about these friends, but she drew her story from more distant threads: That was how it was with the rich landlord's wife and that of the tinsmith. The tyrant evicted the tinsmith, but the two wives, along with the landlady's servant girl, were like sisters. The three women found their common language in planting a vegetable garden, which gave them as much pleasure as a broken window gives a prisoner. Every morning, when the children were at school and their husbands at work, they would gather to see the fruit of their labors, delighting over every young bud. One day they found that their garden had been uprooted to make way for the foundation of a new building. The women stood together in silent sorrow.

Things are the same the world over, she said after a pause, even in faraway France. Have you ever noticed how lonely Emma Bovary is in Flaubert's novel? she surprised me by asking. With whom could she share her distress?

They say that your translation turned *Madame Bovary* into a book of your own.

Well, for two years it was the center of my universe. I lived the story and its characters.

A few words from the book arose in my memory, and I wondered if Dvora had modeled her life on Emma Bovary, or if she had modeled her protagonist on herself. I remembered Dvora's translation of Emma's protracted breakdown after her lover's flight: "Her detachment from everything had become so complete, her language was so sweet and the look in her eye so haughty, her behavior so mercurial, that there was no longer any way of telling where selfishness and corruption ended and charity and virtue began." Could this not describe the character of Dvora Baron?

When did you translate the novel? I asked aloud.

While Yosef was still alive, she answered; I began the work before the end of 1930, and after more than two years the book was published. Not many people know that Tsipora was also translating a very important book at the same time, *Kristin, the Daughter of Lawrence,* by the well-known Scandinavian author Siegrid Ondst, who won the Nobel Prize for her work. It made a big impression when it appeared in the original in the early 1920s. Tsipora's translation, from the English, was also praised when it came out in 1936; but to my disappointment not many people read it.

Why did you choose to translate that book in particular? I turned back to our topic.

I loved Flaubert. Do you know what a good story is? One that you have to stop after every passage you read, as if you were sipping fine wine; and when you finish, you feel intoxicated. That is *Madame Bovary.* In the course of the translation I considered learning from Flaubert the "deep breath" of writing a novel, since I had only written short stories, many of them very short indeed. The protagonist's troubles interested me enormously, she said, without expanding. Nevertheless, she immediately added, there was nothing unusual about this work, since I had translated stories from Russian, French, and German. I filled the pages of the *Young Worker* with these, when needed, bringing the native Hebrew reader a taste of contemporary European literature. All of us—the Hebrew writers of my generation—worked at translation in order to bring the youth, who had been raised in Palestine in the lap of the Hebrew language, the literature of the world in their own tongue. It was a sacred task, and it also brought in a little extra income.

Nevertheless, why specifically this novel? I asked again.

You should know the answer to that, she smiled at me. I was drawn to the life of a woman, and this was, after all, one of the finest portraits of a woman in world literature. No one better described the enormous void in the life of a prosperous woman, who lacked even the burden of domestic chores, and who had nothing of her own—no work and no business—so that her life revolved around the craving for love. And love, as a support, is a flimsy reed. See how low Emma Bovary's life sank in her search for love, or sexual satisfaction, if you will. How greatly we erred in laying such importance on sex, including Freud, for those who read his works superficially. He himself was intelligent enough to say that satisfying work is also necessary for happiness and peace of mind.

It would be well if everyone understood that all that remains in married life after the passion cools is friendship and partnership, she continued heatedly. Many marriages could have been saved from irredeemable tragedy. Flaubert knew, as I did, that the weight that is heaped on married life in the name of love is too heavy not to sink it. He also knew that physical love was transient, as he said in the words of his heroine, Emma: "Adultery was the same as marriage—the same boredom—the same banality." In my stories I described women characters whose life improved precisely when they stopped waiting for love; but perhaps, she said, young people cannot sense this until they have been scalded; or is it that only older people are granted this understanding, when their sexual desires no longer press so urgently.

You never translated such a masterpiece again, I remarked.

It was an exalted mission, much larger than I had anticipated, she replied. After Aharonovich's death I was no longer capable of such enormous tasks. In the years after he died I began to work with his friend at editing his letters and articles for publication, which appeared in 1941. In the time that remained from this work and my illness I wrote new stories, some of them quite long, and reworked the old stories for various collections. Perhaps I did not return to translation—although I had a few proposals—because of the criticism of *Madame Bovary*.

But the critics were enthusiastic, I said.

Most of them, but not all. Look, she smiled, critics are not my favorite people. Do you remember the verse, "They made me keeper of the vineyards, but mine own vineyard have I not kept"? That could apply to critics, who write about other people's work without having a dose of their own medicine. Although critics have sometimes taught me about my own work, I always say to my friends that criticism has only three concepts at its disposal—lyric, epic, and romance—and from these ingredients, critics cook up every review.

Many critics praised the translation, she continued when our laughter had subsided. One, however, argued that my work was inaccurate because I was too sloppy and worn out to do it right. That angered me, since I had been careful to arrive at a deep and precise understanding of the work. Recently I was approached to translate Flaubert's other novels, but what is the point? Twenty years have passed since my translation of *Madame Bovary*, it is impossible to find a copy, and no one is prepared to print a new edition.

All in all, I began after I had brought in the teapot from the kitchen and poured from it, it would be hard to avoid the impression that you are the greatest critic of the institution of marriage. There's your translation of *Madame Bovary*, all the gossip about the way you talked about marriage with your friends. It's not too great a leap, you see, to the conclusion that your own marriage couldn't have been one of the better ones.

That rumor has not a leg to stand on, she said. My marriage was quite good, except that Yosef was always exceptionally busy, and I suffered because of it. Nevertheless, you are correct about my position on marriage in general. I frequently observed how damaging marriage could be for a couple, how much better off they would have been separately, especially the woman. I have seen women lose their spouse, and after the initial pain had subsided, they stretch their wings for the first time in their lives.

Marriage is especially difficult for an artist, she continued. We have agreed that the imagination develops in people who were introverted in their childhoods. People like these cannot easily fit into the framework of family life; and if they do, it will affect their creativity. There is little hope for a man or woman who has reclusive tendencies, and a fragile talent that requires solitude, to acclimate themselves to domestic life. Sometimes they can find a spouse who protects them, prevents anyone from disturbing their work, frees them from daily household chores and the material aspects of life, takes upon himself the contact with editors and publishers. But that is very rare.

It seems to me, I continued her thought, that the chances of a male writer finding a wife who will shield him from the world are greater than the chances of a woman artist finding such a husband.

Dvora nodded, but said no more.

And Yosef? I asked.

She shrugged, raised her palms in a helpless gesture and sank into her thoughts.

In the beginning he understood the strange need I had—to be both independent and protected—and his intentions were good; but in the final analysis he was an activist, and his public service ate up the best part of both our lives.

Nevertheless, I said boldly, you don't seem as angry as you sometimes have been.

Do you mean my friends who quote me as saying that every husband murders his wife? she said scornfully. Or that one should send a condolence note—not congratulations—to a woman on her wedding day? Well, a person must watch what she says.

I was silent, thinking about the bride at the Jaffa port at the beginning of autumn. How much time had passed since then, and how often my perspective on Dvora Baron had changed in that time. And then Dvora surprised me by speaking in a constricted voice.

But why am I trying to deceive you? If I do not reveal everything, what is the point of everything we have built together?

What do you mean? I asked, agitated. Wild guesses flashed like lightning through the darkness. Was she finally going to reveal to me the secret of her marriage, some lover, or her lesbian proclivities? None of these seemed likely.

You may have noticed that most of those things I said, the translation of *Madame Bovary*, also some of my harshest stories about marriage, she practically whispered, were written after I understood that Tsipora was ill and would never marry.

Why? I asked, startled by the direction of the confession.

Do you really not understand? I am a mother, after all. The girl grew into a woman, and was I blind? Not only was she devoid of charm in her own eyes, so she presented herself as a woman whom no man could ever desire, but her body was also afflicted with an incurable hereditary disease; if she married and had children, she could pass it on to her descendants. If you had ever seen her when she returned so injured from the street, from where she had fallen, poor woman, and lain on the pavement until she regained consciousness. Dark smudges on her cheeks, as scratched as an alley cat, and apologizing that the biscuits she had brought had broken, she said, falling into a long silence. Even if Tsipora were not my only daughter, she said, compassion, they say, is my profession.

What's the connection? I asked.

So, she said with a mixture of pain and anger, how can a mother comfort her adult daughter when they learn that she will never be able to have a family of her own?

By heaping scorn on marriage and praising single life? I tried.

Dvora nodded slowly and kept silent.

Do not mistake my words. I did not, after all, reverse my opinions completely, and I have never lied for Tsipora's sake. Nevertheless, whenever I could I stressed—even without noticing it—how much luckier she was than married women who were enslaved to a husband and house. In that way I saw myself as shoring up my daughter's strength, helping her to accept her destiny.

Gradually I molded her character until she could stand on her own two feet, despite her bitter lot, she continued. True, I gave her no opportunity to form ties with people her own age, and some suspected me of sadism for that, she said bitterly. Others said that I encouraged her dependence on me for my own sake, and what would happen to her, poor thing, when I died? But in reality all my thoughts were directed toward giving my only daughter an inner life that could sustain her after my death. She learned how to make do with little, to respect freedom, learning, and work. She learned about solitude, and about how a good book could ease that burden. She learned languages from me, and also translation, editing, and typing, so she can earn a decent living, I hope. She learned not to wait for a man to save her, because there is no such man on the horizon. Beyond that, she learned from her mother to scorn marriage.

Dvora fixed her burning eyes on me as if to ask: And what do you say to that?

So you feel you have prepared her to live according to her abilities, I asked, amazed.

Correct, Dvora responded. I have explained myself once and for all, she said, so let there be an end to those who would testify that I have enslaved my daughter to the will of a crippled, eccentric, selfish woman.

Those rumors never made sense to me.

Fine, said Dvora, but no smile lit her face. I have left one story unpublished, she continued, because of its especially harsh criticism of marriage—I thought it would lead to conclusions about my marriage. Tsipora was the one who edited it, and we spoke about it often. I have sometimes thought that it was written for Tsipora alone, she whispered. Of all the stories I have written in the last few years this is the only completed story I have kept from the public eye.

Can you tell me the plot? I asked.

Certainly, she said. This story too is based on tales I heard by the well in my town. It is about a beautiful young woman, an orphan, who is compelled by circumstances to marry a rich man who adores and spoils her—but cannot win her heart. You will live like a queen, her poor aunt promised, and that decided it. But the young girl was lost among the luxuries of her husband's house, for she had been sold to a man who was like a block of wood to her. The touch of his body was horrible to her and made her long to die. After every time he came to her, she would hurry to the nearby river, strip off her clothes, and plunge into the water, trying to cleanse herself of the pollution that clung to her. She would lie on her back in the middle of the river, spread her arms as if to embrace someone, and slowly float downstream.

It was that bad? I wondered.

Dvora ignored my comment. Finally the man fell ill, certainly from heartbreak, for he was a good man and had nothing but kind intentions.

Like Madame Bovary's husband, I said; like Yosef, I thought. I knew that Dvora would never confirm my suspicions about her bad marriage.

Then, as he neared death, they suggested to her that she accept a divorce from her husband, so that she and his brother be spared the necessity of marrying each other according to the levirate law. She stood by her husband's bed, as the rabbi directed, and received the divorce papers from the sick man's hand. That was something, believe me, she said, since a man who dislikes his wife can legally divorce her, while a woman who finds her husband hateful has no recourse but to tie a rope around her neck and hang herself.

That sentence sounded familiar, maybe from the story about Fradl, I thought. Unlike many elderly people, Dvora Baron almost never repeated herself in our conversations.

Here she was given her divorce as a gift, Dvora said in amazement. Now, she continued, when she no longer owed him anything, she was happy to care for him on his sickbed after the members of the rabbinical court had permitted her to do so. She prepared healing foods until he got out of bed and stood on his own two feet. Then, when she was asked if she wished to marry him again, she said in a voice that filled all the space in the world: "No." At sunrise she left with a small bundle on the road that led to her hometown.

That was her hour, Dvora concluded, charmed by her own story, for every person in the world has their hour, for which this hour was created.

And that is your lesson for your daughter? I asked.

Dvora withdrew like a snail into its shell.

Would you like me to go? I asked after a while.

No, she answered. Our conversation is difficult for me. Only very few of my friends, most of whom have died, knew this secret, she said, her thin hands moving on the blanket as if scrambling for a way out.

What else would you like to tell me? I asked gently.

I might feel better if I told you about a couple I knew who lived in beautiful harmony. A crippled woman lived beside her window by the town square. That was Muscha, who had fallen ill immediately after her wedding and had not left her bed since then, and Nachum the town photographer, who was her husband. His store was next to their house and when she became ill, he tore down the wall that separated the house and store, so that she could always see him. A ray of light emanated from his eyes to her, and from it she lived. He always sensed what she needed at any moment. He set up a washbowl so she could wash herself just as if she were standing before the sink. At noon he would let her serve the food, drawing the table to the bed; and in the evening, when Zusya the servant girl came to air out the bed, he would lift her carefully and carry her to the couch in his arms. I will pamper and worship you, he had sworn when they first met, and now he fulfilled that promise every day.

When spring arrived the bed was moved to the window. From there she could see people moving about the square, accompany with her gaze the workers going out to the melon fields each morning, and then, with their family, await their return. She could see the innkeeper going about her business, and further on, the owner of the dairy setting jugs of milk along the fence. That was how she passed her days. Sometimes in the middle of all that she would remember what was wrong with her and grow dizzy and weak, as if she had peeked over the edge of an abyss; but then Nachum would send forth his radiance to her, and she clung to it and regained her equilibrium.

It was bad when Nachum left on errands. When he was delayed, the shadow of death was cast upon her. The square before her eyes lost its tangibility, and uprooted from her existence, she wilted like a plucked flower. A barren ruin, a heap of debris; but when he came in, she returned to among the living. Her husband was her support until the end of his life.

It was this disabled woman who managed to find such a warm and supportive relationship, which lasted for life, I said with amazement, wondering who would be first to draw the comparison between the bedridden Muscha and Dvora.

Perhaps precisely for that reason, said Dvora. Perhaps her own will was so meager, she was grateful for anything that was done for her.

If so, an utterly passive, weak, and dependent woman will better succeed at maintaining the marriage bond, I said.

Dvora smiled at me with her characteristic tolerance. Now, really, Amia, she said, you know that such generalizations are useless.

But you sometimes use them, I protested.

She shrugged and chuckled. I am allowed.

Oh, I don't mind being a perfect fool to you, I continued. After all, you can always reject my suggestions.

So what other suggestions do you have? she asked, cajoling me.

I stepped happily into the trap: You see yourself in Muscha, and the character of Nachum expresses your longing for the ideal, loving caretaker.

Again you are correct; but where else would an author find material? The imagination is nothing but a quiltmaker. Obviously there are personal elements, or perhaps it is the opposite: I wish to live the plot I imagine for my characters.

Look, she said, since my childhood I have seen many people, men and women alike, who fell ill and spent the rest of their lives in bed. The first was the water carrier, who was not old at all, who rested in the shade of the pear tree in the courtyard after his legs ceased to carry him; at the end of the summer I saw how his mother covered his spindly legs with warm autumn leaves, with their healing properties. In the gulch there were a few miserable creatures who crawled on their bellies when they could no longer walk. And then there was Muscha, who lived beside the window.

Tell me about the world of a person who passes their life beside a window, I said.

The feeling is of sitting by the side, she began immediately. Some who sit by the window are bound to memories of their childhoods, or happy marriages that are long gone. But I, when I sit by the window, I see living people around me. Even in my childhood, when I was not allowed into the neighbor's garden or the estate across the river, beyond the terrifying snarl of the dog guarding the gate, I made do with sitting across the way and looking in at what was happening inside. I read things through the window as in a book, and forgetting myself, I race on to see the rest of the story: when those who left will return, who will accompany the little girl home from kindergarten, why the apartment across the way remained shuttered that morning.

Because I did not leave the house, she said, contact with strangers became more difficult. But there were still people for whom I was happy to open my door: those who were not frightened of me. I loved seeing children, infants with wide eyes who did not recoil from me, fresh-faced students who listened to my stories and told their own. I leaned against the pillows and played with them, and the room would become a play-ground, in which they could swing or make necklaces from seeds, imagining they were shiny pearls. A few of them brought me their compositions to read, she said wistfully.

When they all left me and the house returned to its desolation, I would sometimes feel like a heap of rubble no one has any use for. Sometimes I would sit by the window and imagine that those who walked by every day had grown tired of seeing me there, framed by the window, gazing at them with gloomy eyes. They must imagine that I begrudged them their sturdy legs. It was especially infuriating when there was some family celebration in the courtyard, and my dark, mournful face would float above the merry crowd like a black stain against the bright background of their lives. Even while Aharonovich was still alive a woman once entered and demanded to know why I was in bed, darkening the lives of my entire family. If I could only cry, I would feel better; but the tears within me have frozen.

I put out my hand, grasped her dry, cold palm. From peals of laughter to the depths of the despair was only the shortest of distances! I thought.

I wanted to ask you something, I said, when her face had become serene again.

Ask, she said in a heartier voice.

Is it true that you didn't see a doctor, didn't try to get better?

Certainly I consulted doctors, and which of them did not visit, whether I wished it or not? Doctors of all varieties, orthopedists, dentists, ophthalmologists. My nephew, who became a famous professor of medicine, also sent the greatest specialists. This year I turned sixty-eight years old and as you see, many of my friends who were stronger than I are no longer, while I continue to survive. But none of the doctors did the slightest good, she said decisively; an ordinary person who gives advice to a sick person is liable to harm them, a doctor even more so, and a professor a hundred times more than that, she smiled. I have seen doctors force-feed their patients with various "fashionable" drugs, paying no attention to the patient's ability to absorb them, like seamstresses dressing a woman according to the latest style, and not her figure or taste. I have had my fill of doctors.

And now I want to get up, she said suddenly.

I helped her sit up, and watched as, very slowly, with a grimace, she put her long legs, in heavy woolen stockings, down from the sofa. She stretched out an arm so I could help her. I appproached, gripped by fear, and stood beside her; she rose, leaning on my shoulder, a head taller than me, skin and bones in a long dress. Slowly we walked toward the door, Tsipora coming from the kitchen and supporting her mother skillfully from the other side.

We can handle this, Tsipora said to me, Thank you, you can go home now.

How did she know we had finished our conversation? I thought. How long had she been home? Was she listening from the kitchen? But when I saw that Dvora was not protesting her daughter's decision, I took my leave of them and went my way.

On the drive to Jerusalem I listened to our conversation on the car's tape deck. The most interesting development, I thought, was Dvora's revelation about how the connection between mother and daughter had influenced opinions about male-female relations. A "folie à deux," I remembered the phrase. The daughter is enslaved to her famous mother who sees herself as ill, although no one knows what's wrong. The daughter accommodates herself to the mother's ascetic habits, refraining from nutritious food, becomes seriously malnourished until she looks like the sister of her ascetic mother. The two of them avoid doctors and medicine in the absence of the one doctor whom they can trust, and decide themselves how to deal with their health. The mother, a compassionate woman, wanting to ease the suffering that sours her daughter's life—a real or imaginary consequence of her daughter's illness—paints so gloomy a picture of life for her that their home becomes the only refuge, a strip of sky blue in a sea of muck. Nevertheless, the mother has—alongside sadness and despair—sensuality and a powerful emotional life, which sometimes bursts through, while the daughter lacks this completely. And so, in their bubble, they are locked away from all that happens outside, choosing the few things that will enter. Sometimes they translate world literature, sometimes they talk like old cronies about the neighbors they see outside the window. But a world of difference divides them: Dvora, who even in her old age is still attractive, is the true artist, reclining on her sofa; while Tsipora clumps around in her heavy boots, with no other mission than to serve her mother.

A double madness? I asked myself, opening my front door at the end of my trip to the excited barking of the dog. Who is healthy and what is sickness anyway? On the kitchen table, a sixth-grade geography workbook and a note from my son, asking me to wake him early so I could help him finish his homework, cut off the tangled thread of my unhappy thoughts.

twenty-fourth encounter

Is that you? Dvora Baron greeted me on a spring evening at the beginning of May, reclining as usual on the couch, covered with a woolen blanket. What have you done with your hair? I did not recognize you. You have not visited for a long time.

I very much wanted to, I said, and I wrote to you, but every time something else came up.

Is there any point in your continuing to come here? she persisted.

It was true that I hadn't been in their house for a long time. The Passover vacation had made it difficult for us to arrange a meeting. I traveled to Europe for a conference and stayed for two weeks, and then Dvora postponed a few times because she was in deep mourning over the death of her close friend Yitzchak Brodny-Bareli. After that, she had been hospitalized for tests, and when she returned home she was scheduled for a cataract operation. The operation had not yet taken place, but Dvora had granted me an invitation anyway—although, Tsipora claimed, she was less well than usual.

I had worried that I would see a deterioration in her appearance, but I didn't notice any. I arrived with a large package of sugar cubes I had bought for Dvora in Switzerland. The light in Dvora's room was dim, and she looked like a nun in a medieval saint portrait, the kind I had just seen in Italy. But it was impossible to miss the angry note in her words when she said: I am an old woman, and no one is interested in me.

You know it's not like that, I protested. What about our strong friendship? I asked, using my experience of dealing with clients after a break in the course of the treatment imposed by the therapist. I knew this was not therapy, and I worried about the consequences of this break in our meetings, which had been prolonged far beyond my intentions.

Look, she said heavily, perhaps I was not meant to live for so many years. The members of my generation who immigrated to Palestine when I did, the transitional generation of the desert, did not live long lives, and most of them have already died. And now Brodny is gone, too. He was very dear to me, she said in a hard voice, and he cared for my daughter as a father, and now we have been orphaned anew, Tsipora and I.

Do you know the famous poem of Yitzchak Katzenelson? she suddenly asked, and in her singing voice she began to recite the Yiddish words of the poem:

> Locked is my door
> No one knocks, as before
> No one comes anymore. . . .

Can you understand? she asked.

Certainly, and saw her surprise. I translated while Dvora smiled, finally pacified.

When I arrived at the hospital for tests I felt it clearly, she said, although the most eminent doctors came to visit. Tsipora brought me in an ambulance. They took out the gurney and set it down in a corridor. I lay there for a long while, no one approached me and no one looked at me, just another poor old woman from the street. Her voice was tearful and she was repeating herself, which was unusual. No one recognized me, no one knew me, knew who Aharonovich was, what we had done. I lay on the gurney, it was in the corridor. After a few hours one of the good women who read to me regularly came to visit, and was amazed to find me there like that—and not in a room—like a beggarwoman. I am Odysseus, I told her. If a person comes back to the world after twenty years, who will know him?

Once, as I was sitting by the window, she continued, I saw a mangy dog in the yard who had been abandoned by her owners. She trudged around the courtyard with that feeling, so familiar to those who have reached their lowest point, that everyone has suddenly ceased to notice them. People look down past them, or worse, stare disdainfully. I felt all that lying on a gurney in the hospital corridor.

I also thought about the moon while I was in there. Once there was a lunar eclipse, she explained, but on the city streets people hurried along through the darkness, humming the theme song of the film they had just seen. No one raised their eyes to see the wondrous sight of the moon hiding and then emerging. I thought, then, the moon must certainly feel like a poet who writes something beautiful and no one notices. Now it knows what that is like.

We were silent for a long time before she continued.

The life of an elderly person who has lost most of her friends is a sad one. How I mourned the deaths of those who were closest to me, who were healthier than I and died before their time. My loyal friend Asher Barash, and now Yitzchak Brodny. Deaths that came like a thunderbolt. Sometimes in the evening I hear a heavy tread on the stairs and think that soon the door will open and they will enter.

I sat sunk into my chair, unable to find a response.

The life of an elderly person is a sad one, she repeated as if in lamentation, and no one has any use for it. How much more so an old person with a healthy soul in a broken body. My hands lay like this on the blanket like useless implements, unable to hold even a pencil. If I wish to write I dictate to Tsipora. Amia, tell me, why should I live if I cannot hold a pen in my fingers?

Once, not very long ago, I heard an explosion while I was alone at home. That day I was unable to stand on my legs at all. I crawled out of bed, like an animal, like those creatures that creep on their bellies, and crept into the kitchen. On the floor, which apparently had not been swept in the last few days, were onion peels and garlic skins and a layer of dust and the grit of pollution. A woman crawling through the garbage. I could see that the walls had not been painted in some time and a lattice of cracks had formed. I could see spider webs. I lifted my eyes to the uppermost windowpane and the strip of blue through it, and I asked: How much longer? How much further would I have to carry this life of mine?

That was certainly an awful moment, I said, but you don't always feel so desperate, do you?

It has grown worse, she answered. In the first few years I had visitors, and sometimes the prospect of a visit would cheer me and I would push aside the medicines and feel like a healthy person. This house, which seems so gloomy, has seen so much laughter, heard so many witty, worldly conversations. When I was alone I often listened to the radio or to music. Nothing lifts one's spirits like a good book or good music. Beauty is dew for the soul, reviving it after the night.

Music is a source of strength for me too, I said. I often come home and the first thing I do is put on some music to fill the emptiness inside me or the house. Music has never disappointed me.

Sometimes I found in myself consolation for someone whose fate was worse than my own, Dvora said. Many women I knew had lost sons in the War of Independence, and these women had an open invitation to my house. One of these was Yocheved Bat Miriam, my friend the poet. How difficult the visits of these mothers were, and when they had gone, I was left brokenhearted—although in their presence I tried to find the strength to comfort them. Rivka Guber, who lost two sons in the war, was different. She took comfort in the legends I presented to her; while I leaned on her strength, she had the ability to get up when her life lay in ruins, to adopt an immigrant child, to launch the settlement of Lakhish in the Negev desert, and rebuild herself through this. She was always my role model.

In moments of despair I would remember my childhood, she said, her eyes shut, my mother and father, and I tried to draw comfort from their strength and faith. And so with the other characters I remembered, like the bricklayer in our town, a man dogged by loss, but who nevertheless arose every morning and reverently recited: "I thank you, O King who lives forever, for returning my soul to me, with great compassion." Since childhood his face was always before me. I was still a tender child, under my mother's wing, and I did not know that the sentence decreed upon the bricklayer was the decree of most people on the face of this earth: to labor, toil, trample the mud, to suffer, wound ever tighter in the branches of that magical tree called Death. How amazing it is when one poor soul manages to leave a little light or warmth for those who follow.

She sank into a weary silence. Her face had taken on an olive cast, and within it her eyes, open now, burned like a pair of Sabbath candles. Eyes that her admirers had described since her first youth; and although they could barely see and were sunk in a drawn face, in a body that was ever closer to utter collapse, they had not lost the power to enchant. I gazed as in a temple, thrilled to be so close to such unspeakable power.

It seems to me that in your seclusion you became a kind of symbol, I hesitated, a high priestess of suffering; people came to you with their pain, to which was added your own—and how could you ease such an ocean of sorrows? For myself, I can only rid myself of depression, my own and others', by being active, going out, seeing people, window-shopping, seeing a good movie, losing myself in my work. But you never had that kind of escape.

Recently I have felt a longing to go out among people, to see the city, Tel Aviv, and the country and its inhabitants, she said dreamily.

Was she finally going to leave her house? I wondered, amazed. But before I could speak, she continued: There are good days too, when I enjoy writing, a good review, the letters I receive, hours of music and moments of laughter, meeting with a friend. I too have found respite in work, and even now I still write a little, although mostly I rework stories I have already written for republication. I personally supervise the editing and proofreading, cover designs, translations into English or French. And from time to time a prize falls into my lap, although I never submit my stories to contests. That is life: the good and bad are stirred together like barley soup, as I always say, she laughed, her face shining.

The time has come to finish the story of my life, she said quietly and undramatically, and my heart skipped a beat and I could think of nothing to say.

Between morning and nightfall, she continued, between the moments of laughter and the despair of old age, this ordinary life of ours, Tsipora and mine, has unfurled itself. The sicker I grew and the more my freedom was curtailed, even within the house, the more I found a loyal and loving support in Tsipora. For all these years she cared for me with unending devotion, to the point of neglecting herself—she, whose health was never good. More than once her physical condition deteriorated, and she spent months in the hospital trying to regain her strength.

When was Tsipora in the hospital? I asked with concern.

Many times, she answered sadly. Starting at about the age of thirty, that is, beginning with the Second World War. I can remember her extended stay in the hospital during the food scarcity; I think that was during the World War. She was also hospitalized during the War of Independence. Of course it was Tsipora who stood in line to receive our rations of flour, sugar, biscuits, our half-liter of kerosene for heating—the bare minimum we needed for the house. We had no use for most things they rationed, but the municipality would not accept substitutions. They did not know the name Dvora Baron, and our suffering was great. Our friends from the agricultural settlements helped as much as they could, and Brodny and his associates at the Workers Bank responded to our requests; but nevertheless, those were difficult times of financial distress and petty worries. I shrink from even talking about things like this, she said dismissively.

When Tsipora's hospital stays were prolonged, she did not cease to worry about who could take care of me in her stead. All I asked is that she not leave prematurely, that she stay until the doctors could find the proper treatment. In any case we had housekeepers to ease Tsipora's burden, and at times like these, they increased their efforts. My conversations with these ordinary women kept me abreast of what was happening in the country, but Tsipora's absence was still difficult for me. The house felt empty, pervaded with a petrified stillness like Fradl's house before her divorce. I often asked my friends not to come when Tsipora was absent.

How I grieved for my daughter, she continued, and the torments they put her through—and for what? As I have told you: They know nothing, the doctors. I could not stop worrying about her health; but she asked for nothing for herself, and her concern was only for me: Is mother eating? Are they sweetening her tea? Are the rooms being aired? I had to calm her by writing long letters about the dedicated girls who were filling her shoes as best they could, boiling the egg for precisely five minutes, preparing the cereal or rice or potatoes exactly right. I enjoyed reading her beautifully written letters, in which she described the other patients in much greater detail than she spoke about herself. If a few of my doctor friends had not visited me with news of Tsipora's condition, I would have known nothing. I sent my friends to visit her, mailed newspapers and books to the hospital, and wrote to her about what was happening with the neighbors, the small events I witnessed in the street and the visitors who had come to ask after her. When both Dr. Manya Merari and Dr. Einhorn, my friends, assured me that Tsipora really could benefit from the arduous treatments she was undergoing, I tried to shore up her strength to bear them.

In the first years of my illness young girls would come to help around the house, and I am reminded of one of them now. She was very beautiful, and when I invited her to eat with us, she said that she wished to begin working immediately. She was tired of being idle, she said, she had just arrived by boat and had a long rest. She energetically filled the bucket with water and went scrubbing her way through the rooms, as if she were going after some stubborn stain. When I asked about her family, she said that her mother had remained in the shtetl by herself, and she herself was so homesick it was as if the ground had fallen away from under her feet. But she arose early the next morning to open the door for the milkman and light the oven and scrub the pots, and the house rang joyously with her presence. When I felt bad, she managed the house on her own, bargaining with the peddlers, making sure the laundry was done right, even taking over the household accounts. But eventually she found herself a pioneer and went off with him, and she never even returned to visit.

People are busy with their lives, you know, I said, fervently promising myself that I would never neglect this house as long as Dvora lived.

You are too busy, you young people, she said with the trace of a chuckle. In general, the world is not what it used to be. Things do not have the stability they used to, the cloth they make today is flimsier, and the radishes and onions—they have lost their sharpness. Even people have emptied out: there is no faith in their hearts and they rush from place to place for no clear reason. Before, a Jewish man would pray three times a day and make a blessing over his meal, earn his bread and even set something aside for a future day through Torah study and charity; now, when someone gets up in the morning, he rushes to the shower, and while gulping his coffee he swallows his salad and runs, not even managing to put a hat on his head. The woman fusses with her clothes and hair, and if she has a spare hour, she spends it in idle conversation or sitting in some playhouse.

I laughed and said, But you are not among the believers yourself, Dvora.

True, but at least I remember what once was. In the last few years the city has exploded with people, she continued, until the screeching buses and screaming airplanes have closed in on us. To where? What is the hurry? People once went places on foot or in a wagon and there was time to see things. Philosophers would walk slowly, thinking their thoughts as they strolled. And today? Notice how noisy it is inside the house, how the walls vibrate from the traffic.

I had not noticed any particular noise, actually. On the contrary, the apartment had always seemed isolated from its surroundings, but I didn't argue.

I came here to escape the suffocation of a different neighborhood, said Dvora, to live beside the serene and fragrant orchards. But at the end only one open space remained, across from my window—an unusual spot among the rows of urban walls. Only from this lot could I draw enough breath. It sated itself on sun and raindrops and grew what it could in the way of grass and plants and a few bushes, which were more solidly rooted than they looked. Flocks of birds would sometimes stop in the vacant lot on their migrations, scrabbling joyously around this strip of living earth, and in the autumn the Arab shepherd would climb through the broken fence with his flock. He would lead his sheep to the green pasture, take out his flute and play a shepherd's tune, as if for me. The tune made me homesick for the days before the earth was ruined, when it still lay open to the sky and grass and fruit trees grew upon it, as God had ordained to sustain man and beast.

I could not travel to see other landscapes, she continued, so the lot brought back to me a piece of that childhood landscape that glimmered like a paradise in my memory, and which I would never see again. In the spring I barely moved from the window. I only half-lowered the folding shutters, to cut off my view of everything outside the vacant lot, setting off the place for myself alone. Then I lived among the butterflies and beetles and tribes of alley cats who found refuge in the lot from the murderous monsters that roared down the streets. There they basked in the sun or rolled about the warm grass with that simple pleasure only animals know in this world.

When the weather was good the vegetable dealer would bring his horse there in the evening, and the horse would chew his fodder with the perfect contentment of a laborer, at the end of a long day, eating a well-earned meal. At night the crickets would chirp a song of praise in their glassy voices for whoever had made the grass and dew and darkness—one of those hymns that is revealed to poets with ears to hear it, like Basya's brother from our town. I would look through the window and see all this, and my heart would open wide and tremble.

But I knew that, with my bad luck, I did not merit a miracle patch like this one. In nightmares I would see the hand of destruction suspended over the lot. And I arose one morning, not long ago, looked outside, and saw: The lot lay supine before me, dead. Its bushes and grass had been torn up, and a man was passing over it with a bulldozer, uprooting the last few blades. Even before the day was over, the lot had been leveled. Through two openings that had been cut in the fence vehicles roared in with horns blaring, trucks and motorcycles and taxis, a herd of beasts of prey with blazing eyes. The strip of sky above them grew hazy and a cloud arose, filling the air with dust and the stench of rubber and gasoline. It was a parking lot, and at night, after their petroleum souls had sunk into slumber, the cars seemed like a petrified herd of primeval beasts in the moonlight. All I could do was fan myself with a handkerchief, struggling for a breath of air.

So what sense is there in my staying alive, you tell me, she concluded, without fear or complaint.

I am not afraid of dying, she said, while I was still searching for the right words. To what can a person's life be compared? To a railroad jour-

ney. If a person traveling on a train worries about the train being derailed, they will not see the beauty rushing by. In life, it is better to look
at the sights and forget the dangers.

This philosophy of yours is new to me, I said. You were the one who
always said that you lived with premonitions of impending doom.

That was when I was young and my life and the lives of the people
around me still had some worth; but today, at my age, I have lost the
sense of that worth, and with it the sense of danger. Nothing remains
for me to fear. Even the past seems distant, I seem to have finally left it
behind. There are only two things I regret, she said firmly, that I did not
send Tsipora to school when she was little, and that I allowed my legs to
waste away. But so it was fated, apparently. I am content with myself and
with the world.

Especially now that you have nearly finished telling me your story, I
thought, without daring to express what I was thinking.

A sick and housebound woman like myself, she continued, who no
longer has a hand in what happens outside her room; I am like a soldier,
who fell behind his unit during a march. He is cut off while his friends
move onward in their rows, and so the distance between him and his
friends grows ever greater. Some of them come to visit their wounded
comrade; but their eyes are always sliding toward their watches. One
does not wish to "disturb" me, another has an urgent meeting or someone is waiting outside. From their colognes or the expression of anticipated pleasures I know that they are on their way to some entertainment.
When they leave, barrenness descends upon me, and deep within me the
bitter taste of disappointment rises, too familiar now.

You are trying to find some comfort for me, she smiled, reading my
thoughts, if only the comfort of this faithful watch, which keeps on beating like the heart of a loyal pet. But from here on my highest goal is to
meet my death gracefully. I have seen a few people do that.

I pushed aside my terror, reminding myself that I would have to share
even this chapter with her, and with dignity, as she was doing. Tell me,
I begged.

There was Chaya-Fruma, of whom we have spoken. When she felt her
death was approaching, she found a good home for her cow, who had been

her closest companion on earth, and she swallowed the medicine she knew would shorten her suffering. My mother told me that together with the bonds of sleep she was wrapped in a radiance that poured light on her as from an invisible sun, and by this marvelous light my mother understood what awaits those who had been burnished with suffering in this world.

Grandma Henya's end was like that, too. She prepared for her death with moderation and reason, as was her way. She, who had no children, prepared her own "eternal clothes" so they fit correctly, and accepted a promise from her nephew that he would recite the Kaddish in her memory. When she felt one morning that she could no longer get out of bed, she asked that the sheets on her bed be changed and candles lit. But since it was Passover, she strengthened herself and said: "Why should I ruin anyone's holiday?" When the moment finally came, she allowed herself to fall asleep on the pillow beneath her head, and those who were caring for her said that she returned her soul to heaven as pure as when she had received it.

How do you know these stories? I blurted out.

I have long been meditating on a proper death. Even here, in this country, I happened upon a few. I heard about a pioneer who fell ill with malaria and would not recover. I was told that one night his ten-year-old daughter awoke to the sound of someone singing, a joyous song. She arose and walked into the next room and saw her father with something like rays emanating from him, filling up the room; everything around— the table, the chairs, the books—radiated too, as if they were sharing the joy. She called her mother, and when she looked, she told her daughter that they were seeing the godhead. In the morning when the father awoke, trying to warm himself up because the malaria was making him shiver, he joyfully related that he had seen his holy grandfather and family rowing toward him in a boat, and he asked to be given his good clothes so he could go and greet them; with that, he departed this world.

Suddenly I remembered my mother's death and the sign she gave me that it was approaching. My heart surged as I said to Dvora: Maybe my mother belongs among these stories. She died ten years ago.

Dvora fell silent and listened.

After her heart was damaged, I made a habit of telephoning every morning and asking how she felt. I called from work, right after I got to the office. I would find my mother still in bed, reading a book or the paper, after my father had brought her coffee in bed and left for work.

I remember well a winter morning when I arrived at the office soaked from the rain. Still taking off my coat and scarf, I dialed my parents' number. My mother picked up immediately, as usual, but her voice was sad and soft. What happened? I asked. Do you feel sick? She answered, "No, I just had a bad dream last night." I asked her to tell me. It was the first time in my life my mother had told me a dream the next morning—although she knew I had a professional interest in dreams. This was my mother's story: "In the dream I saw my younger sister Bella, the most beautiful of us sisters, who died, as you know, in Auschwitz with everyone else. In the dream I saw my sister wearing a white dress, stretching out her arms to me and calling me to come to her—but I could not reach her, for some reason, I just couldn't."

I heard the tears in my mother's voice. Why couldn't you? I asked. "I don't know," she said, "she was in a different world. Maybe she was asking me to save her from death, and I couldn't rescue her."

I don't remember what I said to my mother, I continued my story to Dvora Baron. Maybe I said that it would soothe her to have told her dream, and maybe I comforted her with the fact that Bella was now a part of her, and this Bella, the internal one, she could certainly protect. The conversation ended as usual with the promise that we would speak again that afternoon.

The next day was Mother's Day, and I came to her with a bouquet of anemones—red, white, and purple ones—which cheered her up. We did not speak of the dream. On the third day after the dream, on a rainy morning, a few minutes after she had arrived at the volunteer headquarters for a meeting about founding a shelter for battered women, her heart stopped. She just fell down and died. Later I remembered the dream and thought that she had been given a sign from that world, and that now she was certainly with her sister Bella.

We sat quietly, and in the silence I saw my mother before my eyes. What would she say now, to the two of us? I thought to myself, she would certainly have shown her impatience at this idleness, a woman lying in bed like that for years, for no good reason. "How could you think only about yourself?" she would ask her. "After all, there's a lot of work to be done!"

While I was still imagining this encounter, shielding Dvora from my mother's directness, Dvora suddenly asked, Are you like your mother?

The way we look, I answered, the look in our eye; but for the rest of it—I don't know. I'm a little thinner, I responded lamely.

I have sometimes thought, Dvora surprised me by saying, that women like us find support primarily in their fathers, pushing our mothers aside.

What do you mean by "women like us"? I asked.

Women who work and create, finding their own place in the world, which is a man's world, of course. I have often thought about how my father was my support in childhood and gave me the permission to study as a son. He created a special place for me in the family, and that was how it all started. Even after his death he was the figure I raised before my eyes in times of trouble, from which I drew advice or comfort. It is sad, but apparently unavoidable, that my mother's concern and dedication never turned into a similar source of strength for me. What do you think? she turned to me. In your generation there are many more women who took destiny into their own hands.

There are studies that show, I said, that the father's acceptance and encouragement are decisive factors in a daughter's success—not the mother's. In my family it was also my father from whom I acquired the drive to succeed. Only recently have I understood that my mother was also a talented and unique person in her own right—not only as my father's wife. When I grew older, I had a lot of support from her nevertheless. She was proud of me and I respected her, and I never told the story of that dream to anyone until now.

Why not? she asked.

I don't know, there are secrets that maintain their power only as long as you keep them. Once a young man told me a dream he had about his friend who had been killed in the war, that his friend came to him and they sat on the steps of the kibbutz dining hall and joked about the fig-

ures of the girls—exactly as they had in real life. He didn't talk to anyone about his dream, the young man told me, because he thought that
if he kept it to himself, it would be more likely that his friend would
come back in a dream the following night, which would ease the sharpness of the loss. But the miracle did not recur, so he finally allowed himself to tell me about the dream.

It is easy to tell you things, she said.

Is there something else you want to tell me? I asked, as if I felt our
story approaching its end.

There are nights when the years rest heavily upon me, she said. Sometimes I see the nightlight near my bed as the flame of the candle in my
father's house, flashing and hinting something to me, I know not what.
Sometimes I see myself as the sole survivor of a tribe that has been
destroyed one by one, like a tree whose limbs have been lopped off, leaving only scars and a phantom pain where they had been. From somewhere a damp, chill wind blows in and penetrates my room, and I can
hear the distant echo of a cry from the open mouths of freshly dug
graves. The house seems a flimsy hut perched one step from the abyss.
God of Sarah, Rebecca, Rachel, and Leah—I remember my mother's
whisper in times of danger. What happened? she suddenly asked, as if
she had noticed the shudder that gripped me.

You don't have to be your age to feel that way, I said.

You know what I mean then, she said. I remember when we spoke of
that.

I was amazed by the clarity of her memory—for I had already forgotten having revealed my secret to her, it must have been at one of our
first meetings—I couldn't quite remember.

Well, mostly since my husband died, I answered, there is a black pit,
which only I can see, and it is with me all the time, always one step
ahead of me. When I remember its presence, I know that I must make a
true effort not to slip. It's the same step that separates you from the
void, as you just said. Sometimes I'm tired and I say to myself: Fine, I'll
sink into the black hole and that will be the end of the story.

But you do not, she said, with surprising firmness.

No.

And how do you make sure not to stumble? she asked.

I turn up the volume of the music. Concentrate on the bird swaying on the branch outside my kitchen window. Drive like mad up the road to the Augusta Victoria Hospital and gaze at the desert stretching behind Mount Scopus. Sometimes I think of my son waiting for me at home, about a man I love meditating on the Jaffa beach. Then, it's as if a door had opened and my mother enters in a flood of light, radiating goodwill, and the pit recedes.

Dvora nodded: It is not bad to die, Amia, certainly not at my age. Life and death are like seasons, coming and going in turn, like the waves on that Jaffa beach of yours, she smiled understandingly. As when the rains rage, until no one can leave the house. And then one day the snow falls persistently, until the puddles and mounds of garbage are covered and the sky brightens.

Again she's in her childhood town, I thought; and she continued dreamily, her eyes fixed on the ceiling. Then the wheel turns again: spring comes, and the river cracks and the fruit blossoms; and again summer, with its colorful fruit. And so in a human life: In the morning one prepares for market day, the sugar, the kerosene, and jars of herring; and at night peace descends on everything, and only one man returns his soul to his Creator this night. And again morning, and the dead man is brought to burial, his relatives accompanying him with sobs; and the wagons are already returning from the graveyard, and soon the neighing horses and ringing bells are heard, and the first wagons draw up to the market square. And so the circle turns over and over again.

I could see her drawing deep into herself before my eyes; and along with it growing and expanding in perfect clarity, eyes radiant and wise. Was she finally achieving the precious balance between consciousness and the unconscious—past, present, and future like the river of life itself? She was turning her back on us and toward her own garden, now at the end of her journey.

This time I have read your thoughts, Dvora, I thought as she continued: That is how I wish to depart this world. I see the coming days. My heart will go weaker, my face ever paler, and my hair will glow white on my skull and to those who pass my window, will seem like a halo. I will sit on an easy chair for hours, seeing again the orchard and the grove of pines, and at twilight I shall watch over my childhood, which was also graced with a fading light like this. The narrow path I traveled in life will wind between dreaming and waking, dusk and dawn, high walls and angry hedges to the right and left; but I will gaze only before me, onward, to the marvelous rose garden awaiting me where the walls end. I will remember the old books in the attic that sweetened my lonely hours, and my pure-eyed mother and the smell of the kitchen and the nut trees in the courtyard that were a canopy against the rain and sun, where I once learned to gather points of light dancing in the shadows.

She shut her eyes. Our silence lasted for a long while. She did not answer when I asked if I could bring her something from the kitchen. The blanket rose and fell rhythmically, and I arose and left the room.

"Where I once learned to gather points of light dancing in the shadows," I repeated to myself on the stairwell. I tried to draw another sentence from my memory, to console myself; and only in the car, on the way home, did her beloved voice sing in my ears, only to me: "Thanks to these embroideries an eternal spring began to bloom."

epilogue

After Dvora had spoken with me about her death, there was an unspoken agreement between us that her story was at an end and there was nothing more to add to it. I continued to visit Dvora Baron's house without a tape recorder all that summer, and I visited Dvora in the hospital when she was hospitalized shortly after our last conversation. Surprisingly, Dvora took no interest in what I was doing with the material I had collected, and only Tsipora asked me from time to time how the editing was going, as if "editing" was what my work came down to. But the two of them were very taken up with Dvora's health, which deteriorated all summer, and the matter of Dvora's story ceased to concern them.

In the first few weeks Dvora's condition was surprisingly changeable. Some days she seemed to be growing stronger. She intended to try walking again, and hoped the operation would improve her sight enough for her to get back to her translation of a Thomas Hardy novel, work that might alleviate the financial pressure in the house. One day she came out of her room to greet me, looking beautiful in a dress I had never seen, patent leather shoes on her feet. She walked with difficulty, leaning on a cane, and she said with a brave smile: Now this is walking. Then she sat in an armchair and spoke optimistically about her literary plans for the future. But it seemed to me that these were the last flashes of life visiting her weakened body like a dying spasm, and most visits found her melancholy and pale, lying in bed, as if she was looking death in the eye.

Dvora Baron's cataract operation took place in the Tel Hashomer Hospital at the end of June 1956, and was considered a success. The second hospitalization, following a high fever, began on August 13 of the same year, and the tests showed a disturbance in the brain. Dvora Baron lost consciousness a few days later, and died on August 20, 1956. She is buried at the edge of the writers' section in the old cemetery on Trumpeldor Street in Tel Aviv.

Her daughter, Tsipora, liquidated the household possessions. She transferred the proceeds to Rivka Guber, who founded a rest home for writers in Dvora Baron's name in the town of Lakhish. Tsipora herself chose to live in dire poverty, despite the attempts of a few family friends to help her out, devoting herself to the literary estate of her two parents, to aiding—with no financial compensation—in the editing and publication of the writings of a number of family friends, and to working for the indigent blind and others. In 1971, between the New Year and Yom Kippur, in an attic apartment in which she lived alone, Tsipora met her death from a uteral hemorrhage, apparently the result of prolonged malnutrition. Her body was found three days after her death. "A saint," she was called at the gravesite by the cleaning woman, an Iraqi immigrant, whom Tsipora had taught to read and write "as if she were my mother."

For long months my conversations with Dvora Baron were the center of my world. They accompanied me each morning to my work at the university, I spoke of them with my children and friends, and at night they visited me in my dreams. During the day I heard the rustle of the long white dress of the young Dvora, strolling with a parasol through the woods of Lithuania, her deep voice as she spoke biblical Hebrew with her students—young boys gazing at her with longing eyes. At night I saw her beside me by the light of a round green lampshade, bent over pages crowded with letters, struggling to express her stifled rage over the injustices done to women, carving out a single Hebrew sentence that could ring true to her musical ears. For many months she was with me.

On the anniversary of her death, early in the morning, I left my house in Jerusalem to find the grave of Dvora Baron in the old cemetery on Trumpeldor Street. I had not stopped on this street, so close to my childhood house, for many years. My father prayed at the synagogue across from the cemetery during the whole period we lived in Tel Aviv, and on Friday evenings I would accompany him there. This morning it was desolate and shut down, and there was no one around but the boys from the Ankori Vocational School in their blue shirts, hanging around their parked cars and talking loudly. The cemetery gate was locked too, and I sat on the railing of the house across the way to wait for the guard to arrive at nine, as the sign promised. A young man with curled side-locks arrived in a taxi, shot a hostile glance at the boys across the street, and hesitated before greeting me, a woman in pants, waiting for him at the gate. But when he heard I was looking for the writers' section, he eagerly offered to help me locate the grave in the small, manicured cemetery. The boys made him angry, he explained, the way they came to the cemetery to smoke and play hooky. Section 4, row 11, number 4, he announced after checking his list, and hurried to lead me there. Dvora Baron Aharonovich, clear black letters said on an unadorned gravestone. A few rows over Bialik and Tschernichovski, the giants of the nation, lay under monumental stones. Dvora Baron, the sole female author of her generation, was at the very edge.

In the bed of broken soil over the grave stood a truncated date palm, with dried-out, dead fronds. Who planted a palm tree here? I asked the guard. "No one plants palm trees here," he answered, "the wind blows the seeds, and they plant themselves." He pointed to a tree with a thick head of fronds on a grave up the path, and another, a young one, breaking through between the cracks in the walkway. "But someone cut down the palm tree that was blossoming here," I commented. He shrugged. He wasn't the gardener here, and in any case, he was too young to remember. But a tender new palm recently sprang up in my friend's garden in Jaffa, I thought. I left a small stone on the grave of the writer and parted from the guard with a smile.

The autumn arrived, and with it obligations demanding my return. I took a final vacation at the end of the holiday season, a farewell to summer. I walk barefoot with my friend Aviva on the warm sands of the beach at Ma'agan Michael. Soon the sun will set, and the birds rush toward the nests of approaching night.

I tell Aviva about Dvora Baron, about her loneliness, her death, her daughter, her stories, my own story that is nearing completion.

"It isn't necessary to solve every riddle," Aviva says to me.

For a moment I'm alarmed. She's hit the target. I remember Rilke, in Dvora's voice, saying: "Love the question, young man, no less than you strive after the answer." Then I suddenly recall the unfinished notes Rachel Eitan left after her death—question marks in the riddle of Dvora Baron, and the wonderful quotations in Nurith Govrin's book from members of my own generation, talking about the writer's character— although they had never met her face-to-face.

In Ruth Almog's book, *Death in the Rain*, it is written: "And in one of those houses once lived an amazing invalid named Dvora Baron, who enslaved the members of her family to her illness, which may have been imaginary, the one whom no one reads anymore. Flaubert survived and she passed away."[1]

And the lines from Moshe Ben-Shaul's poem:

> I thought I would write about the author Dvora Baron
> Whom I loved
> Bony and pale, dying in her bed . . .

> I thought I would write about the author Dvora Baron
> I thought I could see her
> I thought I could be
> A chapter in the chapters of her life . . .
> What would I write about this woman
> I don't think I know . . .
> The wheel of the eye a blackening kernel of wheat
> Her hands covered
> And a yellowish paleness at the edge of the picture.[2]

The riddle remains, I hope, I said to Aviva.

And so we sat in silence on the fine sand, and above the island of birds the sun descended and slowly set, and the sky filled with red.

JERUSALEM 1990–91

1. Ruth Almog, *Death in the Rain* (Jerusalem, 1982), p. 33.
2. Moshe Ben-Shaul, "I Wanted to Write About Dvora Baron," *Achshav* 51–54 (1987), pp. 207–10.

Fradl

BY DVORA BARON

Fradl

_____

DVORA BARON

FULL OF CHARM, BUT ALSO sorrowful in spirit, was the woman Fradl in Chana's hometown, whom fate had dealt with bitterly and she struggled with it mightily for years.

She was the daughter of one of the best local families, and she had a large house in the community alley that she had inherited from her parents, who died in her childhood. Her relatives, in whose house she had been raised, were the ones who, when the time came, found a mate for her—an educated boy from the next town who was also of good family. And the two were bound together with a betrothal celebration and the remittance of the dowry, and after the wedding, they came to live in the big house that was in the community alley.

A few elegant pieces of furniture were brought from the provincial capital, and the woman had clothes sewn for her in the big-city style, and in them she walked from room to spacious room, in which reigned order and cleanliness and a frozen stillness.

The lacy curtains here bestowed a pale light, something like the afterimage of snow, and even the silver bowls in the cupboard glinted with a frosty, whitish shine, and the woman, as she gazed out every once in a while at the alley, which was darkened by poverty but radiated the joy of life, seemed as if she were warming herself in that radiance.

A school for the children of the poor had been founded at that time, and her husband—Avraham-Noach was his name—volunteered to teach arithmetic there. Aside from that he also had some business, commercial matters, which he had taken up at that time, and he spent most of the hours of his day buying and selling. And when he came home for the meal, he would read the newspaper or some book, an activity best done quietly. So nothing could be heard here other than the clink of silverware and china as they ate. Afterward the tablecloth was carefully shaken off and the woman went off somewhere, to her embroidery, or else she stepped out at dusk to the bench beside her house. Here, she sat, with her kerchief bound modestly around her head, a young woman of charm and goodness but without that secret joy one sees in a woman's face in the first flush of married love. And when the neighbor women around discerned this, their hearts went out to her, but the rabbi's wife, a woman of intelligence, said: "She is still 'empty,' therefore she sorrows, her hands will be 'filled' and respite will come to her."

And it would be impossible not to mention here the widow Sarah-Leah and her son Chaim-Raphael, who also lived in that alley, and their vegetable garden that bordered on Fradl's yard.

They also had a spacious house with a grassy yard where wildflowers grew in abundance in the summertime. And Fradl, in her childhood, had often come to play there. The kind-hearted Sarah-Leah had fed her sugar cookies with cherry jam and had embraced her tenderly, with a wistful sorrow, since she herself had not been blessed with a daughter. Her son Chaim-Raphael, already past his bar mitzvah then, had also attached himself to the little girl during the hours when he was out of school, swinging her in the swing in the corner of the garden or pushing her doll carriage that had been brought for her from the city. He would loosen one of the screws and send the carriage flying down the paved path, while they, her little hand in his palm, ran after it laughing so brightly and merrily that even the mother, Sarah-Leah, would momentarily forget the sorrow of her widowhood at the sight and laugh right along with them.

And so the years passed, and the little girl, who went off to live in her relatives' house after her parents died, became a young woman and went out for walks with Liebka, the daughter of her uncle Isser Levin, and with Reyzl, the daughter of her aunt Chana, in their skirts and cotton-knit shirts. Chaim-Raphael also matured and grew tall, and was already doing business with agents and landowners, for like his father, Yerucham-David, he too was in the grain trade.

He only saw Fradl from time to time—in the market square or in the linden avenue, and then he would incline his head to her politely. At such moments, his cheeks would flush red with excitement, while her face remained closed and cold.

His friends, who saw into his heart, would go off with him on summer Sabbaths toward the Countess's wheatfields, where they knew the girl would be walking during those hours. But when they happened upon her on one of the trails, she would flutter by as if she had not seen them; and the scent of her perfume, mingled with that of the field, would make the boy dizzy. He finally decided in his own heart that he would no longer even step foot beyond the bounds of the town, and he distanced himself from his friends, who had witnessed his weakness, and began to spend more time with the agents and dealers in the marketplace. From them he acquired a sharp and joking tongue—something a sensitive person wields, in most cases, to conceal a wounded heart—and on the Sabbath, when the Torah was being read in the synagogue, he would go down to where they sat behind the pulpit to talk. And his mother, as she saw from behind the lattice how he stood there exposed and small among his peers, most of whom were wrapped in the prayer shawls worn by married men, her heart wept within her.

For years the old man Shmuel-Meir, who was a longtime friend of the widow's family, would come over there after Sabbath had ended for a glass of tea. In the past, when Yerucham-David was still alive, a pleasant sense of well-being would reign over those evenings, along with that unique spirit, in which the sacred and the profane mingle.

People were still dressed in their Sabbath finery, but steam from the simmering samovar was already rising over the table, and the host and his guest, over glasses of tea, played chess on the checker-

board that was set into the middle of the table. Their combat was
pleasant, without the storminess of war, punctuated by rabbinical
proverbs or jokes, and in the meantime Sarah-Leah, the strand of
pearls around her throat, was preparing the post-Sabbath meal in the
kitchen or she was arranging the Sabbath goblets in the glassed-in
breakfront with a silvery tinkle that eased the heart.

Now there was gloom in the house.

Sarah-Leah's pearls were tucked away in the moneylender's strong-
box, and the breakfront, without the glitter of the silver vessels, stood
cold and shadowy; only the luster of the friendship of the old
man Shmuel-Meir had not dulled. Diligently stirring the watery tea
he was served, just as if it had been sweetened as before, with a generous hand, Shmuel-Meir would ask Chaim-Raphael how his business
was going and pass along some advice—he was a man of experience
with a good sense for such things—and then, in order to raise the
spirits of the two of them, he would talk about what he had seen
and heard in the course of the week. Out of respect for him they
would listen attentively, and even contribute a few words from time
to time, although their minds, as could be seen from the expressions
on their faces, were often drifting far off from such matters.

Once, after such a tea party, during which the old man had heard
more of the surging of their hearts than he did of their words, he
went into the shop of Isser Levin, the man in whose house Fradl had
been raised, and made the suggestion that to his mind seemed perfectly appropriate. For the person in question, Chaim-Raphael, was
a fine vessel, and the families on both sides have long and distinguished pedigrees—the match would be like a graft of two strong
grapevines.

But the proud grocer answered with such an emphatic "No" that
the old man recoiled, as if someone had thrown a stone at him, and
walked out without a farewell, and he carried that humiliation in his
heart for a long time.

It was different with Sarah-Leah, who showed no signs of anger
when word of the story reached her, and who continued to speak
with members of the Levin family with as good a temper as before,

and she also treated Fradl warmly when she returned to live next door—although Fradl, actually, seemed somewhat estranged—and from time to time would bring her homemade pastries or preserves. The neighbor women, who saw this, were amazed at her good nature, and some of them noted that although she was named after two of the biblical matriarchs, by her deeds she was equal to all four of them together.

In the third year of her marriage Fradl gave birth to a son, and the dark house, which had always seemed to be shadowed by a cloud, rang out with joy.

Aunt Chana closed her millinery shop and arrived to tie on Fradl's apron, and very soon the smell of cinnamon and warm honey suffused the house.

On the clothesline, in the yard, all the infant clothes that had been tucked away for a long time were hung for all to see, and in the evening the nighttime prayers of the little boys from the cheders rang out, and Mirl, the child of Chana's old age—she was as young as the little boys were—passed out sweets with an embarrassed smile.

It was a great moment when the child, during the circumcision ceremony, was named for his mother's father, Barukh-Leyb, who was called the Strongman for the bravery of his heart, and who had passed away in the prime of his days, before his time.

When the weakened Fradl's cries joined those of the infant, Avraham-Noach looked at her with eyes moist with pardon and trembling, and the rabbi's wife, who was among the invited guests, said that now the flaw had been set right and the bond between the two of them would henceforth be solid.

Now came days that were like the days of half-holiday, for those to whom an eldest son has been born.

The fancy tablecloth had not yet been removed from the table, and relatives and friends who stopped in were treated to wine and confections, amidst preparations for the celebration of the "redemption of the first-born son," when the infant would be a month old.

The custom of the Levin family was to celebrate this ritual with a great banquet and invited guests; so the large pots were taken down from the kitchen shelves, and from the nearest town the woman Toybe, a seasoned cook, was brought over. Then the child fell ill.

In the evening the sound of women cooking up a storm could still be heard from the kitchen and by the morning Avraham-Noach could already be seen running with galoshes on his bare feet to the doctor; then the sound of weeping echoed through the rooms and the house was plunged once again into shadow.

An infant who dies before he reaches his first month is not mourned according to the customs of mourning, so the rooms were cleared of everything with which they had been filled. The servant-girl took all the appetizers and cakes down to the poor people in the gulch, which now would not be needed, and Avraham-Noach began to go out in public again. He worked at his business and went to the community house for a little conversation, or he went down to the town garbage dump to visit Zanvil Elke, who had recently returned from the Talmudic Academy and was always ready for a game of chess. From a square of cardboard they cut out the pieces that would represent the pawns, the knights, and the bishops, and sent forth these troops against each other with the cool poise of seasoned military commanders. Sometimes they sat over the board so far into the night that the footsteps of the butchers sounded as they walked to the slaughterhouse after midnight, at which point Elke, the mother, would awaken and begin grumbling about how they were wasting her kerosene. Then, the guest would get up, unwillingly draw on his coat, and go.

"Mixed-up" Gitl, Fradl's neighbor on the kitchen side, once saw him steal into the house through the back entrance, and then from inside came the sound of words and a moaning cry, and the next day she told the women about it at the community bench, where the relations between the two spouses was by now a frequent subject, and little Chana, who was playing there, listened to the story.

In that place, in those days, they did not believe in shielding the eyes of a child by throwing an elegant prayer shawl over life's nakedness. And so, along with the song of sun-dazzled birds and the scent of dew-drunk plants, she also absorbed impressions of daily life, bits

of local color, of heart ache and joy, which in the course of time—
when they had been refined and illuminated by the light of her intellect, and experience had bound them into lifestories—became for her,
in the solitary nights of her wandering, a source of pleasure and comfort.

In those days Fradl was no longer as beautiful as she had once
been, the light in her shining light blue eyes had been dimmed, and
her body, like a plant that has not been watered for many days, had
gone slack and lost its flexibility, and one could see from her knitting, as she sat on the bench outside, that she kept it up only for the
sake of appearances, for the stitches did not match up and the spool
of yarn grew no smaller.

Sometimes in the afternoon hours Aunt Racha, the wife of Isser
Levin, would come by. She was a woman as intelligent and tough-
minded as he was. Then she and Fradl would go into a small side
room, where they would remain for a long time. When Fradl came
out to see her visitor to the front gate, her face looked as if it had
been washed after a cry.

Once Avraham-Noach's sister came for a few days from the district capital for a visit. She was elegantly tall with uncovered blond
hair she wore in thick curls, and when she was at her brother's side,
his face glowed, as if it were reflecting her radiance. On the Sabbath
the two of them sang the Sabbath hymns together, as they had in
their parents' house, he in a deep bass voice and she in the tones of
a harp.

For the first time since the man had come to live in that house,
the sound of singing emerged from there, and the neighbors, in the
course of their Sabbath strolls, drew near and saw Fradl, standing at
the front door, still and cold in a dark kerchief that cast a pall across
her face—a shadow.

Aunt Chana, who had some acquaintance with the visitor since she
often traveled to the provincial capital on matters relating to her
store, came the next day for a visit, for she had heard that the
woman was preparing to depart. And when she saw Fradl prostrate

with melancholy, a bandage tied to her aching forehead, she drew the city woman into the next room and asked her, speaking laconically because of the constraints of time, if she could do something to help her, for certainly she could see what was becoming of the woman.

But Avraham-Noach's sister, fixing on Aunt Chana with her intelligent eyes, responded with another question: What could she do? When things had come to such a pass, she said, was there anyone who could assume responsibility for another in affairs of the heart?

After a slight hesitation she added with a sigh, very seriously, that in her opinion it would be better if they were to separate. Neither he nor she had any other real alternative, she pronounced, and with that she walked out and went along her way, for she heard her carriage arrive.

After that it became perfectly clear to the members of the family that there was no hope left for the woman, and Aunt Racha, her confidante, made no attempt to shield Fradl from that fact. But she, like a sick person of whose life the doctors had already despaired, tried a number of other various remedies: she had a few dresses made up, as people did then, in fiery colors, although they only accentuated her pallour; and when she was told that a man likes a woman with some flesh on her bones, she began to fill herself up with fortifying foods: fattening cereals and thick cream soups.

On the step at the entrance to the kitchen was where she usually sat, swallowing slowly from the full bowl with such a grimace of distaste that whoever saw her would be unable to touch that particular food again.

It was especially difficult to see her in her servility when she hurried forward to bring him, her husband, his coat or umbrella because it had begun to rain—which he rejected, incidentally, with a gesture of protest—or when she squeezed herself to the side, in order to make room for him, when she saw him coming as she sat on the step.

The post or the door against which she was leaning became at that moment a depression into which she pressed herself to become yet a little smaller and more insubstantial, and at those moments, in the headshake of those who watched her, there remained no compassion, only scorn, the emotion aroused in us by the hated one in the Scriptures, like Leah who defiles and humiliates herself by chasing after a little husbandly affection.

Those whose hearts were no longer touched by the fate of the woman watched her struggles only because they were curious, the way one might follow such a character in a novel. And there were some among them who really found in it the stimulation and spicy plot of a romance. For after all, did they not also have before their eyes the figure of Chaim-Raphael, the neighbor, with his "deafness" toward everything that touched upon the matter of marriage; he, whose afflicted face made him seem like a person for whom life was an uncharted wilderness.

With what careless abandon he stood on the dilapidated bridge, at the very height of the breakup of the river ice, and how eagerly he pursued every opportunity, as a member of Hospice for the Poor, to care for sick people afflicted with contagious conditions.

During a fire, he was seen jumping into a burning building in order to save a few petty household items, and his mother Sarah-Leah, when she saw that he was tarrying inside, climbed up herself onto the ladder that led to the opening.

Afterward she stood on the nearby grassy field and smothered the places on his clothes that were still smoking; then, the old man Shmuel-Meir approached them and rebuked the young man angrily, which was not his usual way. Have you forgotten the commandment 'And you shall guard your own souls?' he said. And he, with a twisted mouth, looked at him and laughed a strange laugh, like Crazy Chaim-Zelig during a heat wave.

Once, it was in the summertime, Avraham-Noach suddenly became ill in the middle of the night.

It seemed to him as he slept that someone was stabbing him in the side with a knife, and when he awoke he felt as if that entire part of his body were about to split open, and he was seized by a choking sensation and deathly terror.

Fradl, who had also awakened, got out of bed and stood over him

in alarm; so as not to be oppressed by her questions, he tried to restrain himself and swallow the pain, but when it grew stronger he
asked for a doctor to be called, and Fradl—the servant-girl was sleeping in her own house at the outskirts of town that night—went outside and looked in both directions, mentally weighing which way to
turn. But since the nearby houses all stood closed and shuttered, as
if estranged from her, she turned and climbed the porch steps of the
factory owner's house, and as she had before in the time of the catastrophe, when her mother and father had left her, she knocked softly
on the glass door there. The man inside—as if he had been awake
and waiting for the knock—immediately dressed, took up his stick
to defend himself against dogs of unfamiliar streets, and went to get
the doctor. He also went to the pharmacy to buy the medicines, and
then he sat by himself in the big room and waited, in case he should
be needed for something else.

When the servant-girl came in at daybreak, she was amazed to
see the strange neighbor sitting, absolutely still, eyes closed as if he
were dreaming. She walked over and extinguished the lamp that was
burning at the side of the room, at which point the man turned gray,
awoke, arose, and walked out.

And as her husband rallied and he could take from her hand some
small sustenance, Fradl's spirits were revived. She herself swept and
scrubbed his room, and drew aside or raised or lowered the curtain
on the window as he desired; she walked about in light house slippers to keep down the noise, looking as if she were floating on air.

From the attic she took down the folding chair, in which one
could both recline and lie down, and as soon as the patient could get
up and stand on his legs, she took this reclining chair to the side of
the yard where the climbing vines from the widow's garden cast
their shade. She also brought out one of the little ottomans so that
the man could eat his meals on it as if it were a table.

But as soon as the man took a whiff of fresh air, he stood up and
crossed the synagogue square at a diagonal and, to the astonishment
of the people watching him, walked down toward Zanvil Elke's room
at the edge of the garbage dump.

He was still unsteady on his feet, but his game partner, who came out to greet him, supported him as the two of them walked over to the shack where the wild dogs emerged to circle him, and a dust cloud from the garbage of the community whirled about him in the breeze.

Now the servant-girl could put the dishes back in their places and walk around the rooms in her nailed shoes without fear of disturbing anyone's rest.

At that time Aunt Chana was about to leave for the village of Kaminka to attend an engagement party at the house of one of her relatives, and Fradl went to help her with the preparations for travel. In the course of that day she was not seen in the alley, until the neighbors were sure that she, too, had gone off with her aunt. But later that evening, when "mixed-up" Gitl approached the shared fence, she saw a kind of housedress lying there on the other side. Thinking that a piece of laundry had been left there, she stooped down and was about to pick it up when the dress moved. What revealed itself from within it convulsed before her like someone in the spasms of death. Then the God-struck woman clapped her hands together and ran quickly to the community house, where a few Talmud students were passing a friendly hour, and called out in a horrified voice: "Come and look how he butchered her now."

She gestured toward Avraham-Noach, who was among the group seated there.

The rabbi's wife, who understood that the woman had been "visited by the spirit," called to her in soothing tones: "Gitl, Gitl," and she drew her behind the partition of the women's section and spoke to her with coaxing, pacifying words until she calmed down.

But the people there, around the table, could not find the thread of their conversation again, and one by one, they got up and left, as if in shame.

At about that time Mordechai Katz bought the tar furnaces in the Kochticzy Forest from the Zarczya farm, and invited Avraham-Noach to be his manager and bookkeeper. He accepted.

A house had not yet been set up for a family, so the man prepared to go out there on his own for the present, and he packed up everything he thought he would need as Fradl stood by his side and helped him.

It was something of a shoal this, amidst the angry waves surrounding them, and they, exhausted from their struggles, both took their rest on it. For in his mind's eye, he already saw himself in the refuge of the abundant fields of Zarczya, and felt the contact of men with whom he shared a bond of affection.

Fradl passed the pressing iron over his linens, and in a special basket prepared all sorts of pastries for him, which were good for snacks. On the day of his departure, she accompanied him to the hotel at the edge of the town, where the farm's carriage awaited him. And this time the two of them walked together, abreast, not as on their holiday visits, when he would race ahead of her or dawdle, following far behind.

While the driver was dealing with the horses in the yard of the hotel, he loaded his suitcases in and prepared a place for himself to sit, and when the wagon finally departed toward the high road he turned toward the place where she stood and waved his fine handkerchief at her. This noble gesture was engraved within her as a token of goodwill, a sort of waving of a white flag to signal the desire to bid for peace.

As one among the many women whose husbands were off somewhere in distant regions, she began to live a "paper life": she waited for the postman or for the carriage-drivers who passed by the Kochticzy Forest, where the tar furnaces were.

The letters she received were short, but they were of value to her, and she read their lines and between the lines, in an attempt to find something there that could resonate with the feelings in her own heart.

In the autumn he moved to the new place and he promised to come home for Passover, but then it happened that the way home was blocked due to a flooded river and the visit was postponed to the

Shavuot holiday. Then the man who was supposed to take over for him fell ill, and again, he was unable to set a date for his arrival.

In any case the house was neat and ready at every moment. The storehouse was full of all sorts of food that could keep and the furniture was draped with holiday covers; to keep the other rooms tidy, she ate her meals in the kitchen, at the edge of the table—a provisional eating, as on the eve of a holiday, when the important meal is reserved for later on, for the anticipated celebratory hour.

At the same time, she dressed in her good clothing and was found more and more at the market—in Isser Levin's store or at her Aunt Chana's—places that had a good view of the high road and where one could see every passing carriage.

And one day the carriage of the Zarczya farm indeed appeared, with the man and his traveling case inside.

Leybl, the child of Isser Levin's old age, was the one who noticed it first, and he ran ahead of the horses to pass along the tidings, and there, in the house, Fradl was already appearing at the front door, her brushed silk headkerchief glistening on her head like a halo.

The master's carriage was brought into the yard and Aunt Chana, practical and efficient, could be seen making her way among the curious and turning toward the community house. The woman, who had not purified herself according to Jewish law before her husband's arrival, was forbidden to him, so the aunt had been sent by her to the rabbi on some matter regarding her ritual immersion, and the response came that she would be permitted to immerse. Then, after the visitor had eaten a little something and rested and gone off to take care of his business, she went out, a small package in hand, to the end of the lane, where there stood, open and heated in one of its sections, the bathhouse.

It would be worthwhile to write a special section about this commandment, and how the daughters of Israel in the small towns fulfilled it.

These shy women, who concealed themselves within their kitchens, how they made their way, when the time was upon them, through the alleyways to the bathhouse before the eyes of the curious, each of whom could call them by name. The kerchief was too small to obscure their flushed, shamed faces, and the ground beneath was stiffened and rigid and so slippery as to trip up the foot.

And behind them, had they not left a house in disorder, a goat waiting to be milked, hungry children crying for their supper, and an unperturbed husband who paid them no mind? He was a moody man, who did not pamper his household or speak soft words to them, and against him the heart swelled with rage. And indeed it was not the desire for a little lovemaking that propelled these women, but rather the holy duty, the inheritance of their mothers, the commandment of life itself.

And these were the women who raised clear-eyed sons, weaned them and fed them on suffering. The sons were washed not with water but in their mother's tears, and they were sated, in the absence of bread, on the sorrow of her love, which they absorbed like nectar of the gods.

There were some among these sons who were overtaken and slaughtered by violent gentiles, but there were also some among them who went out at such times with an outstretched hand and were a shield and savior to their brothers, or else, with the redeemers of their homeland, prepared themselves to work the soil and provide a place to settle for the rest of their nation, who were perched, wherever they were, on the edge of the abyss.

And so Fradl, after she too had passed the tortuous way described above and then come out again after her immersion, fingernails clipped and her hair dripping wet—and the day had not yet completely darkened—she turned to walk along the winding path through the gardens, whose owners had already gone inside by this hour.

At the house, the servant-girl in her wisdom had, in the meantime, provided bread and meat for the carriage driver and water for the horses, and set the table neatly and tastefully, as her mistress would have done, she assumed. The man came in from the street in a flurry and asked that he be given his suitcases because he was going to have to leave. He had already ordered the driver to harness the

horse and had also gone out himself, wrapped in his overcoat, and
Fradl appeared at that instant as she arrived home. He told her he
had something to take care of in the village of Kaminka, and that
there were merchant-men waiting for him there; shortly after that,
the carriage left with a hurried trot through the alley.

Through the clouds of dust the faces of the dumbstruck people
peered as if through a fog, and an anticipatory stillness settled there,
as after a murderous blow had descended on someone, while those
who stand around listen for the groan in reaction, which is the sign
of life.

"Mixed-up" Gitl, who was standing beside the shared fence, called
out in her piercing voice: "You see, I told you he was a murderer,
and now he's really spilled her blood." She pointed toward the window where the red of the sunset was penetrating, and then the servant-girl appeared and pulled at the cords and the curtain fell.

Aunt Chana, who had been called by one of the neighbors, came
and could be heard there, inside, speaking to an unlistening ear, for
the woman, as later was told, just paced back and forth in her room
groaning little truncated groans, from between clenched lips, like
someone trying to overcome their pain. Every time the aunt tried to
come near her she gently pushed her aside, politely, until the woman,
exhausted with grief and the day's exertions, finally went over to one
of the couches, reclined at one end of it, and fell asleep. When she
later awoke, in the morning light, something happened that at first
frightened her, as she told it, because she found her niece sitting at
the table that was still laid out from the day before, hungrily eating
everything that had been prepared there. But after she noticed her
bright face and the clarity of her mind, the woman understood that
something had taken shape within her niece in the course of that
night, the thing that her enlightened daughters later called a turning
point, but which in her opinion was nothing more than the little
common sense the Lord had put in her heart.

The members of Isser Levin's household were surprised to see
Fradl come in, wearing, unusually, a dress of simple cut, one she had
saved from her girlhood days. Going off into a side room, she spent a

long time there with her aunt and confidante. When they finally emerged, the two of them announced together, cheerfully, that it was time to go about arranging a divorce. Uncle Isser was commissioned to act as intermediary in the negotiations with "the other party."

While her uncle was involved with handling the divorce, Fradl slowly but surely "purified" the house. She cleared out everything that had been purchased for his comfort, sold the dresses in which she had adorned herself to find favor in his eyes or gave them away to poor women, and then removed his letters from the desk drawers, those he had sent during their engagement and those he had written afterward, and sent them all up in flames. She piled up the kindling and twigs so the flames would reach high, and she stood and watched his deceit, his empty tokens of love and his broken promises, go up in smoke. And her face, with her pale blue eyes, shone forth at that moment like the face of her father when he, in his time, went out to avenge himself against the gentiles up the mountain who oppressed him continually for no wrongdoing of his own.

The day came when she stood in the community house, before the eyes of all assembled for the ceremony, and received her divorce. She was dressed simply, as in her girlhood, and now that she had regained her recognition of her own worth, she stood straight and tall once again. People said that she was more beautiful than on her wedding day.

After all this, the events came to pass that many had long anticipated: Isser Levin went into the house of the old man Shmuel-Meir and settled the matter that he had suggested to him years before. And with that the fence that separated the lots of Fradl and the widow was removed, and the two large houses at the center of the alley became as one.

Sarah-Leah, whose face regained the radiance it had once held in good times past, now lavished treats on Fradl even more tenderly than she had in her childhood, and she was the one who raised for her Yerucham-David, her son, a beautiful child who even when he was very young showed signs of the strength of his maternal grandfather, and when the little schoolchildren came into conflict with the gentile urchins, he was always at their head. And Chana, who in the meantime had gone off to distant regions, was told that he was the one, when he grew up, who taught the young men of the town the tactics of self-defense.

For in those days the surrounding gentiles sought pretexts against the townspeople and their thirst for Jewish blood grew. When they gathered and came here with their weapons of destruction, those brave boys went out to meet them, with Yerucham-David, Fradl's son at their head, and they chased them away and the town was quiet.

Designer:	Barbara Jellow
Compositor:	J. Jarrett Engineering, Inc.
Text:	10/14.5 Aldus
Display:	Texas Hero and Aldus
Printer & Binder:	Royal Book